Where Women Run

Where Women Run

Gender and Party
in the American States

Kira Sanbonmatsu

THE UNIVERSITY OF MICHIGAN PRESS   *Ann Arbor*

Copyright © by the University of Michigan 2006
All rights reserved
Published in the United States of America by
The University of Michigan Press
Manufactured in the United States of America
♾ Printed on acid-free paper

2009   2008   2007   2006   4   3   2   1

A CIP catalog record for this book is available from the British Library.

Library of Congress Cataloging-in-Publication Data

Sanbonmatsu, Kira, 1970–
    Where women run : gender and party in the American states / Kira Sanbonmatsu.
       p.   cm.
    Includes bibliographical references and index.
    ISBN-13: 978-0-472-09934-4 (cloth : alk. paper)
    ISBN-10: 0-472-09934-5 (cloth : alk. paper)
    ISBN-13: 978-0-472-06934-7 (pbk. : alk. paper)
    ISBN-10: 0-472-06934-9 (pbk. : alk. paper)
    1. Women in politics—United States—States.   2. Women political candidates—United States—States.   3. Political parties—United States—States.   4. Representative government and representation—United States—States.   I. Title.

HQ1236.5.U6S265   2006
324.082'0973—dc22   2005033819

For my father and mother, Yoshiro and Marianne

CONTENTS

FIGURES

TABLES

ACKNOWLEDGMENTS

More than two hundred state legislators, party officials, activists, office-holders, and other experts took time out of their busy schedules to assist my research. They were gracious to grant me interviews, sharing their insights into their states' politics as well as their personal experiences. In addition, nearly four hundred state party and state legislative leaders from across the country and state legislative candidates from Ohio completed mail surveys about their parties and their experiences. I owe a great debt to all of these individuals. This book would not have been written without their participation. We political scientists depend on the practitioners of politics to share with us what they do and why; in turn, we are quite grateful for their willingness to do so. The interviews and surveys were invaluable for the light they cast on both party practices and the relationship between gender and candidacy. In this book I have only begun to make sense of the points of view revealed in the interviews. To be sure, my analysis makes full use of all interviews and surveys. But in the interests of advancing a concise account of politics in each state, I am not able to give a full hearing to all of the important details from the interviews. I plan to continue to draw on these insights in my future work.

Throughout this project, from my initial ideas through the various stages of data collection, Paul Allen Beck provided immeasurable support and advice. I am grateful for his assistance in making this research possible and for sharing his expertise about political parties.

I owe yet another tremendous debt to the Center for American Women and Politics (CAWP) at the Eagleton Institute of Politics at Rutgers University. CAWP's research piqued my initial interest in women's representation in the states. I am grateful to CAWP for the Research Grant for Junior

Faculty, the invitation to conduct research at the 2001 Forum for Women State Legislators, my year at CAWP as a visiting professor, and their data on women candidates. My many conversations with Sue Carroll and Debbie Walsh shaped my thinking about this project in important ways. I am also grateful to Eagleton Institute Director Ruth Mandel, Gilda Morales of CAWP, and the rest of the first-rate CAWP and Eagleton faculty and staff for their advice and assistance.

A host of individuals advised me in the course of my research or commented on parts of the manuscript: Chris Afendulis, John Aldrich, Herb Asher, Thad Beyle, Barbara Burrell, Dianne Bystrom, Debra Dodson, Morris Fiorina, Linda Fowler, Richard Fox, Claudine Gay, Michael Hagen, Mala Htun, Karl Kurtz, Jennifer Lawless, Jerome Maddox, Gary Moncrief, Pippa Norris, Maureen Rand Oakley, Zoe Oxley, Theda Skocpol, Wendy Smooth, Peverill Squire, and Walt Stone. Maryann Barakso carefully read every page of the manuscript, for which I am grateful. I thank my colleagues at Ohio State for their support and interest in my research and for making the department a great place to work. I benefited from the comments of seminar participants at the University of Maryland, Rutgers University, and Stanford University. Nico Flannery deserves a special thanks for housing me during my trip to the Massachusetts State House. I greatly appreciate the support of my editor at the University of Michigan Press, Jim Reische, and the sage and careful advice of the anonymous reviewers. I also thank Heidi Bruns, Nanaho Hanada, Emily Kerns, Huma Khan, Amanda King, Javonne Paul, Angela Stanley, and Lyndsey Young, for their invaluable research assistance. Lew Horner and the staff at the OSU Center for Survey Research conducted the mail surveys and provided useful advice. I thank the OSU Department of Political Science and College of Social and Behavioral Sciences for research support. In addition, I received a Coca-Cola Grant for Research on Women and Gender from the OSU Department of Women's Studies. I, of course, am solely responsible for the book and any errors within.

As always, I am grateful for the love and support of my family and friends. Meriting a special thanks is my Dad, who read the entire manuscript with an eye to a general audience. The additions of my nephew and niece, Emmanuel and Karina, to the family have made life a lot more fun. I also thank Tim for his suggestions on the book from start to finish. Tim met me—and this project—with his usual good humor and good advice.

CHAPTER 1

Gender and Representation

The presence of women officeholders in local, state, and federal government has increased dramatically since the early 1970s. Nevertheless,
men continue to outnumber women in elective office. In 2005, as we approach the one hundredth anniversary of women's suffrage, women comprise
15 percent of members of Congress and 22.5 percent of state legislators
while men are 85 percent and 77.5 percent of those institutions respectively
(CAWP 2005b). The scarcity of women candidates, rather than a failure of
women to win their races, is the primary reason for the dearth of women in
public office; election results reveal that women candidates typically win their
races at rates similar to those of men. This gender parity in electoral success
has given rise to an oft-repeated slogan, "When women run, women win."
With continuing changes in women's role in society and the adoption of
term limits in many states, women are expected to seek office in even greater
numbers. However, the percentage of women serving in the legislatures has
leveled off in recent years after trending upward for several decades. This
unexpected plateau in the presence of women state legislators is cause to revisit the question of why more women do not run for public office.

In this book, I examine the relationship between political parties and
women's representation. What role do the major political parties play in
shaping who runs for the legislature? How do party practices affect women
candidates? Do party activities facilitate women's election to public office?
Or do parties make women's representation less likely?

It is commonly expected that women's representation will necessarily
increase in the future. As women's role in society continues to evolve, more
women are positioned to run for office. Thus, over time, more women are
expected to achieve elective office. But the presence of women in the state

legislatures is not a foregone conclusion; rather, the likelihood that women will run for office is shaped by politics. Who runs for office is partly determined by idiosyncratic factors such as personal interest, timing, and family. But there is more to the story of who runs for office. In particular, I focus on the institution of the political party.

Much current debate concerns the condition of the political parties in the United States—whether they are weak or strong, resurging or declining. Scholars often argue that parties are peripheral to contemporary elections because primary voters—not party organizations—select candidates. Understanding who runs for office may therefore have little to do with parties. However, other scholars argue that party organizations have grown stronger as the Democratic and Republican parties have become more competitive.

I will argue that political parties are, indeed, consequential for who runs for and wins office. Parties often use candidate recruitment as a political strategy, inserting themselves in what might seem to be a purely personal decision. First, parties can encourage office seeking by individuals who might not have otherwise done so. Second, parties can discourage candidates from entering a race. Finally, parties support candidates in the primary. Therefore, understanding who runs for office—including whether women run for office—may have much to do with party. Few scholars have examined what parties seek in candidates and whether gender factors into the parties' electoral strategies. But attention to political parties is critical for understanding women's candidacies. By focusing on parties, I enter an existing debate about how parties connect to women's opportunities for office.

The conventional wisdom is that stronger parties and greater party control over the nomination can increase women's representation, while candidate-centered elections and weak political parties put women at a disadvantage. Because politics remains a predominantly male profession, parties can increase the presence of women candidates through their candidate recruitment efforts. They can also help women win election by acting as gatekeepers and restricting the party nomination, easing women's access to the general election. Because women have fewer personal resources than do men, women stand to benefit from party efforts to play a more significant role in choosing the party nominee.

Both recruitment (party attempts to encourage candidates to run) and gatekeeping (party efforts to influence the nomination) arguably serve as indicators of party organizational strength. However, I find that stronger party organizations have a negative effect on women's representation: fewer women run for and hold state legislative office where parties are more likely to engage in gatekeeping activities. I argue that more restrictive candidate selection processes and gendered social networks reduce the likelihood that women will be recruited. Moreover, party leader doubts about women's electability make it is less likely that women will be handpicked for important races. Greater party involvement in the recruitment of candidates has no consistent positive or negative effect on women's representation. Thus, different aspects of party organizational strength have different implications for women's candidacies.

The similar success rates of men and women candidates have led some to conclude that candidate gender plays a small role—if any—in who wins elections. By these accounts, the dearth of women in office has little to do with gender. Yet my research suggests that the level of women's representation has much to do with gender. Because women have been so much less likely to seek public office than men, gender remains consequential for candidate recruitment. Party leader beliefs about women's electability vary a great deal by state. In most states, the viability of women candidates is thought to depend on the district. Thus, the view that "When women run, women win" is not universally held across states and parties.

We cannot assume that potential women candidates will become candidates. Gender continues to structure social life—and political life—in important ways. Much research suggests that men and women take somewhat different paths to public office. As a result, the presence of women legislators depends on the condition of those mechanisms that facilitate women's path to office. Women are much less likely than men to hold leadership roles within their parties, a fact that has implications for candidate recruitment. Just as party decisions about whom to contact and mobilize have consequences for which citizens participate in American politics, party decisions about who should be encouraged to run for office have consequences for which citizens serve as legislators.

DEMOCRACY AND REPRESENTATION

The numerical presence of women in elective office merits investigation for a number of reasons. On one hand, legislators are more likely to vote with their political party than their gender group. On the other hand, however, the presence of women in office has consequences for representation. The "descriptive representation" of women, or standing for women, in Hanna Pitkin's framework, is related to the "substantive representation" of women, or acting for women (e.g., Thomas 1994; Dodson and Carroll 1991; Mandel and Dodson 1992; Swers 1998; Bratton and Haynie 1999; Carroll 2001; Bratton 2002b; Swers 2002; C. Rosenthal 2002; Dodson forthcoming). Gender is an independent and significant predictor of legislative behavior, even when powerful explanatory variables such as district characteristics and ideology are taken into account (Swers 2002). Gender differences in agenda setting are particularly prevalent: women legislators are much more likely than men to work on legislation that is important to women as a group and more likely to make that legislation a priority.

Whether women are represented in legislative institutions also contributes to the legitimacy of the political system (Darcy, Welch, and Clark 1994). The shortage of women in elite politics can be described as "women's underrepresentation" in elective office, given that women constitute a majority of the population. As Phillips (1991) notes, women's underrepresentation itself provides evidence that gender is a relevant feature of the social structure and that women's experiences must differ from men's. Gender differences in social position appear to necessitate the representation of "women's interests" (Sapiro 1981). As descriptive representatives of women as a group, women legislators can improve the substantive representation of women's interests by improving the quality of deliberation; according to Mansbridge (1999), representatives of disadvantaged groups can enhance communication within legislative bodies as well as between representatives and constituents. In short, the presence of women in deliberative bodies provides an opportunity for more fair and effective representation (Phillips 1995).

In addition to the many ways in which gender influences men's and women's daily lives, gender differences in legislative behavior may reflect the different paths that men and women take to elective office. The work of women legislators across party lines is also often the product of conscious effort and strategy: women legislators meet together informally as well as formally through women's caucuses in many state legislatures and in Congress (CAWP 2001c).

How institutional factors affect the ability of women legislators to substantively represent women motivates a growing body of research (e.g., Bratton 2002a; Beckwith 2002). A critical mass of women may be needed before women can act for women. As women approach parity in the legislature and move beyond token status, they may be less constrained and better able to act for women (Kanter 1977; Thomas 1994; Thomas and Welch 2001). Yet even a small number of women can have an impact on women's substantive representation (Crowley 2004).

One of the most striking findings from this body of research is women legislators' strong belief that they have an obligation to represent the interests of women as a group (CAWP 2001c; Reingold 2000; Carroll 2002). Men legislators are much less likely to feel this obligation. This gender difference may be fueled by life experience, the expectations of voters and other political actors, and the electoral connection between women legislators and women's organizations and women voters. According to Carroll (2003a: 22), women's organizations—both within legislative institutions and external to the legislature—act as linkage mechanisms, "connecting women officeholders to other women and to a more collective vision of women's interests." Moreover, "in the absence of close ties to women's organizations, it seems likely that fewer women legislators would be active advocates on behalf of women."

Women voters are more likely than men to want to see more women in public office (Cook 1994), and some evidence indicates that women voters are more likely than men to vote for women candidates (e.g., Zipp and Plutzer 1985; Plutzer and Zipp 1996; Seltzer, Newman, and Leighton 1997; Dolan 1998). In turn, the presence of women as candidates and officeholders can increase women's civic engagement (Burns, Schlozman, and Verba 2001). Once elected, women are uniquely positioned to enhance the ties between women in the mass public and policy-making.

Thus, normative concerns about democracy and equality and growing evidence of gender differences in legislative behavior make the question of women's underrepresentation a compelling one. I focus on a critical stage of the representation process: candidacy. As Fowler argues, much about our political life turns on who runs for office:

> Politics in the United States depends on candidates to provide leadership, to foster vigorous competition, to ensure that a wide range of interests in society has access to political power, to uphold the principles of popular sovereignty and individual rights, and to give expression to citizen demands for policy change. (1993: 37)

The presence—or absence—of women candidates has implications for what interests are heard in American politics. Indeed, the descriptive representation of women can give rise to the content of women's interests (Mansbridge

1999). Descriptive representation also conveys social meaning to the citizenry as a whole about the political equality of women as a class and the appropriateness of women's participation in the public sphere (Sapiro 1981; Phillips 1995; Mansbridge 1999).

GENDER AND STATE LEGISLATIVE OFFICE

The focus of my investigation of women's representation is the state legislature, where political careers often begin. In his landmark study of political ambition, Schlesinger (1966: 72) identified the state legislature as a base office and "a natural breeding ground for political ambition." His analysis of the backgrounds of statewide leaders in the first half of the twentieth century revealed that the legislature was the single most common prior officeholding experience. Today, the legislature remains a stepping-stone to statewide and congressional positions. Meanwhile, for the majority of state legislators, the legislature is their first elective office (Pew Center 2003). Thus, understanding why more women do not run for the legislature and understanding where women run has long-term consequences for women's officeholding at higher levels. How women fare in state politics is also increasingly important given the devolution of policy-making responsibilities to the states.

At first glance, that men outnumber women as political candidates may seem unremarkable: women have always been less likely than men to run for office. Yet looking across the United States, it is evident that the relationship between gender and officeholding is anything but fixed. The percentage of state legislative candidates and state legislators who are women ranges widely across the American states. In South Carolina, for example, only about 9 percent of legislators are women (see table 1.1). But women comprise 34 percent of legislators in Maryland (CAWP 2005d).

One might expect women to be least well represented in those regions of the country where traditional gender role arrangements are more common. Such an account might explain why women are fewer in number in southern states than in other states. But the low representation of women in Wyoming and Pennsylvania is inconsistent with such an explanation. Moreover, the states with the highest proportion of women legislators represent a range of geographic regions and ideological views. And though an overall increase has occurred in the proportion of women serving in the legislatures,

TABLE 1.1.   Percentage of State Legislators Who Are Women

More than 30%	24–30%	18–24%	15–18%	Less than 15%
Maryland	Minnesota	Florida	Tennessee	Oklahoma
Delaware	Connecticut	Maine	Rhode Island	Wyoming
Arizona	Hawaii	New York	Indiana	Mississippi
Nevada	Oregon	North Carolina	Louisiana	Pennsylvania
Vermont	Illinois	Missouri	Arkansas	Kentucky
Washington	Idaho	Michigan	North Dakota	Alabama
Colorado	Wisconsin	Iowa	South Dakota	South Carolina
Kansas	Montana	Texas	New Jersey	
New Mexico	Massachusetts	Ohio	West Virginia	
California	Nebraska	Utah	Virginia	
New Hampshire		Georgia		
		Alaska		

Source: CAWP. Data are for 2005.

the American states have experienced change at different rates (E. Cox 1996). Indeed, in nearly one-third of states, women constitute a smaller proportion of legislators in 2005 than they did in the wake of the 1992 elections—the "Year of the Woman" in which a record number of women won seats in Congress.[1]

In most areas of political participation, women participate less than men (Burns, Schlozman, and Verba 2001). Yet women outparticipate men in politics in one respect: women are more likely than men to vote (CAWP 2004). This evidence suggests that gender does not inherently constrict women to a lesser role than men in politics. Furthermore, changes over time and variation across states mean that the current relationship between gender and officeholding is not a permanent feature of our political life. Instead, the dearth of women candidates requires explanation.[2] My focus on women's representation therefore concerns women's descriptive representation. I investigate a neglected aspect of women's representation: the relationship between parties and women's candidacies.[3]

---

1. Data on women legislators are from CAWP Fact Sheets, various years.

2. Women comprised 19.6 percent of Republican and 22.7 percent of Democratic general election candidates for the state House between 1986 and 1994 and 14.6 percent of Republican and 19.7 percent of Democratic state Senate candidates (Seltzer, Newman, and Leighton 1997: 146).

3. Political parties are arguably a "missing variable" in the study of women and politics (Baer 1993).

WOMEN AND THE POLITICAL PARTIES

Women's participation in the major political parties has been a struggle for inclusion. The Democratic and Republican parties were not initially sympathetic to woman suffrage and indeed mainly presented obstacles to suffrage. According to suffrage leader Carrie Chapman Catt, women won the right to vote despite rather than because of the two major parties (J. Freeman 2000: 61). On the eve of suffrage, both major parties rushed to mobilize women voters, creating women's auxiliaries and women's campaign divisions at the state and national levels and counting on party women to mobilize women voters (Harvey 1998). The Republican party created a Women's Division in 1918, while the Democratic party established a Women's Bureau in 1916 (Andersen 1996). In 1924, the Republican party enlarged the Republican National Committee to include men and women from each state; the Democrats had included a woman associate member to the Democratic National Committee from each state in 1919 (Andersen 1996).

Thus, even as the parties made it more difficult for women to gain suffrage, they also acted in anticipation of women's enfranchisement (J. Freeman 2000). Indeed, J. Freeman observes, "By 1920, women were already in politics and had been for quite some time. Women got suffrage *after* they proved themselves to be an important political force. Suffrage was a consequence as well as a cause of the movement of women into politics" (3).

Winning the right to vote in 1920 did not automatically mean that women could seek public office, however; being male remained a legal qualification for holding office in some places (Andersen 1996). Rarely did the debate for or against suffrage turn on women's pursuit of public office (Cott 1987). But the parties were not necessarily interested in fielding women candidates. A 1922 editorial in the *Woman Citizen* opined,

> It is clear that the barriers in the way of women being elected to any political office are almost insurmountable. The dominant political parties do not nominate women for political office if there is a real chance for winning. Political offices are the assets of the political machine. In general, they are too valuable to be given to women. They are used to pay political debts or to strengthen the party, and so far the parties are not greatly in debt to women, and it has not been shown that it strengthens a party to nominate them. (Cott 1987: 110)

Women who ran for office in the 1920s were not thought to be politicians; instead, their political involvement was thought to be spurred by issues—in particular, social reform and "housekeeping" policy change (Andersen 1996). In other words, women were perceived to be in politics as an extension of their domestic responsibilities rather than out of political ambition.

Through the twentieth century, party women populated women's divisions and women's clubs, establishing themselves as the workhorses of the party. Women helped with campaigns, educated and mobilized other women, staffed party headquarters, raised funds, and trained women leaders (Harvey 1998; J. Freeman 2000). But even as they made a place for themselves within the parties, they faced resistance; control of the parties ultimately remained in the hands of men (J. Freeman 2000). Loyal party women were rewarded, disloyal party women were removed, and pressing the concerns of women as women remained quite difficult (J. Freeman 2000). Even in the 1970s, studies of local party organizations revealed a gendered division of labor, with women more likely to be engaged in the daily maintenance of the organization and men in charge of candidate recruitment and party strategy (Fowlkes, Perkins, and Rinehart 1979; Margolis 1980).

Women's roles within the party organization would change with the modern women's movement. Pressed by the National Women's Political Caucus and feminists organizing within the party, the Democratic party reformed its presidential nomination rules in 1972 to increase women's presence as convention delegates. In 1980, the Democratic National Committee adopted rules requiring "50-50," or equal gender representation on party committees at the national level and on the state committees—rules that remain in place today (J. Freeman, forthcoming). Many critics viewed the reforms as empowering activists at the expense of party regulars (Crotty 1978, 1983). On the one hand, "amateur Democrats" were likely to be women and apparently clashed with the male-dominated "professional" party members (Wilson 1962). In the 1950s, party reformers had challenged party regulars in local Democratic clubs (Wilson 1962). On the other hand, the Democratic party's reforms are perhaps best understood as essentially creating a new party elite that replaced the party regulars (Baer and Bositis 1988). Moreover, the distinction between amateurs and professionals within political parties may be overstated (Stone and Abramowitz 1983; Maggiotto and Weber 1986; Carsey et al. 2003). Indeed, party women and men do not evidence different levels of amateur style (Baer and Jackson 1985).

The Republican party did not mandate changes to its delegate selection rules, but the Republican National Committee is still composed of one man and one woman from each state in addition to the state chair. Each state also has gender balance on the national convention committees, and many Republican state committees have gender balance as well (J. Freeman, forthcoming). Thus, despite feminist groups' closer alignment with the Democratic party and antifeminist groups' affinity for the Republican party (J. Freeman 2000; Wolbrecht 2000), both parties use gender quotas. Indeed, the idea of ending the gender quotas on the convention committees does not even merit discussion within the Republican party (J. Freeman, forthcoming).

Both parties have used their national platforms to pledge their support for women candidates (Sanbonmatsu 2002a). Yet despite gender quotas on many Democratic and Republican party committees, neither party has supported such a reform with respect to candidacy. At the same time, a growing number of countries and political parties around the world have adopted quotas to increase women's representation in legislative bodies (e.g., Lovenduski and Norris 1993; Norris and Lovenduski 1995; Dahlerup 1998; Caul 1999; Klausen and Meier 2001; Caul 2001; Htun 2004; Baldez 2004; Jones 2004). As I discuss in more detail in chapter 2, how political parties shape women's candidacies in the United States—in the absence of quotas for women candidates or legislators—has received scant attention among scholars of women and politics.

DATA AND METHODOLOGY

The fifty states provide a natural laboratory in which to examine the determinants of women's officeholding and the connection between party activities and candidacy. I use a multimethod approach and several different sources of data to determine if the activities of the major parties are related to women's representation (see table 1.2). Together, these approaches enable me to examine the relationship of women's candidacies to the parties with several research strategies.

TABLE 1.2.   Data Sources

Data Set	Sample	Time Period
Case studies (personal interviews)	AL, CO, IA, MA, NC, OH	2001 and 2002
Elections data	AL, CO, IA, MA, NC, OH	2002
Women's representation in the states	All states (lower chamber)	1973 to 2003
State Legislative Leader Survey	All states (lower chamber)	2002
State Party Leader Survey	All states	2002
State Legislative Candidate Survey	OH	2002

I conducted case studies of party recruitment practices and the status of women candidates in six states that represent a diverse range of party activities: Alabama, Colorado, Iowa, Massachusetts, North Carolina, and Ohio. In each state, I conducted semistructured personal interviews with state legislators, legislative leaders, state party officials, activists, and other elites. The interviews concerned recruitment for the legislature, party strategies regarding candidate gender, and perceptions of barriers and opportunities facing women candidates for the legislature. The case studies enable me to make comparisons across the states and the two parties within each state, examining the party's role, if any, in shaping women's representation. I supplement the case studies with additional interviews conducted at the Center for American Women and Politics 2001 Forum for Women State Legislators.[4] I conducted a total of more than 240 personal interviews.

Women's candidacies are not usually studied with qualitative methods. However, studying gender can benefit from the use of qualitative methods, among other approaches (Carroll and Liebowitz 2003). The barriers women face today in politics, as in other professions, may be informal ones. Personal interviews are a valuable technique for studying attitudes about gender, the subtleties of which may be more difficult to gauge through other approaches such as phone or mail surveys. Given the subjective nature of the calculations involved in the personal decision to run for office, perceptions are important. Perceptions are also critical to understanding potential women candidates' ability to attract informal support prior to entering the primary.

Interviews also represent a useful methodology for collecting data on the parties' informal and formal practices and their electoral strategies. We know relatively little about the parties' recruitment practices for the state legislatures. In addition, we lack a knowledge base about party leader beliefs about women's electability and whether those beliefs vary across states. These beliefs may help explain why women are more likely to run for the legislature in some states than in others.

For the case-study states, I also examine the pattern of women's candidacies and analyze their success rates in state legislative elections. The elections data enable me to compare the presence and success of women in both

---

4. At the forum, I conducted a small number of interviews with women from California, Georgia, Maine, New Hampshire, and Washington—states that complement the diversity provided by the six case-study states. I discuss these additional interviews in chapter 7.

parties in each state and examine the extent to which women enter the primary for open seats.

I also conducted a mail survey of party leaders in the lower house of the legislature in all states, modeled after the interview schedule used in the case studies. The State Legislative Leader Survey includes questions about the involvement of the legislative caucus in candidate recruitment activities as well as questions specifically about women candidates. I conducted a similar survey of state party chairs and executive directors—the State Party Leader Survey—that was sent to all fifty Democratic and Republican state parties. I use the survey data to analyze the effects of party activities on women's representation in the lower chambers of the legislatures. I also analyze the effects of parties on where women run as general election candidates.

The party leader surveys are unique in several respects. First, they include more detailed questions than past studies have about the nature and extent of state and legislative party activities in state legislative elections. Second, the surveys tap party leader beliefs about candidate emergence in the state, including the extent to which candidates are thought to be self-starters and whether interest groups recruit candidates. Third, the surveys concern candidate gender, including questions about party leader beliefs about women's electability and whether men or women candidates have an electoral advantage.

I supplement the party leader surveys with a mail survey of major-party state legislative candidates in Ohio. This State Legislative Candidate Survey enables me to compare the paths that men and women take to the legislature and to examine candidate views about the electoral significance of candidate gender. As the case-study state with the strongest political parties, Ohio should confirm the conventional wisdom that strong parties enhance women's representation.

I also analyze an original data set of state-level variables to examine the relationship between parties and the presence of women in the state legislature in a multivariate framework. This data set, which extends from 1973 to 2003, includes party factors in addition to control variables that are thought to explain cross-state variation in women's representation. I use these data to examine the effects of existing measures of party organizational strength on women's representation in the state legislatures.

Throughout, I devote significant attention to the role of the legislative party. Observers often cite the national-level parties' legislative campaign committees as evidence of the increasing strength of the Democratic and

Republican parties (Herrnson 1988). Scholars have also studied the function, origins, and activities of the state counterparts of these committees, known as state legislative campaign committees (Gierzynski 1992; Shea 1995; C. Rosenthal 1995). The rise of legislative campaign committees may constitute evidence that the parties are becoming stronger (Gierzynski 1992). Then again, perhaps campaign committees "are best viewed as independent, election-driven machines, little different than campaign consulting firms" (Shea 1995, 6). Because responsibility for candidate recruitment appears to have shifted to the legislative caucuses (Shea 1995; Moncrief, Squire, and Jewell 2001), an analysis of the legislative party is important to understanding how parties today shape women's opportunities for office. Indeed, studies reveal significant contact between state legislative candidates and the party prior to the primary election (Frendreis and Gitelson 1999; Moncrief, Squire, and Jewell 2001). Yet we know very little about the extent and nature of caucus involvement in candidate recruitment (Gierzynski 1992).

Chapters

I propose a framework for studying the relationship between gender and parties in chapter 2. In chapter 3, I introduce the case studies and surveys and begin to analyze the role of parties in recruiting and nominating candidates. I turn to the place of candidate gender in the parties' electoral strategies in chapter 4. In chapter 5, I compare perceptions of the barriers and opportunities facing women candidates across the case-study states. I conduct a quantitative analysis of the relationship between party factors and women's representation in chapter 6. In chapter 7, I summarize my findings and draw on interview evidence beyond the case-study states to revisit the view that women are disadvantaged by weak party systems. I conclude with a discussion of the implications my research holds for current debates about parties and candidate emergence as well as debates about women's representation in American politics.

CHAPTER 2

Gender and Candidacy

Supply, Demand, and Political Parties

Running for office is not a common act of political participation—among either men or women. Yet many individuals do run for office. Some have always aspired to a career in politics and need no invitation to run. For these individuals, politics may best be described as a vocation. Other candidates are more aptly described as made rather than born. Being asked to run may transform an ordinary citizen into a politician. More often than not, this less-planned path to office is more likely to characterize the political careers of women than men. In part because politics has traditionally been a male domain, men are more likely than women to plan to run for public office.

One institution that is in the business of encouraging candidacy is the political party. Recent evidence indicates that political parties in the United States are growing stronger and that they actively recruit candidates. Yet it is frequently argued that parties lack influence in candidate selection—that contemporary elections are candidate centered and party organizations are weak. This debate about whether political parties are strong or weak has particular relevance for women's representation. As Burrell (1994: 308) notes, a weak party system with candidate-centered elections can be both a plus and a minus for women's candidacies. On one hand, women may stand to gain from a system wherein parties—institutions in which women wield influence—control the nomination. On the other hand, women may stand to lose in such a system. Indeed, the potential problems of closed candidate-selection processes are evident in the creation of women's political action committees (PACs) aimed at ensuring that women are not overlooked in their attempts to win the party nomination.

In this chapter, I consider the mechanisms by which political parties may affect women's representation. Because the scarcity of women candidates is recognized as a central cause of women's underrepresentation, I focus on the parties' role in shaping the decision to run. I examine party goals with respect to candidate recruitment and discuss the ways in which gender may intersect with these goals.

I begin the chapter by discussing the limitations of existing accounts of women's underrepresentation. Past studies have emphasized two main determinants of women's underrepresentation: the problem of incumbency and gender differences in the informal requirements for public office. Incumbency is a structural barrier that limits the opportunities of any new group seeking representation, including women. In addition, women have historically been underrepresented in those occupations that typically lead to running for office. Both explanations have merit. However, despite much research on this question, the gender gap in who runs for office remains a puzzle.

THE PUZZLE OF WOMEN'S REPRESENTATION

A prime suspect for understanding why more women do not hold public office is the voter: perhaps the underrepresentation of women in office indicates that voters are unwilling to elect women.[1] However, voter prejudice is no longer thought to be a barrier to women's candidacies. Studies show that women are not disproportionately likely to lose their races (Darcy, Welch, and Clark 1994; Burrell 1994; Seltzer, Newman, and Leighton 1997).[2] For example, Darcy and Schramm (1977) found that gender had little or no effect on the performance of men and women candidates in general election races for the U.S. House of Representatives in the early 1970s once incumbency status was taken into account. Burrell (1994) reached similar conclusions about both primary and general election races for the U.S. House.

Studies of state legislative races have achieved similar results. Women and men performed similarly in general election races for the legislature from 1986 to 1994 (Seltzer, Newman, and Leighton 1997). In House races, for example, Seltzer, Newman, and Leighton (1997) find that men and women

---

1. The literature on women and elections is vast. For comprehensive reviews, see Carroll 1993; Darcy, Welch, and Clark 1994; Flammang 1997; Niven 1998; Carroll 2003b.

2. One recent exception to the general rule that women and men succeed at similar rates after incumbency is controlled is a study by Delano and Winters (2002). They find that women gubernatorial candidates are slightly disadvantaged compared to men.

won their races at about the same rates. Of incumbent candidates, 93.8 percent of men and 93.6 percent of women won; 53 percent of men open-seat candidates and 52.2 percent of women open-seat candidates won, as did 9.7 percent of men challengers and 10.9 percent of women challengers (80). The authors conclude,

> When women run, women win . . . as often as men do. Our study found no difference between success rates for men and women in general elections. Based on the overwhelming weight of the data gathered, the conclusion is clear: A candidate's sex does not affect his or her chances of winning an election.

> Winning elections has nothing to do with the sex of the candidate, and everything to do with incumbency. (79)

Gender parity in candidates' success rates has given rise to the conventional wisdom that women win when they run.

Gender inequality with respect to campaign finance has also been ruled out as a source of women's underrepresentation. For similar types of races, the campaign receipts of women and men tend to be comparable, showing no signs of gender disadvantage (Schlozman and Uhlaner 1986; Burrell 1990, 1994; B. Werner 1997). The idea that women are not financially able to compete with men candidates is, arguably, a myth (Seltzer, Newman, and Leighton 1997). Indeed, women candidates have outperformed men in some cases (Burrell 1994).

Meanwhile, it has long been argued that the sexual division of labor contributes to women's underrepresentation in elite politics (Carroll and Strimling 1983; Carroll 1993; Dodson 1997; Thomas 1994). Despite changes in gender roles, women continue to hold a disproportionate share of household responsibilities.[3] Women face greater hurdles than men do in pursuing political careers—as with any career—because of gender differences in caregiving obligations and societal views about women's role in the private sphere. However, scholars typically cite incumbency and the social eligibility pool as the main barriers to women's representation.

The electoral advantage enjoyed by incumbent politicians poses a structural problem for women candidates. Carroll (1994: 120) argues, "The truly

---

3. For a recent example of the continued gendered division of labor in the home, see Burns, Schlozman, and Verba 2001.

critical impediments to greater success at the polls—the staying power of incumbents and the lack of larger numbers of open seats—are factors individual women can do little to change." For example, Burrell (1994) concludes that the scarcity rather than the performance of women candidates explains the low numbers of women in Congress. Darcy, Welch, and Clark (1994) also argue that incumbency provides the major explanation for women's underrepresentation. Most incumbents win reelection, and most incumbents happen to be men. Thus, more women would hold office if there were more opportunities for women to run in winnable races.

Another major obstacle to women's representation is socialization and particularly occupational segregation: "This is a structural explanation that posits that changing the occupational distribution of women would influence their recruitment to public office" (Darcy, Welch, and Clark 1994: 108). The underrepresentation of women in fields such as law and business, which often lead to careers in politics, provides an important explanation for women's underrepresentation in elective office. As more women enter these fields, the numbers of women in public office should increase.

Women's access to higher offices should also increase as more women fill local offices.[4] It is commonly believed that the proportion of women in office will necessarily increase over time: "As we see the results of the 'pipeline' of women who have entered public office begin to pay off, and as women continue to become more powerful and prevalent in worlds outside the home, the numbers of women in public office will no doubt continue to rise" (Seltzer, Newman, and Leighton 1997: 91–92). Thus, according to past accounts, the problem of women's underrepresentation will resolve itself with time. Indeed, Darcy, Welch, and Clark (1994: 126) projected that women would constitute the majority of nonincumbent state legislative candidates by 2006.

Yet the limitations of our understanding of women's underrepresentation are becoming increasingly clear. Despite the continued gains of women as a group in education and occupational status and despite the enactment of

---

4. In the 1992 Census of Governments (U.S. Department of Commerce, Bureau of the Census 1994), 24 percent of local government elected officials reporting gender were women. Of all local offices, women were most likely to be found in school districts, where 31 percent of officials were women. CAWP (2005b) reports that in 2005, women comprise 15.9 percent of mayors of cities with populations greater than thirty thousand.

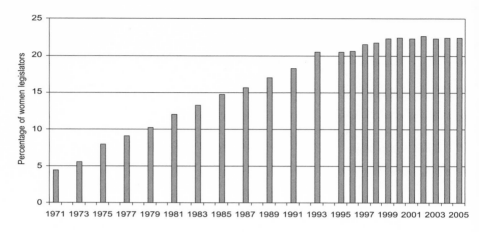

Fig. 2.1.   Percentage of women in state legislatures, 1971–2005.
(Data from CAWP 2005d)

term limits, women's representation at the state legislative level has reached a plateau in recent years (see figure 2.1).

Many scholars as well as proponents of term limits expected state legislative term limits to lead to an increase in women's representation. The logic behind this expectation is simple: women are most likely to increase their numbers in office through open seats because most incumbents are men, and term limits create open seats. However, term limits have not had the large, positive effect on women's representation that many anticipated (Bernstein and Chadha 2003). For example, women's presence in House seats declined after term limits were implemented (Carroll and Jenkins 2001). No woman ran in the primary of either party in about 40 percent of all House seats vacated as a result of term limits in 1998 and 2000 (Carroll and Jenkins 2001). Although women's presence in the state Senates increased in 1998, it stayed the same in 2000.

Thus, the current stagnation in the level of women state legislators defies most predictions. Women and men may be equally likely to win their races, but our existing explanations for why women are so much less likely than men to run for office are deficient. Incumbency and the social eligibility pool remain important explanations, but these factors alone cannot account for the dearth of women candidates.

The presence of women in the social eligibility pool appears to be a necessary but insufficient condition for women's representation (Niven 1998).

Indeed, most state legislators arrive at the legislature without prior elective officeholding experience.[5] Carroll explains,

> There are many, many more women in the *eligible pool* from which candidates are drawn than there are candidates. Women are active in politics in sizeable numbers—as party activists, as convention delegates, as staff members for other politicians, as community activists, as leaders in civic and community groups, as members of appointed boards and commissions. Yet, few of these women seek elective public office. . . . To develop a better understanding of why few women run for office, we need to examine what happens *before* primaries, i.e., the preprimary candidate selection process. (1993: 214–15)

Meanwhile, the mere presence of women in the pool does not automatically lead to candidacy: in a recent national study of potential candidates by Fox and Lawless (2004), women were less likely than men to have ever considered running for office. Accounting for changes in gender roles and generational replacement also cannot explain current patterns: the gender gap among young elected officials is even more dramatic than the gap among state legislators. Only 14 percent of today's elected leaders under age thirty-five are women (Mandel and Kleeman 2004).

Moreover, despite the conventional wisdom that no barriers remain to women's election to office, other evidence suggests a more pessimistic view. About one-third of state legislative candidates agreed in a recent survey that it is more difficult for women to put together the necessary resources for a competitive campaign (Faucheux and Herrnson 1999), including 70 percent of women respondents and only 25 percent of men polled. In another survey, women in local elected office in Ohio, New Jersey, Tennessee, and California identified local party leaders' gender bias as a barrier to women's state legislative candidacies: 64 percent of locally elected women believed that party leaders discouraged potential women candidates from running for office (Niven 1998). In addition, potential women candidates are less likely than their male counterparts to report having been asked to run for office (Fox and Lawless 2004).

Men may also be more likely than women to translate local officeholding

5. A Pew Center on the States (2003) survey found that 59 percent of state legislators had no previous officeholding experience. Twenty-five percent of nonincumbent state legislative candidates surveyed by Moncrief, Squire, and Jewell (2001) currently held elective office.

experience into a career in the legislature. This possibility is suggested by Pennsylvania, which ranks among the lowest in the nation for women's representation and where women in local elected office are disproportionately found in bookkeeping and clerical offices (Fastnow and Levy 2001). It is not clear if this gender distribution results from self-selection or some other process, but this case illustrates the tentative relationship between local officeholding and state officeholding. Women may not increase their numbers as legislators if their gains at the local level occur in offices that are less likely to lead to the legislature.

One institutional change that has occurred since the 1960s with potential consequences for who seeks office, including whether women seek office, is legislative professionalization. The state legislatures have become increasingly professionalized as demands on the legislatures have increased and legislative compensation has risen (Squire 1988; A. Rosenthal 1989; Thompson and Moncrief 1992; Squire 1992, 1997). One indicator of this professionalism is the rise over the past several decades in the percentage of legislators who describe themselves as "full-time" legislators (Bazar 1987). With greater professionalism, the state legislature has increasingly become a stepping-stone to Congress. It is quite common for members of Congress to have experience as state legislators, although remaining in the legislature has also become more desirable in many cases (Fowler and McClure 1989; Berkman 1994).

This increase in professionalism has the potential to diversify the legislature. In the 1960s, Schlesinger (1966: 17) observed that the "open character of political opportunity in the United States forces the politician to treat public office as an avocation. . . . The politician needs another means of support, preferably one compatible with officeholding." A legal practice can usefully be combined with the part-time aspect of legislative service (Hirsch 1996). As the legislatures have become more full-time institutions and pay has increased, there are arguably more opportunities for the candidacies of individuals other than the typical white male lawyer (Squire 1992).

Legislative service may also be a particularly desirable occupation for women. A number of drawbacks exist to running for any office, including the legislature, and legislative service may be less attractive to potential candidates because of the opportunity costs of serving. But public service should be an attractive career option for women: there is no reason to believe that it is more attractive financially to men than women and some reason to believe that the reverse is true. As Maddox (2004) argues, given that women face a disadvantage relative to men in the labor market, the opportunity cost of being in the legislature is likely to be lower for women than for men. Indeed, women state legislators are significantly less likely than men to be employed outside the legislature while serving (Maddox 2004).

Women and men officeholders also tend to have different backgrounds (e.g., Carroll and Strimling 1983; Thomas 1994; Burrell 1994; Gertzog 1995). For example, women state legislators are less likely than men are to be lawyers (CAWP 2001c). Women have typically come to elective office from different occupations—and from a more diverse set of occupations—than men, although men's and women's paths to office have converged to some extent in recent years (Gertzog 1995; Thomas 1994; Burrell 1994; Dolan and Ford 1997; Gertzog 2002). Therefore, the social eligibility pool of women differs somewhat from the pool of men.

In short, women remain underrepresented in elective office several decades after the emergence of the modern women's movement despite the dramatic increase in the numbers of women with the informal requirements for office as well as the new openings created by term limits. New research strategies are needed in light of the limitations of past research. Most scholars have studied the fate of candidates rather than potential candidates and have looked at successful candidates (i.e., party nominees) rather than losing candidates (Carroll 1993; Niven 1998). But a focus on the success rates of women party nominees may not represent the experiences of women at much earlier stages in the process, particularly before the primary (Carroll 1993). I will turn next to the role of parties prior to the primary.

THE PROMISE OF POLITICAL PARTIES?

Are political parties the solution to the problem of women's underrepresentation? The idea that parties can remedy women's underrepresentation stems from the assumption that candidacy in the United States is purely a matter of self-nomination.[6] For example, Norris and Lovenduski argue,

6. See Fowler 1993 for an important analysis and review of the literature on candidacy. One weakness of this literature's focus on ambitious politicians is what Fowler describes as the "neglect of the contextual and structural features that determine the candidate pool" (180–81). Fowler argues that variation across states in the presence of potential candidates and their qualifications has been neglected, as has the role of elites—including parties—in deciding which candidates to support.

In most states parties have lost their gatekeeping role: the rise of primaries in the last two decades means party bosses no longer pick candidates in the traditional smoke-filled rooms. The function of candidate selection has been transferred to primary voters. Politicians are self-nominating; they offer themselves as candidates, raise money, create publicity and make the key decisions about how to generate votes. Since parties no longer play a major role on the "demand-side," the literature has shifted to focusing on the supply-side of the equation: why candidates choose to campaign within a particular local context. (1995: 22)

Political recruitment can be considered in terms of supply-side and demand-side explanations: the supply-side factors encompass the eligible candidates and their motivations and resources, while the demand side includes the role of gatekeepers and the criteria party leaders employ to select candidates (Norris 1993, 1997).

This "entrepreneurial system" of candidacy—where candidates are viewed as self-nominating—may not be ideal for women candidates (Burrell 1994: 189). Instead, many scholars have proposed that a stronger party role in nominating candidates and less reliance on primaries would increase women's representation (Darcy, Welch, and Clark 1994; Burrell 1994; Caul and Tate 2002). Caul and Tate (2002: 238) summarize the conventional wisdom: "While a strong empirical case has yet to be made for the claim that strong political parties lead to higher levels of women's representation, most scholars agree that weakening the control of parties will impede the growth of female representation in legislative office."

This optimistic view of parties is premised on the belief that the bias of party leaders has long been obsolete:

> One explanation for the small number of women candidates is that women who are potential candidates believe that voters and party elites will not support them because they are women. This fear may have had some basis as recently as twenty-five years ago, but it is certainly no longer the case. Nonetheless, if some potential women candidates believe this, they will be discouraged. (Darcy, Welch, and Clark 1994: 178)

In this view, there is no reason to believe that party elites are biased against women. Party receptivity to women candidates can arguably be gauged with election results. For example, Clark et al. (1984: 149) explain, "While it may not be possible to observe systematically the deliberations leading to the recruitment and support of candidates, it is a simple matter to examine the results of these deliberations." Party support of women candidates is evident in the statistics that women typically win their races at the same rates as men and in the fact that women are not disproportionately slated to run as sacrificial lambs in unwinnable races.

Burrell's (1994) analysis of campaign finance and congressional candidates yielded similar conclusions: the Democratic and Republican parties were equally likely to fund men and women party nominees. Therefore, parties do not put women at a disadvantage; instead, the benefits of parties are apparent:

> Party organizations are no longer negative "gatekeepers" for women candidates. But neither do they control the nomination process which could facilitate the nomination of more women candidates. Women who seek office have to compete in an entrepreneurial world of independent candidacies. They have to operate in a weak party system. Ironically one can see that as both a plus and a minus for women candidates. But overall, stronger parties should advantage women candidates. (Burrell 1993: 308)

Women should benefit from a system where those active within the party organization—rather than primary voters—select candidates. Relying on party committees and conventions instead of primaries would make the level of women's representation in the United States more similar to other countries: "Women and sympathetic men party activists would be in a stronger position to support and sponsor potential women candidates" (Darcy, Welch, and Clark 1994: 189). In a weak party environment, an individual can run for office without coming through the party organization. With the direct primary, it is easier for self-starter candidates because the party cannot prevent them from running (Seligman et al. 1974). Therefore, the nomination should arguably be returned to the party, giving individuals an incentive to become active within the party organization:

> If parties are strengthened in the United States, then women's candidacies for public office should be facilitated and perhaps enhanced. Evidence from other countries and the transformation within our own parties indicate that party organizations are no longer the enemies of women politicians with ambition for public office. They are an organizational base of opportunity for women as opposed to the present, more entrepreneurial, system that characterizes contemporary American elections, even though women did well in such a system in 1992. (Burrell 1994: 191)

Cross-nationally, the ability of women within the party to press for women candidates seems to depend on centralized control of nominations. Norris (1993: 324), for example, explains that in "informal-localized systems" of recruitment such as in the United States, "it is difficult for the central party leadership to play a major role—whether positive or negative—in the recruitment process." If they received more control over the nomination, parties could ensure that women were recruited and nominated.

Parties can bring women into the process and help them overcome barriers that might result from socialization, the historic underrepresentation of women in politics, or women's lack of access to important social networks: "Parties provide a vital linkage mechanism for women and other traditional outsiders who do not have the business and social connections often associated with a successful campaign, personal connections that men are more likely to possess" (Bledsoe and Herring 1990: 220). Caul and Tate echo this viewpoint:

> It is easier for parties to encourage and recruit female candidates for nomination if party committees and conventions have more control in the nomination process. Strong parties can prepare and train potential candidates, compensating, therefore, for women's relative disadvantage to men in terms of the personal resources that they are able to bring to the campaign. (2002: 239)

However, whether stronger political parties inherently advantage women as a group remains to be seen. The parties have not necessarily promoted women within their ranks to become party leaders or candidates (e.g., Clarke and Kornberg 1979; J. Freeman 2000; Baer and Bositis 1988). The women's movement arguably was needed to diversify the party leadership. Indeed, social movements can help outgroups gain access to leadership positions:

> Political parties have long been recognized as essential for democracy. This is because parties *accumulate power,* yet remain *permeable* to political movements. But elite cadres also tend toward *oligarchy.* Because of the exclusion of some groups from political influence, *social movements arise* as a periodic phenomenon *that* like political parties, *promote democracy by developing new elites.*

> Elite status is furthered by *information,* and a closer link between elites and masses is forged when *political participation* is informed. Thus, *voting* is a necessary, but insufficient, condition for democracy. Also essential for the democratic representation of interests are social movements, which

arise from social out-groups, while entrenched interests may achieve representation through the pressure group system and political movements. At the juncture of these elements is interest *intermediation*. It is the organizational function of the party elite cadres to intermediate between partisan support groups in the electorate and the party-in-office. (Baer and Bositis 1988: 85)

Women's groups including the bipartisan National Women's Political Caucus and women's PACs such as the Women's Campaign Fund, EMILY's List, and WISH List have recruited, trained, and funded women candidates, helping to elect record numbers of women. These organizations formed, in part, as a response to the perceived failure of the parties to promote women's candidacies (Hartmann 1989; Burrell 1993). The activities of women's groups and PACs may still be at odds with party goals in some cases (e.g., Franke-Ruta 2002). As Burrell (1994) acknowledges, women's groups helped to elect a record number of women to Congress in 1992 in a system without party control of nominations.

Meanwhile, in E. Cox's (1996: 12) view, "More than any other single factor, it is the closed nature of the political structure that has impeded the election of women to political office." Historically, a qualitative distinction has existed between the vote—"when women voted, no existing voters lost their voting rights" (11)—and public office: "Positions of influence were inherently scarce and existed in a 'closed' system of 'back room' politics of the political parties and their nominating conventions. In that environment, if a woman achieved elected office or other position of influence, that deprived a man of the position" (12). Indeed, the move to a direct primary at the turn of the twentieth century was intended to make candidate selection more democratic and more representative (Merriam 1922).

Evidence that parties may reduce women's opportunities for office comes from several sources. Strong party organizations are negatively related to the presence of women in the legislature (Nelson 1991; B. Werner 1993; Sanbonmatsu 2002c). In addition, women candidates have been slated as sacrificial lambs to run in difficult races (Carroll and Strimling 1983; Carroll 1994). Surveys have also gauged party support for women's candidacies (P. Freeman and Lyons 1992), with lack of party support cited as a problem for women candidates (Carroll 1994). In addition, the case of New Jersey is suggestive that stronger parties bear a negative relationship to women's representation: New Jersey, known for its powerful county parties, ranked forty-first out of the fifty states for women's representation (CAWP 2005c;

Fitzgerald 2003). Only four women serve as chairs of New Jersey's forty-two county party organizations (CAWP 2005c).

Women candidates' success rates may mean that the parties treat men and women candidates equally. But the gender disparity in who seeks office may mean that the parties do not treat men and women equally. The dearth of women candidates may represent the outcomes of party recruitment deliberations and therefore lack of party support for women candidates (Carroll 1994). Further consideration of the consequences of party activities for women is needed.

DO PARTIES MATTER?

Despite its status as the conventional wisdom, the idea that strengthening parties will increase women's representation has yet to be demonstrated. Before I turn to a more detailed discussion of how parties may be related to women's opportunities for office, it is important to consider the role of parties more generally and whether parties are relevant to understanding anyone's election—men's or women's. I focus on the perspective of ambition theorists. From this perspective, parties are not typically regarded as influential in the candidacy decision.

The crux of the issue is whether most candidates come forward to run on their own—essentially recruiting themselves—or whether other actors such as parties play a major role in recruitment. Maisel et al. summarize the different ways in which a candidate may decide to seek the nomination:

> At one extreme is the traditional group-based concept of candidate recruitment. In this case some external force, normally a political party, tries to influence a potential candidate to run for office. The party, or other external force, attempts to influence the potential candidate's decision-making. At the other extreme is candidate self-selection. In this case a potential candidate "emerges" on his or her own and then considers a run for office, assesses chances, and makes decisions independent of political party opinion or other external forces. In between are various "mixed" cases in which potential candidates might be encouraged to run or might "self-recruit," but in either case party and other external forces are part of the decisionmaking process. (1990: 153)

The ambitious politician's decision to seek office is arguably a function of the benefits of the office, the probability of winning, and the cost of running (G. Black 1972; Rohde 1979; Jacobson and Kernell 1983; Brace 1984;

Abramson, Aldrich, and Rohde 1987; Stone, Maisel, and Maestas 2004). In the theory outlined by Maisel et al. (1990), potential candidates decide to run based on the objective context, subjective context, perceived chances of winning, and personal costs. The authors argue that parties may try to influence the potential candidate's assessment of the subjective context— perhaps by discouraging others from contesting the nomination, promising help to the campaign, or suggesting that entering the race will further the candidate's future political career. In these ways, the party may try to shape the candidate's perceptions of winning. But the decision to run is believed to ultimately lie with the candidate, which makes the party's ability to influence that decision limited. Maisel et al. are skeptical that the party can play a significant role in the decision of potential candidates to seek office:

> No matter how hard party leaders try to increase their influence, their efforts, our model suggests, will meet with only limited success. A number of the factors important in candidates' determinations are simply beyond the control of political parties. (1990: 157)

However, as Maisel and his coauthors note, it is the role of party leaders to find candidates:

> We do not know precisely how to define the population of potential candidates for any office. To a large extent that is the job of party organization. But once those candidates have been defined—or, as is frequently the case in American elections, once they define themselves—party leaders can have an impact on their decision either to run or not to run only in certain ways. (156–57)

Thus, potential candidates weigh the costs and benefits of seeking office. To a large extent, this decision is a personal one. However, parties can shape who runs for office by seeking out and encouraging candidates to run who otherwise might not have considered running for office. A major limitation of ambition scholarship is its primary focus on the decision calculus of incumbent politicians rather than the initial decision to seek office (Fowler 1993). This limitation is particularly significant when we consider women's political careers; as I discuss later in the chapter, women's initial decision to run for office is more likely than men's to involve recruitment. In short, although ambition theory typically treats the ambitious office seeker as a given, party leaders may create ambitious politicians (see Fowler 1993; Aldrich 1995). In addition, parties can influence the perceived probability of winning by supporting candidates in the primary.

STRATEGIC PARTIES

Before turning to specific hypotheses about how parties may affect women's candidacies, I discuss party goals with respect to candidate recruitment and the role of parties in nominating candidates. I make a conceptual distinction between two types of party activities: recruitment and gatekeeping. By *recruitment,* I mean seeking out and encouraging candidates to run; by *gatekeeping,* I mean discouraging candidates from running or supporting one candidate in the primary.[7] Encouraging candidates to run does not necessarily imply discouraging other candidates from running or taking sides in a primary, though it may involve selecting among potential candidates. Distinguishing recruitment from gatekeeping can help to specify the mechanisms by which parties affect women's representation. Indeed, part of the reason for the mixed results of past studies of gender and parties is that scholars have examined different types of party activities.

When do party leaders seek to influence the recruitment and nomination of candidates? Following Downs (1957) and Schlesinger (1975), I view the party as a team of ambitious office seekers. The goal of the party is to capture office. Given this goal, party leaders have two main incentives to influence candidate selection. First, party leaders may recruit candidates because they need candidates to run on the party label. Seligman (1961: 77) explains: "The recruitment of political candidates is a basic function of political parties: a party that cannot attract and then nominate candidates surrenders its elemental opportunity for power."

Candidate recruitment is one component of party organizational strength, as theorized by Gibson et al. (1983). At the heart of their definition of party organizational strength is the idea that the party has an "enduring headquarters operation" (198) and that it pursues activities to further electoral goals. In addition, "strong parties require both organizational complexity and programmatic capacity" (198). One important aspect of these programmatic activities is candidate recruitment, which helps the party win office and "cultivates an important clientele for the party organization" (203).

The minority party may be more likely to be short of candidates than the majority party because a seat in the majority may be more desirable, on average, than a seat in the minority party (Nelson 1991; G. Cox and Hartog 2001). Because the attractiveness of the legislative institution may also

---

7. Kazee (1994: 167) terms discouraging candidates from running "derecruitment."

shape the supply of candidates, there may be a greater need for recruitment in less professional legislative settings. In addition, in areas of a state where the party has few supporters or a weak organization, there may not be a candidate unless the party recruits one (Jewell and Morehouse 2001; Moncrief, Squire, and Jewell 2001). Thus, the party may need to seek out and encourage candidates to run due to a dearth of candidates.

Second, because party leaders want to win a majority of seats, they have incentives to recruit, train, and nominate the best candidates (Riker 1982; Aldrich 1995). In competitive races, for example, the party wants the strongest candidate possible (e.g., Herrnson 1988; Maisel et al. 1990; Jewell and Morehouse 2001; Moncrief, Squire, and Jewell 2001). The party may choose among candidates by taking sides in the primary. Or the party can help a chosen candidate avoid a primary by discouraging other potential candidates from entering the race. I consider these types of activities to be evidence of gatekeeping by the party. The power to choose the party's candidates arguably lies at the heart of the concept of party strength (Ware 1988).

Moreover, as Aldrich argues, the party may need to regulate ambition in the best interests of the party:

> For elective office seekers, regulating conflict over who holds those offices is clearly of major concern. It is ever present. And it is not just a problem of access to government offices but is also a problem internal to each party as soon as the party becomes an important gateway to office. (1995: 22)

> Ambition theory is about winning per se. The breakdown of orderly access to office risks unfettered and unregulated competition. The inability of a party to develop effective means of nomination and support for election therefore directly influences the chances of victory for the candidates and thus for their parties. (24)

Promoting the interests of the party as a whole may entail choosing among ambitious office seekers. C. Cotter et al. (1984: 7) explain, "The capacity of the party to function in a competitive electoral system is conditioned to a significant degree on the range and quality of candidates running under the party label." In its efforts to win a majority, the party does not want just any candidate to run on the party label; instead, the party wants the strongest candidates.

Thus, party leaders have a greater incentive to influence the nomination when there is more competition between the two parties. Picking and choosing among candidates presumes a sufficient supply of candidates. Where gatekeeping by the parties is very high, I assume the supply of candidates allows party leaders to be selective. Recruitment may imply gatekeeping if candidates only seek the nomination if they receive the nod from party leaders. In that case, recruitment means handpicking candidates, and the parties likely would seek to discourage any primary competitors. Elsewhere—in less professionalized legislatures, for example—recruitment may be necessary because there is insufficient interest in running for the legislature; absent party leader efforts to persuade potential candidates to run, the party might not contest state legislative elections. Party recruitment of candidates does not always imply gatekeeping, however; party leaders may encourage a candidate to run without promising support in the primary and without discouraging others from running. Therefore, the party may recruit candidates but refrain from acting as a gatekeeper.

These candidate recruitment activities are not unlike party efforts to mobilize the mass public to participate in politics (Rosenstone and Hansen 1993). Political parties recruit citizen participants as a strategy to win elections. Citizen participation may be spontaneous, not requiring recruitment. But most citizens report being asked to participate in politics, requests that help explain participation (Verba, Schlozman, and Brady 1995). Indeed, recruitment is quite common for more familiar forms of political participation such as voting and working in political organizations (Verba, Schlozman, and Brady 1995). The political parties mobilize voters selectively, recruiting people they know and those who are likely to participate. As Rosenstone and Hansen (1993: 7) explain, these recruitment patterns are consequential: "Thus, in deciding who to mobilize, political leaders help to determine which people participate. . . . Their strategic choices determine the shape of political participation in America." Likewise, in its pursuit of its goal of winning office by recruiting candidates, the party is shaping the composition of political institutions.

CANDIDATE GENDER

Why should party involvement in the recruitment and nomination of candidates have implications for the gender composition of legislatures? My hypotheses about how party activities affect women's representation are based on the historical fact of women's underrepresentation in politics and women's continued underrepresentation as both candidates and officeholders. I posit that the primary reason that candidate gender remains a significant factor in American politics today is that women were historically prevented from seeking office.

The modifier *woman* before the word *politician* indicates that women remain an atypical group of politicians (Dolan 2004). For example, in only ten states have women ever constituted at least one-third of the legislature; in only half of the American states have women ever constituted one-quarter of the legislature.[8] In some states, such as Colorado, where the first women state legislators took their seats in 1895, casting ballots for women candidates is not unusual. In other states, such as Alabama, voters and women themselves are much less familiar with seeing women state legislative candidates. Meanwhile, the presence of women in higher office is even less common than the presence of women state legislators. In all of U.S. history, only twenty-eight women have ever held the office of governor (CAWP 2005a). Only 2 percent of all members of the U.S. Congress since 1789 have been women.[9] Thus, gender continues to serve as a marker for whether a candidate or politician is typical.

Recruitment

Women's status as a historically underrepresented group with respect to candidacy leads to two hypotheses about how party activities will impact women as a group. First, I hypothesize that party efforts to encourage candidates to run will be positively related to women's representation, other factors being equal. Precisely because women have traditionally been less likely to run for office than men, candidate recruitment by the party may lead more women to think of themselves as candidates. When parties seek out and encourage candidates, individuals who have never considered becoming candidates may be asked to run. Although ambition theories commonly take the existence of ambitious politicians as given, the party's recruitment of candidates can create ambitious politicians. In this hypothesis, I assume that the parties recruit candidates without respect to gender. However, this activity has important implications for women in particular.

Scholars of women and politics have long observed that women candidates

---

8. Data are from CAWP Fact Sheets, various years.
9. This statistic is from <http://www.cawp.rutgers.edu/Facts2.html>.

commonly run because of issues, often coming to electoral politics indirectly through some other political involvement (Diamond 1977). In a recent study of state legislators, men were much more likely than women to report that they had always wanted to run for office (Thomas, Herrick, and Braunstein 2002). Women were much more likely than men to report that they became interested in political careers as a result of community involvement or an issue. Women were also likely to report first aspiring to office at an older age than men (Thomas, Herrick, and Braunstein 2002).[10] Indeed, studies commonly find that women candidates and officeholders are older than men (Johnson and Carroll 1978; Carroll and Strimling 1983; Thomas 1994; Squire and Moncrief 1999; CAWP 2001c). This gender gap in age may result partially from women's caregiving responsibilities. However, it may also result from gender differences in planning political careers and the indirect path that women usually take to elective office.

The underrepresentation of women in office has implications for how potential candidates view their chances of winning. Women's decision calculus about running for office may differ somewhat from men's because women may be more worried about their chances for success.[11] For example, women potential candidates in a national study were less likely than men potential candidates to think they would win (Fox and Lawless 2004). Women were also much less likely to have considered running for office than men. This gender difference may result partially from women's beliefs about gender stereotypes and discrimination. Indeed, in designing their electoral strategies, women in politics frequently anticipate and proactively address the stereotypes that voters, the media, and other political actors hold about women candidates (Kahn 1996; Fox 1997). As Squire and Moncrief suggest, women may need more encouragement because of such concerns:

> The reason for this is open to speculation, but one plausible interpretation is that many women still perceive the electoral arena as inhospitable to their gender. If this is the case, then it makes sense that they would re-

10. Moncrief, Squire, and Jewell (2001) found that men candidates were more likely than women to have planned their candidacy at least a year before the primary. On gender differences, see also Constantini and Craik 1977; Bledsoe and Herring 1990.

11. Fulton (2003), for example, found that the probability of winning had a greater effect on the decision to seek a congressional seat for women state legislators than for men state legislators.

quire more encouragement (or at least encouragement from more sources) before they are willing to cross the threshold of candidacy (i.e. the point at which they make the decision to run). (1999: 16)

In addition, studies reveal that women officeholders are more likely than men to have been recruited (McLean 1994). Moncrief, Squire, and Jewell (2001), for example, found gender differences in how nonincumbent candidates arrived at their decision to run for the state legislature. Men were more likely than women to report that running for office was entirely their idea, and men were less likely than women to report having received encouragement to run from state party officials, local elected officials, and legislative leaders. Women were more likely than men to report encouragement from other sources as well. Moncrief, Squire, and Jewell argue,

> Currently, women do not usually face the larger obstacles to candidacy that existed a generation ago when party organizations seemed to give them little support. But they are more likely to need encouragement from party leaders or others to run for office. Therefore, much of the burden for recruiting women legislative candidates rests on the party leadership and on groups that are trying to increase the proportion of women in public office. (2001: 118–19)

In sum, the historic underrepresentation of women and continued dearth of women candidates suggests that more party involvement in recruitment will be positively related to women's representation. Women appear to need more encouragement to enter what has traditionally been a male-dominated domain. Moreover, that women remain atypical politicians and are less likely to plan political careers suggests that the self-recruited individual at the heart of ambition models may not characterize the experiences of most women in politics. The activities of political institutions such as parties may be particularly important to explaining women's representation.

Gatekeeping

The second hypothesis I will examine is that gatekeeping activity is negatively related to women's representation. When party leaders take sides in a primary or seek to avoid a primary, I hypothesize that party leaders will prefer a male candidate over a female candidate, all else equal. Precisely because women have historically been underrepresented as candidates, party leaders should be more uncertain about the electability of women and should therefore prefer male candidates. When the party acts as a gatekeeper, I assume that the party has a sufficient supply of candidates: more gatekeeping implies that the party can have higher standards about candidacy. All else equal, I expect that strategic parties will choose a male candidate over a female candidate in competitive races.

This hypothesis borrows from Diamond's (1977) theory about gender and legislative professionalism. In an area with high political competition for office—more likely in professional than nonprofessional legislatures—Diamond argues that recruiters can be selective: "In this high-demand—and typically professional—situation, the political recruiter can select prospective candidates by eliminating those contestants who do not meet a set of specific criteria: sex, occupational background, and political experience become relevant" (5). The situation of low demand differs:

> The noncompetitive situation is likely to be the nonprofessional situation. When the demand for the product is low, the seller cannot be choosy about prospective buyers. The political recruiter in a low-demand situation cannot ask that potential candidates possess specific qualifications; the politically inexperienced—even women—become acceptable. (4)

Diamond's theory suggests that party leaders will be less likely to turn to women candidates when they can pick and choose among potential candidates.

If party leaders believe that women are an electoral risk, the leaders are unlikely to select a woman candidate for a single-member district, where there is only one party nominee. Norris explains that party list systems can facilitate women's representation precisely because multiple nominees are chosen:

> In single member constituencies local parties pick one standard bearer. Therefore selection committees may hesitate to choose a woman candidate, if women are considered an electoral risk. In contrast, there is a different "logic of choice" under proportional systems where voters are presented with a list of candidates for each party. Here parties have a rational incentive to present a "balanced ticket." With a list of names it is unlikely that any votes will be lost by the presence of women candidates on the list. And their absence may cause offence, by advertising party prejudice, thereby narrowing the party's appeal. (1993: 314–15)

As Norris explains, "Where competition for seats is strong, 'out-groups' face more difficulties challenging the status quo" (315). If there is an adequate supply of candidates and competition between the two parties is high, a woman candidate may not be the party's first choice.

Because the party can encourage more than one candidate to enter a primary, I do not expect that uncertainty about women's electability will preclude the parties from recruiting women candidates. But uncertainty about women's election should typically preclude the selection of a woman party nominee precisely because choosing the party nominee is a zero-sum game. The primary goal of the party is to win office. Given this goal, if the party has its choice of candidates and can only nominate one, the candidate with the group membership associated with greater electoral risk is less likely to be selected. Because of the relative newness of women candidates, party leaders should perceive the average woman candidate to be a greater electoral risk than the average male candidate.

Thus, I expect that gatekeeping will have a negative impact on the presence of women candidates and legislators. Where party leaders seek to influence the nomination and restrict candidate entry, a woman is less likely to be the candidate of choice than a man. Thus, while scholars have theorized that both recruitment and gatekeeping are aspects of party organizational strength, I propose that these two activities will have different implications for women's candidacies.

CONCLUSION

The underrepresentation of women in public office is a problem of the scarcity of women candidates rather than a lack of public support for women candidates. Women do not lose disproportionately when they run. On the contrary, women tend to win when they run. Incumbency makes it more difficult for women to win office in large numbers because most incumbent politicians are men. Moreover, men have been more likely to be in the occupations that usually lead to candidacy. Thus, as women's role in society continues to evolve, so too should women's role in politics.

These existing accounts of women's underrepresentation leave many questions unanswered. Why are women still less likely to seek office than men? Why have women failed to take advantage of the opportunities created by term limits? Past accounts provide only partial answers to these questions. And while it is commonly asserted that strengthening the political parties will increase women's opportunities for office, these expectations have rarely been tested empirically. Moreover, we have almost no knowledge of gender dynamics at the early stages of candidacy.

How parties affect women's representation merits sustained investigation.

To this end, I have argued for a conceptual distinction between recruitment and gatekeeping activities. I hypothesize that recruitment will benefit women: as a group that has been underrepresented and excluded from politics, women arguably stand to benefit when parties recruit candidates. Yet because women are relatively new office seekers, I expect that party efforts to influence the nomination will have a negative impact on women's representation. Precisely because women have been so much less likely than men to seek office, party leaders should have more doubts about women's electability when other factors are equal. I test these two hypotheses about how party activities affect women's representation in subsequent chapters. But first, I analyze party activities and consider the debate regarding party strength.

CHAPTER 3

The Recruitment and Nomination Practices of the Political Parties

Nominating candidates is arguably the key function of party organizations (e.g., Schattschneider 1942). Yet the direct primary has taken away the party's ability to nominate candidates. Ambitious office seekers no longer have to rely on the party to win. Since the party no longer has "an effective monopoly over the campaign," it cannot command the loyalty of candidates (Aldrich 1995: 274). The party organization can help candidates with polling, access to media and advertising, and funds (Herrnson 1988; Aldrich 1995). But today's candidates have their own organizations. Therefore, "very few state and local party organizations have the political power or resources to control nominations" (Jewell and Morehouse 2001: 56).

However, because state legislative office is often an entry-level political position, parties may be particularly important to understanding how individuals decide to run. Indeed, a recent survey of nonincumbent state legislative candidates found that only 32 percent were pure self-starters who reached the decision to run entirely on their own (Moncrief, Squire, and Jewell 2001: 39).[1] Thus, candidacy in the United States does not appear to

---

1. Moncrief, Squire, and Jewell (2001: 39) divide candidates into three categories according to how they decided to run for office: self-starters who decided to run completely on their own, persuaded candidates who had not seriously thought about running until someone suggested they run, and encouraged candidates who had already thought about running when someone encouraged them to run. Almost half of all candidates in their study reported that they had been approached by local party officials and encouraged to run. About one-third of all candidates reported being approached by local elected officials, one-third by state legislative leaders, and one-third by the state party.

be solely a matter of self-nomination. Many scholars dispute the notion that party organizations lack influence in candidate selection, arguing that both state and local party organizations have increased in strength (e.g., Gibson et al. 1983; Herrnson 1988; Gibson, Frendreis, and Vertz 1989; Frendreis, Gibson, and Vertz 1990; Frendreis and Gitelson 1999; Aldrich 2000; Buchler and LaRaja 2002; Francia et al. 2003).

This chapter investigates the political parties' organizational strength. Before assessing how parties may affect women's candidacies, I need to first understand whether parties affect candidacy at all. I draw on personal interviews from six states and mail surveys of party leaders from all fifty states to examine party activities in state legislative elections. To what extent do the parties recruit candidates? Do party leaders support candidates in the primary? The measures of party activities that I establish in this chapter will be used in subsequent chapters to determine how parties affect women's representation.

I argue that parties play a large role in shaping who runs for the legislature. Most state and legislative party leaders recruit candidates. Indeed, in some states, recruitment is thought to explain why many candidates decide to seek a state legislative seat. In most cases, party leaders are not looking for just anyone to run on the party label; they want the best person. Even if a declared candidate has entered the race, party leaders will continue to recruit until they believe they have the strongest candidate. Where the party is committed to a neutral stance in the primary, early intervention and discouragement of candidacies is that much more urgent.

In short, the party nominee is often too important to leave to chance. Formally endorsing a candidate or taking sides in the primary is less common than recruiting candidates, but some parties do engage in these gatekeeping activities. The evidence in this chapter suggests that parties are much more active in recruiting and nominating candidates than is commonly acknowledged.

I begin the chapter by describing the cases and the methodology used in the interviews. I then present detailed case studies of six states, including details of how and why the parties recruit candidates. I supplement the interviews with a survey of Ohio state legislative candidates. Finally, I turn to the legislative and state party mail surveys to look across the nation at party activities. I also examine the determinants of cross-state variation in party activities.

TABLE 3.1.   Case Study Summary, 2001

Legislative Professionalism	Both Chambers Democratic	Split Control of Legislature	Both Chambers Republican
High	Massachusetts		Ohio
Medium	North Carolina	Colorado	Iowa
Low	Alabama		

CASE STUDIES

Case Selection

I use case studies of six states to analyze whether—and, if so, how—party-recruitment practices shape women's opportunities to become candidates for the legislature. I conducted semistructured personal interviews with state legislators and state and legislative party officials as well as other political actors. The interviews concern party activities in state legislative elections and the status of women as candidates for the legislature. I also conducted background research and analyzed state legislative election results for all of the cases.

I chose a set of states that would capture a diverse range of party-recruitment practices. These states—Alabama, Colorado, Iowa, Massachusetts, North Carolina, and Ohio—were selected to maximize variation in party competition and legislative professionalism (see table 3.1).[2] Competition and the desirability of the office should explain the extent to which party leaders recruit candidates and seek to influence the nomination. More

2. In addition to these six states, I interviewed seventeen women state legislators from California, Georgia, Maine, New Hampshire, and Washington at the CAWP 2001 Forum for Women State Legislators. I chose these states to complement the six case-study states in terms of professionalism and party competition. California is arguably the most professionalized legislature in the country, with the highest annual salary. California legislators earned $99,000 in 2001, compared to $32,000 in Washington, $16,000 in Georgia, and $10,800 in Maine (Council of State Governments 2002). New Hampshire is the least professionalized: legislators there earn just $100 per session. Georgia and Maine's legislatures are regarded as citizen, while Washington is considered hybrid (Hamm and Moncrief 1999). In 2001, Democrats controlled both legislative chambers in California, Georgia, and Maine, while Republicans controlled the legislature in New Hampshire. Washington Democrats controlled the state Senate, but the two parties held the same number of seats in the House and therefore shared control. I discuss these interviews in chapter 7. Because I interviewed only one New Hampshire legislator and two Georgia legislators, I have limited information about those states.

TABLE 3.2.   Partisan Composition and Legislative Professionalism, 2001

	AL	CO	IA	MA	NC	OH
Democratic share of House seats (%)	64	43	44	86	52	40
Democratic share of Senate seats (%)	69	51	40	84	70	34
Total House seats	105	65	100	160	120	99
Total Senate seats	35	35	50	40	50	33
Base salary	$10/day	$30,000/ year	$20,758/ year	$50,123/ year	$13,951/ year	$51,674/ year
Term limits	No	Yes	No	No	No	Yes
Year term limits took effect	—	1998	—	—	—	2000

Source: Council of State Governments 2002. Term limits information is from the National Conference of State Legislatures (<www.ncsl.org>).

competition should spur more organization, and vice versa (Key 1949; C. Cotter et al. 1984; Aldrich 2000). Because the cases represent different combinations of partisan composition and professionalism, they should capture a wide spectrum of candidate recruitment practices.

Of the six states, the two parties are least competitive in state legislative races in Massachusetts (see table 3.2, figure 3.1). The Republican party has comfortable margins in both legislative chambers in Ohio, while the same is true of the Democratic party in Alabama. The remaining states see more competition between the two parties. In addition to party competition, the states represent a range of types of legislative institutions.[3] I classify Alabama as a citizen legislature because of its low base salary, though legislators there receive additional compensation to cover expenses.[4] Alabama also has

3. Kurtz (1992) distinguishes among three types of legislatures: full-time legislatures with large staff and high pay, part-time legislatures with low pay and small staff, and hybrid legislatures that lie in between.

4. Ohio legislators do not receive a per diem. Massachusetts legislators can be reimbursed between $10 and $100 per day depending on how far they live from the capitol. Legislators in the other four states receive unvouchered compensation. Alabama legislators receive an additional $2,280 per month plus $50 per day, three days a week during the session; they are also compensated during the interim and for attending meetings. Legislators in Iowa receive an additional $86 per day, which also applies to the interim. Colorado legislators receive a per diem and between $45 and $99 per day depending on whether they live in the Denver area. North Carolina legislators receive $104 per day. Data are from <http://www.ncsl.org/programs/legman/01table1.htm>. Martin (1994) estimated that legislators in Alabama earned about $30,000 per year.

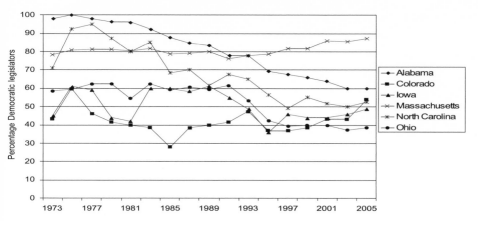

Fig. 3.1.   Democratic share of house seats, 1973–2005.
(Data from Council of State Governments, various years; and
National Conference of State Legislatures, various years)

shorter sessions than the other states: by law, the Alabama Legislature can only meet for 30 days over 105 calendar days.[5] In contrast, the legislatures in Massachusetts and Ohio meet virtually year-round and are considered among the country's most professionalized state legislatures. North Carolina, Iowa, and Colorado are usually categorized as hybrid legislatures, though Kurtz (1992) classified North Carolina as a citizen legislature. Of these three states, North Carolina usually has the longest session length. The Iowa Legislature typically meets from January through late April. Both Colorado and Ohio have term limits. Of the six states, Massachusetts has the lowest rate of turnover.[6]

Interview Methodology

I used the same methodology to select interview subjects in each state. I primarily sought interviews with two sets of individuals I expected would be most knowledgeable about candidate recruitment for state legislative

5. In the first year of the quadrennium (four-year period), the session begins in early March, whereas the session begins in early February in the second and third years and early January in the fourth year. Both House and Senate members serve four-year terms in Alabama.

6. Turnover in the 2002 House elections was as follows: 25 percent in Alabama, 28 percent in Colorado, 39 percent in Iowa, 13 percent in Massachusetts, 30 percent in North Carolina, and 21 percent in Ohio (<http://www.ncsl.org/programs/legman/Elect/02Turnover.htm>).

races: party leaders and staff and state legislators. In each state, I interviewed state legislative leaders and the Democratic and Republican state party chairs and executive directors. With only a few exceptions, I interviewed at least one legislative leader or staff person in the leadership team of each party of both chambers in all six states. I also interviewed men and women currently serving in the legislature or who had previously run for or served in the legislature about their personal decision to run and their experiences as candidates. In addition to the legislators and state party officials, I interviewed members of women's groups as well as other elected officials, local party officials, political activists, consultants, lobbyists, and reporters.

In selecting state legislators, I sought a diverse sample in terms of party, chamber, ideology, tenure, geography, and the competitiveness of the district. I also consciously selected at least some legislators in each state whose biographies indicated significant activity in the party structure. In each state, my sample included individuals newly elected to the legislature as well as at least some individuals whose knowledge of the legislature extended back several decades. I disproportionately interviewed women legislators because of my focus on understanding women's candidacies. But I also interviewed at least one male legislator from both parties in each state; in almost every case, I interviewed at least one male legislator from both parties in both chambers.

In all, I conducted a total of 227 semistructured interviews in the six case-study states.[7] Almost all of the interviews were conducted in person and most were tape-recorded. Most of the interviews lasted between half an hour and one hour, though interviews with party leaders and members of women's groups usually lasted at least an hour. Most of the interviews were conducted on the record. In other cases, I promised interview subjects a degree of anonymity (e.g., remarks are attributed to "a legislator" or "a Republican"), and in some cases the interview was conducted completely off the

---

7. The dates of my fieldwork were as follows: Denver, Colorado, 3–12 April 2001; Raleigh, North Carolina, 25 April–3 May 2001; Columbus, Ohio, 29 May–27 August 2001; Boston, Massachusetts, 5–9 November 2001; Des Moines, Iowa, 25–29 March 2002; and Montgomery, Alabama, 9–12 April 2002. Most of the Ohio interviews were conducted in June 2001. Most of the telephone interviews took place with respondents I was not able to meet with during my fieldwork and took place shortly after my visit to the state. Eighteen interviews were conducted by telephone. Two of the Iowa interviews and one of the Massachusetts interviews took place at the CAWP 2001 Forum for Women State Legislators in Dana Point, California.

TABLE 3.3.   Interview Subjects: Characteristics

	AL	CO	IA	MA	NC	OH	Row total
Total Interviews	26	41	30	30	49	51	227
Party							
Democrats	16	26	13	16	29	23	123
Republicans	7	14	14	8	20	27	90
Gender							
Men	13	13	9	8	14	19	76
Women	13	28	21	22	35	32	151
Interview Type							
State Party	4	5	4	4	6	4	27
Legislators	17	31	21	19	31	33	152
Legislative staff	0	0	3	1	5	4	13
Women's groups	0	2	2	6	3	5	18
Other	5	3	1	0	4	5	18

Note: Categories include current and former state party officials, legislators, and staff. Legislative staff includes caucus or personal legislative staff, campaign committee staff, and consultants hired to work for the legislative campaign committee. The "Other" category includes other elected officials, party officials, candidates, consultants, lobbyists, and reporters. One state party chair was also serving in the legislature.

record.[8] Table 3.3. presents the distribution of interview subjects by party, gender, and type (e.g., legislator, state party, and so forth) for each state.[9]

Table 3.4 provides more detailed information about the background characteristics of the subset of respondents who are state legislators. Collectively, the interviews in each state represent a diverse range of ideological perspectives and paths taken to the legislature.

When I analyze the interview data, I characterize the presence or absence of particular beliefs or points of view in each state and party. I also characterize views as more or less absent—held by "most," "some," or "a few" of my interview subjects. I do not seek to quantify the interview data beyond that, given that the interviews were semistructured. Because the interviews varied in length, I was able to ask some respondents more questions and probe further than in other instances. In addition, although my interview subjects reflect the diversity of each legislature, they do not constitute a representative, random sample.

Parties and candidate recruitment are not the only state characteristics

8. In some cases, I agreed to delay use of the interview material until after the 2002 elections.

9. More details about the methodology and a complete list of interview subjects appear in the appendix.

TABLE 3.4.   Interview Subjects: Legislator Characteristics

	AL	CO	IA	MA	NC	OH	Row total
Leaders	4	12	11	5	10	8	50
Chamber							
House	11	19	14	15	21	25	105
Senate	6	12	7	4	10	8	47
Party							
Democrats	12	20	10	13	16	13	84
Republicans	5	11	11	6	15	20	68
Gender							
Men	7	9	6	5	10	11	48
Women	10	22	15	14	21	22	104

Note: Table includes both current and former legislators.

that might affect women's opportunities for the legislature in these states. As I discuss in later chapters, scholars have found that women's representation is shaped by factors such as public opinion and the presence of women in the labor force. Therefore, I detail additional features of these states in chapter 4.

CASE STUDIES: DO PARTIES MATTER?

How involved are the Democratic and Republican parties in recruitment? What do the parties look for in candidates? In this section, I draw on the 90 interviews I conducted with current or former state or legislative party leaders or staff, which represent about 40 percent of the 227 total interviews in the case-study states. For both parties in these six states, I begin the analysis with an examination of how actively the parties recruit for the legislature in each state. I then turn to beliefs about the relevant pool of state legislative candidates. What are the informal requirements for state legislative office in each state? Because recruitment does not necessarily involve attempts to influence the nomination, I consider the party's involvement at the primary stage. Do party leaders remain neutral in the primary? Or do they take sides? For each state, I also consider the role of interest groups and the local parties. Later in the chapter, I discuss why some parties are more active than others in recruiting and nominating candidates.

I find that the parties' candidate recruitment activities vary significantly across states and the two parties and sometimes across the two chambers. In some cases, the party generally does not concern itself with recruitment.

Respondents in Massachusetts and Alabama, for example, believe that most candidates come forward on their own. Elsewhere, however, party leaders are very engaged in recruitment and consider those efforts quite consequential. Indeed, interview subjects credited candidate recruitment with specific instances of winning the majority in Iowa, North Carolina, Ohio, and Colorado.

The legislative caucus typically has more responsibility for recruitment than the state party does. Long before the election, legislative campaign committee staff or consultants help the party recruit candidates in Ohio, North Carolina, and Iowa. Most of these activities focus on winnable or potentially winnable seats: party leaders generally do not waste time or resources fielding candidates for hopeless races. In some instances, recruitment by the party is thought to explain why a large share of candidates become candidates. Recruiting candidates does not necessarily mean that the party takes sides in the primary, however; indeed, the party may actively recruit precisely because its hands are tied at the primary stage. In sum, whereas scholars of women and politics have argued that the major political parties are currently weak and should be strengthened, my interview data support the view that the parties already play a significant role in candidate recruitment.

North Carolina and Iowa

Individuals run for the legislature for a wide range of reasons. For some people, running for office is a lifelong ambition; the only uncertainty is what office and when. For example, North Carolina Representative Andrew Dedmon first became a candidate when he decided to challenge his state representative. Prior to running for the legislature, Dedmon had been active in the Young Democrats and had planned to run for local office. But he ran for the legislature instead:

> I got into politics because I got mad. I really got mad at a lack of what I perceived to be representation of just regular people. That if you weren't somebody of some influence within the counties that made up my district, you really had no access to your representative. They would say, "Yes, we'll check into it," and that would be the end of it. So that's why I decided to run.

Thus, Dedmon was not recruited. He reached his decision to seek a seat in the legislature on his own. The party did not encourage him to run. Instead, the party mildly discouraged him because the incumbent was a member of his party: "In fact, there was an emissary sent by the party structure to try to dissuade me from running."

However, other state legislators lacked plans to run for office. By recruiting candidates, the party can create ambitious politicians. These recruits may have never even considered running prior to being asked by the party. For example, when asked how she first decided to seek her seat, North Carolina Representative Jean Preston responded, "Well, it was not anything I had ever thought about doing." In its search for candidates, the party may persuade individuals to run who would not otherwise have become candidates. This is especially true of recruitment for the state legislature, where most candidates have no prior officeholding experience.

In Iowa, recruiting candidates typically means identifying and interviewing potential candidates up to two years before the election. Party leaders and their staff contact local elected officials and party activists to see if they are interested in running or know of a good candidate. They sort through names, see what names surface repeatedly, and travel around the state to interview potential candidates. After learning more about the candidates, party officials work to persuade their preferred candidates to run. Assistant House majority leader Bill Dix, the chair of the legislative campaign committee for the House Republicans, explained the process:

> There are a number of different approaches you take, and it varies some from district to district, but generally the policy would be to seek out organizations that can help you identify names that are friendly to your concerns in those areas. We try to find candidates who have been active in their communities, candidates that have taken an interest in public policy—when possible, candidates who have a built-in positive name identification. Things of those nature are factors in determining who we really pursue.

If a candidate surfaces on his or her own, the leadership will make inquiries to see if the person is believed to be a good candidate. And if that person does not seem to be the best candidate, the search continues. The party wants the best horse in competitive races, Republican Chair Chuck Larson Jr. explained; if a candidate who has already entered a primary does not appear to be the horse that can win, they will recruit another candidate.

In sum, recruitment is "extremely important," according to Marlys Popma, executive director of the Republican Party. By Popma's estimates, a quarter to a half of all candidates appear on their own, another quarter are identified easily by making phone calls, and between 10 and 25 percent of candidates require a lot of work to identify. Indeed, only one or two candidates had contacted Andy Warren, the executive director of the Republican legislative campaign committee known as the Legislative Majority Fund, in the 2002 cycle, rather than the reverse. That left many candidates to find: Warren was looking for candidates in about fifty House seats and twenty Senate seats, including Senate seats where state representatives were recruited. Dix said that House Republicans had been looking for thirty-one candidates in targeted races. Fund staff members, the state party chair and executive director, and legislative leaders meet regularly about recruitment.[10]

At the same time, Democrats focused their efforts on trying to win a majority: Republicans controlled the House fifty-four to forty-six and the Senate twenty-nine to twenty-one in 2001. Assistant House minority leader Polly Bukta explained the importance of recruiting good candidates:

> If we're going to take the majority back, we need a slate of *very* good candidates, and we need a *lot* of candidates. We have to have a cushion. We need fifty-one. But you can't just say, "Well, we've got our fifty-one, we can get the majority." That would never work. I know I'm being simplistic when I'm saying that. But you have to have some padding. We figured we had to have sixty-five *really good* candidates to get the majority.

Like the Republicans, Democratic recruitment efforts focused on a large number of seats: House Democrats were looking for candidates in sixty seats, fifteen of which were targeted. Each caucus in the Democratic Party has a staff person to help legislative leaders recruit candidates.[11] Senate minority leader Mike Gronstal estimated that the leadership recruits about 75 percent of Senate candidates, excluding House members who decide to run for

---

10. Republican leaders from both chambers have worked together to recruit candidates in Iowa since 1996. Republicans had taken control of the House in 1992, and four years later, the party's House leaders helped their Senate counterparts win a majority.

11. In the House, the minority leader works with two assistant minority leaders to recruit candidates; in the Senate, the minority leader works with a caucus member who serves as the recruitment chair. In addition, in 2001 the Iowa Democratic party for the first time held meetings across the state to bring together the state party, legislative leaders, and local parties to brainstorm about potential candidates. These meetings were designed to build the local party structure and to involve the state party in recruiting candidates more than in past years. However, responsibility for candidate recruitment lies mainly with the caucus leadership; the Republican state party is more involved in recruitment than is the Democratic state party.

the Senate. Not only are the two parties competitive in the Iowa legislature as a whole, but the districts are competitive as well because of the state's nonpartisan redistricting process.[12] In addition, turnover is higher in Iowa than in the other case-study states, which creates more open seats.

Increased competition between the two parties has also spurred more concerted recruitment efforts in North Carolina. As in the rest of the South, both parties' organizations have grown in North Carolina as the Republican party has become more competitive (Fleer 1994; Prysby 1997). In 1970, Republicans held just 20 percent of House seats and 14 percent of Senate seats (Roederer 1999; Betts and Beyle 2000). Yet in 1994, the Republican Party won control of the House for the first time in the twentieth century, picking up twenty-six seats (Whitman 1996). The Democrats would regain the House in 1998; in 2001, they held a narrow majority (sixty-two to fifty-eight).

Recruitment is an increasingly organized party activity, particularly for the more competitive House chamber. Democratic legislative leaders are assisted by a full-time, year-round staff person—one for each chamber's campaign committee. The staff person for the House Democratic campaign committee, Wooten Johnson, works with the speaker and the majority leader to recruit candidates in a process Johnson likened to the National Football League draft. They rank potential candidates and seek to persuade their first choice to run but in some cases may have to settle for their fifth- or sixth-ranked choice. In past years, Johnson's position was filled only in election years; since 1999, however, it has been a permanent position.

The North Carolina Republican House caucus recruitment committee worked with the state party in 2000 to find candidates for thirty districts, with a focus on about thirteen seats (eight seats were needed to retake the House).

---

12. The states vary significantly in the number of state legislative seats contested by both major parties. In Jewell and Morehouse's (2001: 205–6) analysis of House races between 1984 and 1994, Ohio had the highest percentage of two-party contests (88 percent) and Alabama the lowest (36 percent). The other case-study states fell in between: Colorado, 75 percent; Iowa, 70 percent; North Carolina, 65 percent; and Massachusetts, 42 percent. Only about 30 percent of House seats were contested by the two parties in Massachusetts in 2002. Whether state legislative districts are competitive is a separate question. Jewell and Morehouse found that North Carolina had the most competitive races (41 percent) of the six case-study states in House races from 1984 to 1994. Jewell and Morehouse define competitive as a ratio of 60:40 or better in the general election. Their statistics on competitive races in the other states are as follows: Iowa, 39 percent; Colorado, 36 percent; Ohio, 21 percent; Massachusetts, 16 percent; Alabama, 15 percent.

During the 1980s, Republican legislative leaders first saw recruitment as a way to win the majority. Betsy Cochrane explained that she became involved in recruitment while serving as House minority leader (1985–89):

> My purpose was to try to grow the party. It seemed to me if we were going to become a viable, two-party state that our party *had* to get more involved in recruiting. . . .
>
> I realized to make us grow in the General Assembly in numbers, we were going to have to start helping people want to become a part of us, so they could see we can build towards a majority, and this is the difference we can make as a minority. And so, yes, I got involved in recruiting.

The state party subsequently has become active, and potential candidates are more interested in serving:

> We're not having to do the recruiting in the Republican party like we used to. There are more people coming forward now. But that's because we have elected Republicans and Republicans have become more visible in elected offices, and so people think about running for public office who happen to be Republican.

Republicans' prospects in the Senate are much more pessimistic than in the House: in 2001, Republicans held only fifteen of fifty seats. According to Joel Raupe, assistant to the Senate minority leader, candidate recruitment is quite difficult because the district lines significantly favor the Democratic party: "We're saddled with some difficulty in recruiting candidates because of the district lines being what they are. They're very difficult to win."

Thus, in both North Carolina and Iowa, the parties recruit a large number of candidates in their efforts to win—or maintain—the majority. By looking to local officeholders, interest groups, and other contacts for the strongest candidates, the parties essentially conduct reconnaissance before approaching potential candidates to run. Meanwhile, in safe, open seats, state and legislative party leaders typically expect a primary and do not recruit or seek to influence the nomination.

Massachusetts

One-party dominance has translated into weak party organizations in Massachusetts, and "Republican opposition has been erratic at best" (Mileur 1997: 148); indeed, only about 30 percent of House seats were contested by the two parties in 2002. Of the six states and two parties, the Massachusetts

Democratic party is the least actively involved in candidate recruitment. The state legislature is overwhelmingly Democratic and has been to varying degrees since 1958 (Mileur 1997). According to most Democrats, there is no shortage of Democratic state legislative candidates, meaning that recruitment need only occur on the Republican side. John Stefanini, chief counsel to the speaker, explained that because the Democratic primary is usually the main contest for a seat, the party typically stays out. Democratic Chair Philip Johnston would like to see the party more involved in recruitment and is interested in finding more women candidates and candidates of color. Interest groups, the speaker, and legislators may also occasionally identify candidates. For the most part, however, respondents argued that Democratic candidates come forward on their own.

Republican House leaders meet with candidates and work with the state party to try to recruit candidates. But the state has primary responsibility for recruitment and looks to its state committee to help identify candidates. The party faces formidable obstacles given the Democratic party's dominance and the lack of a strong, local Republican party structure or network of local elected officials. That Republicans hold fewer than 20 percent of seats in the legislature speaks to the party's weak position in the state.

Alabama

The Democratic party also controls both chambers of the Alabama legislature by strong margins. But unlike the Massachusetts case, the two major parties in Alabama have become much more competitive in recent years. Today, local Republican party organizations are stronger than Democratic organizations, and Republican party activists perceive a significant change in their party's strength (P. Cotter 1995). The chair of the Alabama Republican party travels extensively throughout the state to find candidates. The increase in competition means the Democratic party is now involved in recruitment as well, though to a lesser extent than the Republicans. In a marked departure from past years, the House Democratic caucus became actively involved in candidate recruitment in 2002.

Whereas the Democrats largely focused their recruitment efforts on about a dozen open seats, Marty Connors, the Republican chair, focused in 2002 on finding challengers to between sixteen and eighteen Democrats in seats that lean Republican in other races. Connors argued that in general, the best candidates usually need to be drafted because they do not realize they are the best candidates. Though a few Republican candidates were running in districts unfavorable to the party, Connors wastes little time on such districts: "If the fish aren't biting, I'm not spending my time hunting there."

Connors explained how he recruits candidates:

> Well, you've got county chairmen in every county, and then you've got various groups that are traditionally Republican-oriented groups: realtors, homebuilders, chamber of commerce groups—people like that, people who actually produce jobs. So what I'll do is I'll go to our local chairman and I'll say, "Who do you know that can run, who can win?" and I'll go to these various other groups and ask them if they can produce candidates.

Connors looks to see if someone from the local party is interested in running but often needs to look beyond the local party:

> The honest-to-goodness truth is that oftentimes the local party is not strong enough to field a candidate, or they don't necessarily have the deepest influence in a given community. So that's when we'll go to chamber of commerce types or realtors or, you know, other insurance people, and say, "Hey, within your network, is there somebody there?" Then I will go visit them and start the process.

It is apparently easier for the state parties than sitting legislators to recruit because of the high degree of cooperation between the two parties within the legislature. Indeed, the Democratic and Republican House caucuses had agreed not to field candidates against incumbents. This agreement did not preclude the state parties from doing so, however. Because most House members were running for reelection, Marsha Folsom, the executive director of the Alabama Democratic party, focused on targeted seats the party wanted to pull into the Democratic column as well as on keeping the open Democratic seats within the party.

The outgoing member can be an important source of suggestions for candidates because incumbents usually know who is interested in their seats. Indeed, Democratic House majority leader Ken Guin thought that about half of the party's candidates are identified through names provided by the outgoing member. Also, Demetrius Newton, speaker pro tempore of the House, said that many local political groups—including neighborhood groups and ministerial groups—recruit their own members to run. In sum, Alabama party leaders believe that most candidates come forward on their own, although both parties recently have begun to recruit actively.

Colorado

Preprimary endorsements are made through party conventions in Colorado. Candidates must win at least 30 percent of the delegate vote at the district assemblies to compete in the primary (Loevy 1997). Candidates who fail to win the requisite support from the party activists at the assemblies can go directly to the voters, petitioning to get onto the ballot. The use of nominating assemblies has not precluded party leaders from seeking to avoid primaries, however. Recruitment has been central to the Democratic party's efforts to overcome its minority status in the legislature, efforts that succeeded for one chamber in 2000, when the Democrats won a one-seat majority in the Senate. The party continued to trail in the House, twenty-seven to thirty-eight, and lost control of the Senate after the 2002 elections, when the Republicans took a one-seat majority. The Republican Party controlled both chambers of the Colorado General Assembly for almost the entire period from 1960 to 2000 (Loevy 1997; Straayer 2000).[13] In 2005, Democrats held both chambers by narrow margins.

Because it has typically been in the minority, the Democratic party has been more active in candidate recruitment. Both parties have legislative campaign funds but do not hire staff, leaving most of the work to the party chair and legislative leaders. As I discuss later in the chapter, Senate Democrats and the state party targeted ten races in 2000 and selected the candidates in each case. This concerted effort did not include the House, although House leaders recruited candidates for their chamber. The Republican party plays a smaller role in candidate recruitment, with more responsibility for recruitment in the state party than the legislative party.

Ohio

Republicans in Ohio hold all statewide offices and majorities in both legislative chambers (sixty-one to thirty-eight in the House and twenty-two to eleven in the Senate in 2005). They also have a dramatic fund-raising advantage. According to Michael Colley, chair of the Franklin County Republican Party, the rising cost of campaigns and the importance of fund-raising

13. Loevy (1997) observed that Colorado Republicans were better organized overall at the state level and that Democrats typically marshal their resources to support specific statewide offices, a strategy that appears successful. According to Loevy, both parties target roughly between twelve and fifteen of the approximately eighty state legislative seats up for election in a given year.

shifted the responsibility for candidate recruitment from the local parties to the caucuses.

Many interview subjects credited former speaker Jo Ann Davidson with formalizing the House candidate recruitment operation. In the early 1990s when she served as House minority leader, Davidson traveled the state to find candidates and field a candidate in every district. Immediately after an election, the Republican leaders would first look at districts where an incumbent would not be seeking reelection and narrow down a list of candidates, consulting with county chairs and looking at area officeholders. Competitive seats were the next priority, with a focus on how the party could win a seat that it had narrowly lost in the previous election. Finally, party leaders looked to groom candidates for the future in areas they were unlikely to win. They typically targeted between twelve and fifteen races in which the caucus might provide a campaign manager, a poll, and financial support. These efforts succeeded: Democrats lost control of the House in 1994 after holding the body for twenty years under Speaker Vernal G. Riffe Jr., the longest-serving speaker in Ohio history. Republicans have controlled the Senate since 1985 (Curtin 1996).

Republicans described recruitment as "getting the nod" or "being invited to be a candidate." For example, in describing gender differences in candidate recruitment, majority whip James Trakas likened recruitment to being tapped on the shoulder:

> The women candidates kind of recruit themselves, I've found, across the state. And male candidates are kind of part of the tap on the shoulder, "It's your turn," you know, "It's time to go to Columbus and represent us." I found that most women are self-starters. Most [county party] organizations are not as progressive as ours. They generally don't recruit female candidates.

Another respondent argued that essentially all Republican legislators are recruited; the endorsed candidate in the Republican primary was usually recruited by the legislative leadership.

Seeking out and encouraging a candidate to run may still be necessary to defeat a Democratic incumbent. In that case, majority floor leader Stephen Buehrer argued, the caucus will make a conscious effort to go out and identify a good candidate for the district: "Is it a businessperson we need, is it a professional person, you know, is it a union member? Who are we looking for? [Who has] a profile that could win this district? And in some of those cases, you certainly do go out and try to *find* someone."

House minority leader Jack Ford, a Democrat, typically targets five seats in each of three tiers: incumbents who need help with reelection; competitive seats; and long-shot seats. Recruitment begins the day after the election, looking for candidates with name recognition. To fit a particular district, he might seek out a farmer or a candidate of a particular religion or perhaps someone who was a high school sports athlete or local elected official. Though Ford works with the county chairs, they focus primarily on recruitment for county races. The Senate Democrats have an organized effort similar to that of the House, beginning eighteen months ahead of the election and focusing on targeted seats.

In sum, significant variation occurs across the six cases in party recruitment activities. It is not uncommon for Ohio candidates to get the "tap" by the party to become a candidate. By some accounts, all Republican candidates in the state are recruited. The parties' increasingly diligent efforts in places such as Iowa, North Carolina, and Colorado may likewise take the form of a draft: discussions of the relative merits of potential candidates occur beforehand, and the party tries to build consensus on one potential candidate. In Iowa and North Carolina, recruitment involves full-time staff assistance and travel to all parts of the state. Massachusetts and Alabama have had the least extensive recruitment efforts, though the state parties in Alabama are increasingly involved in this endeavor.

Many scholars argue that parties are relatively uninfluential in candidate selection. For example, Maisel et al. explain,

> A political party cannot force attractive, qualified candidates to run for office. Individuals, not parties, therefore control the first threshold in the sequence of activities that ultimately result in the presence or absence of strong competitive candidates. (1990: 155)

Parties cannot force candidates to run; nevertheless, many parties devote significant time and energy to finding the right candidates and persuading them to run. These recruitment efforts often constitute a central component of the party's electoral strategy.

The Pool

Party leaders in different states look for varying candidate qualifications. The diversity of occupational backgrounds among legislators from these six states reflects state differences in legislative professionalism. Not surprisingly,

the states with the highest percentage of self-identified "full-time legislators" are Massachusetts and Ohio, the two most professionalized bodies
(Hirsch 1996). Fifty-five percent of Massachusetts legislators and 47 percent
of Ohio legislators listed their occupation as full-time legislator (Hirsch
1996); in the other case-study states, only between 2.1 percent and 11 percent of legislators identified themselves as full time. Attorneys are also more
frequently found in these two states than in the other cases: 23 percent of
Massachusetts legislators and 21.2 percent of Ohio legislators are attorneys
(Hirsch 1996). Retirees are more common in the less professionalized states.
In North Carolina, 17.8 percent of legislators are retired, as are 10.7 percent
of Iowa legislators.

A 1995 survey of state legislators conducted by Carey, Niemi, and Powell
(2000) reveals that the percentage of legislators who previously held party
office is similar across the six states: between 20 and 35 percent of legislators report having done so. However, the likelihood that a legislator held local, statewide, or judicial elective office varies much more extensively across
the cases: about 50 percent of legislators held such offices in Massachusetts
and Ohio, the more professionalized states. In the other four states, only
20–35 percent of legislators had held such an office prior to serving in the
legislature. The pool of state legislative candidates is therefore much less
rigidly defined in those states. The nature of legislative service as well as the
path taken depends on the case.

Thus, in Massachusetts, local elective office is perceived as an important
credential, particularly among Democrats. The attractiveness of the office,
combined with the party's majority status, ensures more than sufficient interest in serving among potential Democratic candidates. This means that
qualifications are stiffer on the Democratic side than the Republican side.
The state Republican party typically looks to state committee members,
local elected officials, the local party, chambers of commerce, and the business community to help identify potential candidates. The party's first
choice is local elected officials, then appointed officials or former elected
officials; ultimately, however, the goal is to find candidates willing to run.
In the end, the party cannot be particular about which candidates are willing to stand for office as Republicans.

In contrast to states such as Massachusetts, legislative service in hybrid
legislatures such as Iowa and Colorado may seem less attractive and financially feasible for potential candidates. Iowa candidates often have been active in the party structure or have previously held office, and both local office

and the local party are natural places to look for candidates. But neither party views such experience as a requirement for the legislature. Leaders from both parties argued that local elected officials may not be the best candidates because they may have unpopular voting records. Assistant majority leader Dix guessed that about half of candidates were active with the party or held local office:

> I would guess—just off the top of my head, without looking—I would say it's about fifty-fifty. About half of our candidates will be either associated with activist groups, Republican local party activity, or elected officials, and then the balance—50 percent—would be newcomers, people who maybe have been involved and recognize the importance of having good people in policy-making positions that just get involved and engage themselves because somebody comes and asks them to.

Assistant House minority leader Bukta explained that people who have never been involved in political activity can be excellent legislators. Gronstal, the Democratic Senate minority leader, encouraged the activists and party infrastructure with which he consults to "think outside the box" to help him find good candidates who can provide a contrast with the Republican opponent.

Being a local elected official helps but is also not necessary in Alabama, particularly because the Republican party has become competitive in the state only in recent years. Connors, the party chair, looks for candidates with name identification, fund-raising ability, and a volunteer network. The Democratic party relies on its more extensive network of local parties, local elected officials, donors, and other leaders for names. Having local elective experience or being active in the party is not thought to be a necessary qualification.

Background in the party or local office is common but by no means universal in Colorado. Mike Melanson, Democratic party executive director, estimated that about half of candidates come from a background in the party or local elected office, while half lack active involvement. In some areas, the local party believes in "paying one's dues" before becoming a candidate. However, being the favorite within the local party does not guarantee success in the primary.

According to Democratic Speaker James Black of North Carolina, the party has had increasing difficulty finding candidates because of the time involved in serving and the rising cost of campaigns as well as negative press coverage of the legislature. Many legislative candidates come from local office, but Black is also interested in candidates who can raise funds, a view echoed by his Republican counterpart, the House minority leader.

As I discuss later in the chapter, Ohio candidates quite commonly come from previous officeholding experience. However, in the term-limits environment, Antoinette Wilson, a consultant to the House Democrats, argued that there is a need to find "new avenues for additional candidates" and advocated "thinking outside of the box" when looking for candidates.

Not surprisingly, then, prior officeholding experience is perceived as a more important qualification in the more professionalized legislatures. In less professionalized states, name identification and community involvement might be even more valuable than experience in the party or local office. The minority party typically has fewer informal qualifications expected of its candidates. Depending on the size of the party's support around the state, officeholding or even party involvement may not be realistic criteria; identifying nontraditional sources of candidates is that much more important for the minority party.

The relatively small pool of women compared to men who are eligible to run for office is often cited as an explanation for women's underrepresentation. The interviews confirm that in some states, prior officeholding experience often comprises an important part of a legislator's biography. However, the requisite qualifications for the legislature depend on the state. Because most state legislators have no prior officeholding experience, the dearth of women in local office can only partly explain women's underrepresentation in the legislatures.

Efforts to Restrict the Nomination

Not all parties seek to influence the nomination. Massachusetts and Alabama, for example, showed little evidence of gatekeeping. But in several states, including the Democratic party in Colorado and North Carolina, party leaders and staff think that persuading candidates not to run is a central component of the candidate recruitment process. Johnson of the Democratic campaign committee in North Carolina explained, "Part of recruitment is also trying to keep other people out of the election so we don't have primaries." However, the caucus does not become involved if there is a primary.

Ohio in general and the state's Republican party in particular stands at the high end of party gatekeeping. Most of the state's Democratic party leaders think it best to avoid primaries, although their opinion can change depending on the race. For example, Wilson described a process of sitting down with local political leaders and caucus leaders to agree on the best candidate: it is usually best to choose a candidate ahead of time. Because the Democratic party is significantly outspent, a primary is not a good use of resources.

The implementation of term limits in 2000 changed the recruitment process somewhat, given the large number of open seats. About thirty-five members of the House were forced to leave office in that year. More importantly, a leadership struggle created contentious primaries. Indeed, the media described some Republican primaries as "bloodletting" (Hallett 2000). Republican chair Robert Bennett argued that 2000 was unusual in the extent to which caucus and county parties supported different candidates.[14]

The 2002 cycle was more typical except that the Republican party's preprimary activities generated significant public scrutiny. In a secretly tape-recorded phone call, speaker Larry Householder's chief of staff tried to discourage someone from entering a primary for a targeted House seat. After a transcript of the call became public, both the speaker and his chief of staff defended the party's right to dissuade candidates from entering the primary.[15] A potential candidate in another district told the press that he had

14. Davidson recruited candidates as the outgoing speaker, targeting between eighteen and twenty-two races. Davidson had brokered a January 2000 power-sharing arrangement between Representative Larry Householder, who was designated to serve as speaker in 2002, and Representative Bill Harris, who would serve as speaker in 2001 (Leonard 2000a). However, the battle to be the next speaker played out in the primary elections. Householder raised large sums for candidates, and Harris instead sought a Senate seat (Leonard 2000b). According to Buehrer, the majority floor leader, Householder supported declared candidates who shared his ideology.

15. Householder's chief of staff, Brett Buerck, had tried to dissuade potential candidate Doug Mink from entering the primary because Householder was supporting Tim Raussen. Householder had recruited Raussen for the open seat in 2000, and he had come close to winning the seat. Hershey (2002) reported that Householder "defended the purpose of Buerck's call. . . . 'It's just trying to talk some sense into a young man who possibly would have a political career ahead of him,' Householder said. 'At this point, I doubt that he does.' Asked how Mink would get along in the house if he won the primary and election, Householder said: 'I think that's a big if. I don't think he's got a snowball's chance in hell of winning the primary.'" Mink claimed that Buerck said the Republicans had made it easier for Raussen to win the seat through redistricting and removing thousands of African Americans from the district, a charge that Buerck and Householder denied.

been threatened into withdrawing from a primary race, an allegation that the speaker's office denied.[16]

Thus, the speaker continues to play a large role in selecting Ohio candidates. On the Senate side, several respondents said quite simply that primaries do not exist in the Republican party. According to one Republican respondent, even when the caucus claims that no candidate is preferred, one usually is. Organized recruitment efforts in that chamber date back to the late 1970s.

Meanwhile, party competition is extremely low in Massachusetts, leaving little incentive for party leaders to act as gatekeepers. Neither party is very actively involved in trying to discourage a primary or in formally or informally taking sides in a primary. The Republican party usually remains neutral, though the party is currently debating the merits of primaries given its weak condition in the state.

The parties recruit candidates in Iowa but do not help them in the primary. Most of the state's Democratic and Republican leaders stay neutral unless an incumbent is challenged. Some party leaders believe it is best to avoid a primary, but most believe getting involved in primaries to be counterproductive.[17] Asked if he discouraged candidates or sought to avoid a primary, House minority leader Dick Myers explained,

> Well yes and no. . . . *Discouraged* is maybe not the right word for what I do. I do explain to people who's doing what and why and so on and ask some people sometimes to look at whether or not they could compete or whether this is their time. I'll do that. But sometimes I can't be effective. Somebody has just made up their mind that they're going to do it, and that's it.

North Carolina's parties followed a similar philosophy. House minority whip Julia Howard, a Republican, explained that the recruitment committee tries to reach consensus on one candidate and prefers not to have a primary. But the party does not get involved if a primary is held:

---

16. The speaker's chief of staff denied threatening the candidate but argued, "I think it is incumbent upon an organization if somebody's going to get involved in a race we make our intentions known at the outset so somebody can make a fully-informed decision" (Gottschlich 2002). The chief of staff also explained that the party needed to preserve resources for the general election.

17. Party preferences with regard to primary involvement may be more about political culture than party organization (Sorauf 1963). See also Huckshorn 1976.

We would basically try to recruit one individual. With the statement of, "If you find yourself in a primary, hands off—you know, we can't help you." But hopefully we will discourage to the degree that we find feasible, other candidates, you know, that may file just for the sake of filing in the primary. So we try to say, "You know, we have a good candidate over here." But not to any great degree do we discourage. Everybody has the right to run and should be able to.

Likewise, even if the candidate recruited by the Alabama Republican party faces a primary, the party remains neutral. The state party does not get involved in primaries as a general rule, and county parties do not make preprimary endorsements, although local party officials may endorse. The Republican chair thought the endorsements of individual leaders at the local level could be very important, but he said that most counties lacked a "Boss Hog." Alabama's House Democratic caucus prefers to avoid primaries but does not discourage them, according to the majority leader. The Democratic state party is neutral in the primary, and county parties do not make preprimary endorsements. Interest groups, however, do endorse in the primary.

The strongest evidence I found of gatekeeping in Colorado was the 2000 Democratic effort to win control of the Senate. The Senate Democratic caucus and the state party waged a highly organized candidate recruitment and campaign effort with the help of organized labor and trial lawyers. Mike Feeley, the Senate minority leader at the time, explained that the party hired ten full-time campaign managers for the targeted races, which state party chair Tim Knaus said were treated as miniature congressional races.

Candidate recruitment played a central role in the Democratic strategy, which involved identifying candidates to run and discouraging weak candidates from running. Feeley said that the party worked to recruit candidates early in the process, before other candidates could decide to run: "What we learned in past races, past years, was that if you don't start earlier than when we were traditionally doing, all of a sudden you have no choices. The candidates have emerged and they've got the local support." Candidate recruitment was "absolutely critical" and began in February 1999 for the 2000 elections. No primaries were held for the targeted seats, and the candidates were expected to meet certain benchmarks throughout the campaign. These efforts helped the Democrats win a one-seat majority in the Senate that year.

Meanwhile, Republican state party executive director Sean Murphy explained that little recruitment was needed in 2000 because candidates were already poised to run for most of the competitive seats. The party typically tries to stay neutral if a primary occurs because party bylaws prohibit involvement: the party sees its role in the primary as one of a referee. Indeed, by many accounts, contentious Republican primaries reflect the struggle within the party between conservatives and moderates, with each group fielding a candidate in the primary.

House Democrats have been more likely to try to discourage primaries.[18] The caucus walks a fine line when discouraging candidates, minority leader Dan Grossman explained, because it does not want to interfere with the electoral process. Assistant minority leader Jennifer Veiga believes it is better to avoid a primary if a difficult general election race is expected and said that party leaders encourage the most formidable candidate to run and discourage others from entering the primary.

Thus, in some cases, including Democratic leaders in Colorado and Iowa, party leaders expressed a commitment to having an open electoral process. The party's role prior to the primary can be delicate because of possible disagreements with the local party about the best candidate for a race.[19] If the caucus must remain neutral in the primary, or if it prefers to remain neutral, then the party may be more proactive about recruitment. In Iowa, both parties seem to believe that supporting a candidate in a primary—unless that candidate is an incumbent—is probably counterproductive. In other states, such as Colorado, where the Republican party has not sought to discourage primaries, party leaders were reconsidering this approach after losing the Senate.

The Republican party in the North Carolina Senate does not have the option of trying to restrict the nomination. Asked if Senate Republicans had tried to avoid a primary, Raupe explained, "We didn't have that luxury." The caucus was lucky to find candidates for these hopeless races.

A party may want to discourage a primary to save resources or to enable candidates to start campaigning for the general election. One strategy party leaders and staff use to discourage candidates from running is to try to convince potential candidates that they cannot win—that they will not be able

---

18. See Hertzke 1994 on the Colorado Republican party's involvement in candidate recruitment for a congressional race. Hertzke observed the state party's role in discouraging candidates, seeming to contradict the general trend that parties are weakening.

19. See Shea 1995 for a discussion of these dynamics in New York.

to beat favored candidates in primaries or will not be able to win the general elections and consequently should step aside in favor of other candidates. These efforts to discourage primaries do not always succeed. Indeed, some party leaders believe that the best candidate will emerge from the primary, so a primary can ultimately help the party in the general election.

Interest Groups

Party leaders typically work with interest groups when they recruit candidates. This is more common in Iowa, Colorado, North Carolina, and Alabama than Ohio or Massachusetts. In Alabama, party leaders believe that winning interest group support is critical to winning the primary. However, party officials in the other states do not think that interest groups play a large role in independently recruiting candidates; in these cases, party leaders more typically recruit candidates with assistance from interest groups. Party differences in coalitions and therefore the interest groups to which party leaders look for help in recruitment, are often similar across states. In none of the case-study states did those interviewed identify women's interest groups as significant coalition partners with the parties in recruitment.

Leaders of both parties in Colorado perceived interest groups as somewhat active in recruiting candidates in conjunction with the party or in identifying individual candidates. Groups mentioned on the Democratic side included trial lawyer, education, labor, pro-choice, gay rights, and environmental organizations; on the Republican side, those mentioned included the Christian Coalition, pro-life, and business groups. In 2000, the Colorado Democratic party partnered with organized labor and trial lawyers to win the Senate.

Similarly, Republican leaders in Iowa mentioned looking to businesspeople or their spouses. The parties also look to their allied groups and members of the caucus for suggestions, including the Association of Business and Industry, the Iowa Farm Bureau, taxpayer groups, chambers of commerce, and socially conservative groups. When asked whether groups help with recruitment, assistant House minority leader Polly Bukta said, "Oh, yes. There are groups that help us. Labor Congress helps. I'm speaking for Democrats. The teacher's union. Trial attorneys. A lot of the environmentalist groups. And human-service-type groups help find candidates."

Even if an interest group identifies someone from within the organization to run, the party may continue to look. Explained Iowa Speaker Brent Siegrist,

You know, [interest groups suggest a candidate from within the organization] sometimes, and when they do, if it's a good candidate, great. But ultimately you get down to the end, two things happen. One, somebody comes out of the woodwork, it's a banker or it's a lawyer, a teacher, whatever, you call them [the interest groups] up and say, "Well, can you check out this person? We think he or she is okay, but we're not sure." Or, sometimes they'll try to encourage their members and they bring us somebody. If we think they're a good candidate, great, we'll stop looking. If we think we can do better, we'll continue to look.

Although neither party in Alabama takes sides in the primary, interest groups regularly do so. According to Folsom, no clear-cut structure or procedure exists for the recruitment process, although the party communicates with its allied groups—the Alabama Education Association, the Alabama Democratic Conference, and the New South Coalition—about candidate recruitment. Connors, the Republican chair, looks to the local party as well as to groups affiliated with the party, including real estate agents, homebuilders, chamber of commerce groups, and the Christian Coalition, to identify candidates, although he thought the Democrats had more organized groups in which to look for help in finding candidates. Connors explained that some of the party's allied groups are not always interested in helping to find a Republican challenger if they have a good relationship with the Democratic incumbent. He explained the difficulty of unseating an entrenched incumbent in a district that leans Republican:

> Then you run into the problem of, with legislative races, sometimes there's not complete unanimity within the various coalitional groups that you would call upon to get rid of somebody. In other words, one group might like Joe, another group might not. Sometimes you need two or three different organizations, like insurance organizations or whatever to say, "We all agree this guy needs to go." So sometimes I'll be recruiting a candidate and then one of the interest groups will be, behind the scenes, try[ing] to keep you from succeeding.

Interest groups might urge the candidate not to run and withhold their support. In short, Connors explained, "My biggest challenge in Montgomery is not the Democrats, it's the status quo. So beating the status quo is harder than beating the Democrats." Thus, interest groups in Alabama may discourage potential candidates from running. The state's strong interest group system has arguably limited the importance of parties (P. Cotter 1997).

Ohio lies almost at the other extreme. Those interviewed do not believe that interest groups are important in helping the Republican party identify candidates. For example, as executive director Chris McNulty, explained, the party's health makes interest group involvement unnecessary.[20]

Interest groups along with local parties and elected officials may pass names of potential candidates to the state and legislative parties. Party leaders may also call on interest groups for help in evaluating individuals' strengths and weaknesses. With the exception of Alabama, interview subjects thought that interest groups played a fairly limited independent role in candidate recruitment. Interest groups may occasionally recruit their own members to run for the legislature. More often than not, however, interest groups help parties identify and evaluate potential candidates, with each party having a constellation of affiliated groups.

The Local Party

In most cases, state and legislative party leaders report that local party organizations are neutral in the primary, though individual party leaders may not be. The local party can make preprimary endorsements in Massachusetts and Ohio. In other states, the existence and influence of local gatekeepers depends on the area of the state. In Colorado, North Carolina, and Iowa, for example, some areas of the state with stronger party organizations were thought to have local gatekeepers. In Alabama, individual party leaders may support candidates in the primary. However, even when local party leaders get involved, the local favorite does not always win. According to Grossman, the Colorado House minority leader, for example, most local parties try to stay neutral in the primary. Neither the state nor legislative party usually takes an interest in candidates for safe seats; they expect a primary if such a seat becomes open.

Beliefs about the usefulness and importance of the local party in candidate recruitment varied across states and the two parties. In some cases, such as North Carolina, the state party or caucus looks to the local party for candidates or names of candidates. More common was the view that the local parties are weaker today than in the past. For example, Iowa's Siegrist explained why the caucus relies on its campaign committee, the Legislative Majority Fund:

20. See Sorauf 1963: "If the party abdicates control of the recruitment and nomination of candidates, private groups and nonparty elites will take up the task" (53).

The counties enter into it. But the county organizations are not always what they should be, and so we used our Legislative Majority Fund director to solicit names. We talk to our members to solicit names, and the county party enters in there. But in terms of recruiting, by and large we send our people out to recruit. County parties are helpful, but you've got to have somebody else to seal the deal in a lot of cases, tell them what they can expect from the state party or from the House or the Senate.

Of the case-study states, only Ohio's local parties seemed to exercise significant preprimary influence; the interviews there also elicited the common belief that the endorsed candidate was very difficult to defeat. Indeed, both the Democratic and Republican parties in Ohio "have closely approximated the textbook description of traditional party organizations" (Green and Shea 1997: 253). Both major parties have strong local organizations, but the Republican state party has been stronger than the Democratic party. The Republican party is conscious of using the local party organizations to develop a farm team of potential candidates for the legislature, an effort that is expected to become more important because of term limits.

County organizations have the power to make preprimary endorsements, and local chairs may endorse even if the party organization does not. The party may even endorse prior to the filing deadline as a way of discouraging other candidates from entering the primary. However, most of the state's county parties do not make preprimary endorsements. Republican chair Bennett estimated that in about half of primaries without an incumbent, the party has a preferred candidate, and it is difficult to beat that candidate.

The Ohio Republican party does not make endorsements in the primary but becomes involved indirectly because a candidate endorsed by the local party has access to state party resources, including shared fund-raising, assistance with mailings, voter lists, phone lists, and access to computers and desktop publishing. The state party can endorse incumbents running for reelection as well as candidates who are not competing in a primary. The state Democratic party also gets involved in a primary only if the county party makes an endorsement. According to Democratic political director Bill DeMora, it is very hard to defeat the candidate who is endorsed in the primary, although he thought that few counties endorse. But he also thought that in Democratic districts, winning the primary endorsement essentially amounts to winning the election.

The local parties in Massachusetts, which are city and town committees, can make endorsements in the primary. Some respondents thought that these

TABLE 3.5.   Existing Measures of Party Organizational Strength

	AL	CO	IA	MA	NC	OH
Traditional party organization	1	1	1	1	1	4
Local party, 1979–80	−.574 D	−.063 D	.132 D	−.150 D	.194 D	.752 D
	−.621 R	.111 R	.376 R	−.309 R	.260 R	.782 R
State party, 1975–80	—	.405 D	.301 D	.368 D	.386 D	.252 D
	.721 R	.681 R	.608 R	.247 R	.595 R	.808 R

Source: Traditional party, Mayhew 1986 (1 to 5 scale, where low scores represent the absence of traditional party organizations); local and state party, C. Cotter et al. 1984 (higher values indicate greater organizational strength).

endorsements could provide an advantage as well as a disadvantage: endorsements sometimes backfire, and upsets in a primary are not uncommon. Stefanini of the Massachusetts speaker's office thought that a hierarchy existed at the local level in a few areas, including the cities of Boston and Springfield. Otherwise, he explained, "We're not really in Boss Tweed country."

Table 3.5, which summarizes existing measures of party organizational strength for the case studies, confirms Ohio's position among the states with the strongest party organizations. For example, in the C. Cotter et al. (1984) study, the state Republican parties were strong or moderately strong in Ohio, North Carolina, Iowa, Colorado, and Alabama. The state Democratic parties in Massachusetts, Ohio, North Carolina, Iowa, and Colorado were all moderately weak. Ohio, North Carolina, and Iowa had stronger local party organizations than did Colorado, Massachusetts, or Alabama. Of the six states, Mayhew (1986) classified only Ohio as a traditional party organization state— that is, a state that regularly nominated candidates, had a lasting and hierarchical structure, and relied on patronage.

The most common perspective that legislative and state party leaders voice about the local parties is that they are weaker than they once were. Meanwhile, in some cases—particularly in areas strongly held by one party— recruitment is not necessary because local activists or officeholders are ready to step forward. In some cases, the state and legislative caucus turn to local party leaders for advice on recruitment. For the most part, however, the local parties are not perceived as the focal point of state legislative recruitment.

Ohio Survey of State Legislative Candidates

Interviews with party leaders document party activities and provide the party's perspective on the importance of recruitment. I now turn to additional evidence of party activities from the perspective of state legislative candidates.

I find that Ohio candidates confirm the significant party involvement in candidate selection prior to the primary in that state.[21] For presentation purposes in this chapter, I discuss only the responses of incumbent candidates.[22]

According to Ohio incumbent candidates, the parties play a large role in encouraging candidates to run. A series of survey questions concerned the candidate's initial decision to seek a seat in the legislature. About 27 percent of candidates reported that they had not seriously thought about running for the legislature until party officials and/or legislative leaders suggested it. About 37 percent categorized their candidacy as entirely their idea, and 22 percent said they had already thought seriously about it when someone else suggested it. The remaining respondents said they had not thought seriously about running until someone else suggested it—including friends, family, an organization, or local elected officials.

Most respondents discussed their initial decision to seek a seat in the legislature with party leaders—most commonly with local party officials (92 percent), followed by local elected officials (78 percent), leaders in the state legislature (73 percent), and state party officials (52 percent). Of respondents who had a primary the first time they sought a state legislative seat, most reported that party leaders were not neutral in the primary: about 50 percent said that most local party officials informally or formally supported a candidate, and about 65 percent reported that the state party and state legislative leaders took a position.

Candidates were also asked about the party's typical preprimary activities in their district: "In your district, how often do local/state party leaders or

21. The survey was conducted by the Ohio State University Center for Survey Research. All 2002 Ohio state legislative candidates who entered the Democratic or Republican primaries were sent the four-page State Legislative Candidate Survey consisting almost entirely of closed-ended questions. The candidate survey sought primarily to establish the party's involvement in state legislative elections from the candidate's perspective and to compare the responses of men and women candidates. A total of 156 candidates completed the survey, a response rate of about 61 percent. The response rate was similar for men and women candidates. Thirty-five women and 121 men returned completed surveys. Challengers were slightly less likely to respond than incumbents or open-seat candidates. Fifty-one of 97 challengers responded, compared to 54 of 87 incumbents and 51 of 72 open-seat candidates. Resource limitations prevented me from conducting similar surveys of the other five case-study states. See the appendix for more details. I modeled some survey questions after the Moncrief, Squire, and Jewell (2001) study and the Candidate Emergence Study by Maisel and Stone.

22. A total of fifty-four incumbents participated in the survey. Nonincumbent candidates were more likely than incumbent candidates to respond "don't know" on several of the questions about party activities in their district.

legislative leaders *discourage potential candidates* for the Ohio House or Senate from entering the primary?" Twenty-four percent of respondents said "never," 41 percent said "sometimes," 15 percent said "often," and 20 percent said "don't know." Endorsements are also common.[23] About 72 percent reported that the local party in their district sometimes or often makes formal endorsements in the primary, with about 24 percent saying that the party never makes endorsements.[24]

Thus, gatekeeping is quite common in Ohio. In many cases, this means that no primary contest occurs. Indeed, in the interviews, recruitment was frequently described on the Republican side as a process by which candidates interested in running make their interest known, hoping to get the nod or tap on the shoulder to be the candidate.

Summary

Thus, of the six states, the Ohio parties exercise the most influence over selection of the nominee. In Massachusetts, party influence is minimal. Meanwhile, to varying degrees, party leaders in Colorado, Iowa, and North Carolina discourage candidates from running. Typically, aside from Ohio, state and legislative party leaders do not become involved in primary races but might work to prevent a primary. Party leaders naturally use care when dampening potential candidates' aspirations. As a whole, the interview evidence suggests that parties play a significant role in state legislative elections. In chapter 5, I return to these differences in party recruitment practices across the case-study states.

PARTY LEADER SURVEYS

Methodology

Next, I expand my analysis to party activities across the fifty states. I argue that both state and legislative parties are commonly involved in candidate

23. Among nonincumbent candidates, 38 percent did not know how often party leaders discouraged potential candidates in their district. Twelve percent reported that the party never discouraged candidates, but 50 percent said that the party sometimes or often discouraged potential candidates.

24. Nonincumbent candidates were more likely to answer "don't know" to this question about endorsements; 16 percent reported they did not know. Nineteen percent of nonincumbent candidates reported that the local party in their district never endorsed in the primary, while 66 percent reported that the party sometimes or often did so.

recruitment. Moreover, many parties also seek to influence the nomination. Thus, party involvement in candidate selection is not limited to the states where I conducted interviews.

To measure party involvement in state legislative elections, I conducted two mail surveys following the 2002 elections. One survey went to legislative leaders from the lower house of the legislature, while the other went to all state party leaders.[25] The State Legislative Leader Survey concerned the activities of the House caucus in recent state legislative elections with a focus on the candidate recruitment and nomination activities of the legislative leadership team.[26] The State Party Leader Survey was identical to the State Legislative Leader Survey except that the survey questions concerned the activities of the state party in recent state legislative elections rather than the activities of the House caucus. Both surveys also included questions about the candidate recruitment activities of interest groups and other legislators as well as questions about beliefs regarding the electoral significance, if any, of candidate gender.

The State Legislative Leader Survey was sent to a total of 429 leaders; 149 completed the survey, for an individual-level response rate of about 35 percent.[27] I use the leadership team as the unit of analysis because most of the survey questions concern the leadership team rather than the individual leader. At least one respondent from seventy-one of ninety-five caucuses completed the survey, for a caucus-level response rate of about 75 percent. At least one member from thirty-six Republican House leadership teams and thirty-five Democratic House leadership teams completed the survey. The sample includes a respondent from at least one of the legislative parties in forty-five states. The appendix includes a complete list of participating caucuses. Factors such as legislative professionalism, majority party status, and party do not explain the likelihood that the caucus participated

25. See the appendix for additional details about the survey methodology and for question wording. I excluded Nebraska from the State Legislative Leader Survey because it is unicameral and nonpartisan.

26. Resource limitations prevented me from surveying all legislative leaders or leaders in the Senate. However, holding office in the House is often a stepping-stone to the Senate. Serving in the House is not a prerequisite to serving in the Senate, but the House is more likely than the Senate to serve as an entry-level office.

27. I chose to survey the top five leaders in the lower chamber of each state with the goal of receiving a completed survey from at least one member of the leadership team. Because the leadership structure varies across states, the number of leaders included in the sample from each state varied as well.

in the study. However, caucuses from outside the South were more likely to participate.[28]

I analyze the response of the highest-ranking leader in the caucus if more than one leader completed the survey.[29] Thus although 149 respondents returned the survey, the N in the analyses is 71, which is the number of leadership teams in the study. Higher-ranked leaders should be more likely to be responsible for candidate recruitment than lower-ranked leaders and should be more knowledgeable about the leadership team's activities.[30]

The State Party Leader Survey went to the chair and executive director of both the Democratic and Republican parties in all fifty states, for a total of 193 respondents. Of these respondents, 68 completed the survey, for an individual-level response rate of about 35 percent. The two major parties participated at the same rate: twenty-eight Democratic parties and twenty-eight Republican parties completed the survey, or 56 percent of all state parties.[31] The participating parties are from thirty-nine states.[32] If both the executive director and chair of the party completed the survey, I use the response of the chair. Therefore, the N in the analyses of state parties is fifty-six.

28. About half of legislative parties in the South compared to 80 percent of legislative parties from outside the South participated in the study. In part, this differential results from the smaller size of the leadership teams in the South and therefore the smaller number of respondents contacted. When I analyzed the response rate by party, I also found that the party's share of seats predicted the response rate for Republican caucuses only. More Republican chambers were more likely to participate. Given these differences in the response rate, I control for region and for partisan composition of the legislature in the multivariate analyses in chapter 6.

29. In most cases, one or two respondents from a given caucus completed the survey. In about half the caucuses, two or more leaders from the same caucus responded to the survey. On average, two respondents participated. The response rate within each caucus averaged 45 percent. In twenty-eight cases, one leader responded; twenty-one cases, two leaders; thirteen cases, three leaders; six cases, four leaders; two cases, five leaders; and one case, six leaders.

30. For example, if the speaker or minority leader completed the survey, I used that respondent as the spokesperson for the caucus leadership and dropped the lower-ranking leaders from the data set. If the speaker did not respond to the survey, I used the majority leader. In about half the leadership teams, the speaker, majority leader, or the minority leader responded to the survey. According to past research, these leaders are usually responsible for candidate recruitment (Jewell and Whicker 1994). For the caucuses where these leaders did not respond to the survey, I used the next-highest-ranking leader who responded.

31. See the appendix for a complete list of participating state parties.

32. The response rate did not differ for state parties from the South versus those from outside the South.

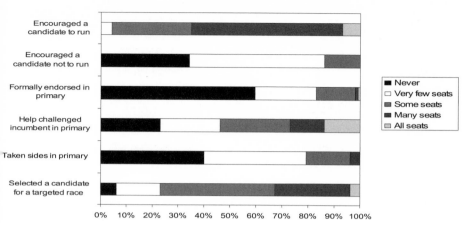

Fig. 3.2. Legislative party recruitment and nomination practices.
(Data from the State Legislative Leader Survey)

The Parties' Recruitment and Nomination Activities

Despite an era of candidate-centered elections, I find that both the legislative party and state party actively recruit candidates for the House and seek to influence the party nomination. Importantly, some parties are more active than others (see figure 3.2). The survey asked leaders, "In House/Assembly elections in recent years, in how many districts has the caucus leadership" engaged in particular recruitment or gatekeeping activities, and for how many seats (never; very few seats; some seats; many seats; or all seats). Most common is encouraging candidates to run, an activity in which virtually all leaders report participating for "some" or "many seats." Half or more legislative parties engage in these activities for at least some seats in the House: selecting a candidate for a targeted race, encouraging a candidate to run, and helping a challenged incumbent in a primary. Some legislative parties reported these activities for many or all seats.

Discouraging a candidate from running is less common, with the majority of state legislative leaders reporting that only in a very few seats did they encourage candidates not to run. Most party leaders (59 percent) report that the leadership does not make formal endorsements in the primary. However, other leadership teams do formally endorse candidates at least some of the time, with 23 percent reporting such endorsements in very few seats and 15 percent in some seats.

Complete neutrality in the primary is not necessarily the rule, however;

the party leadership may support candidates in the primary short of making a formal endorsement. Most leadership teams will help an incumbent who is challenged in the primary; more than half of leaders report such activities in some if not many or all seats. A plurality of leadership teams never takes sides in the primary (40 percent). However, 39 percent of leaders report that the caucus leadership takes sides in very few seats and 17 percent in some seats. Across this battery of recruitment and nomination measures, Democratic and Republican legislative leaders provided similar responses.

State legislative leaders do not report routinely discouraging candidates from running. But most believe it is better to avoid a primary for a competitive race. Party leaders believe it is usually or sometimes better if "the party avoids a primary in a House/Assembly district that is going to have a competitive general election." Only 9 percent answered "no" to this question, whereas 25 percent responded "sometimes" and 66 percent reported "Yes, usually." State party leaders expressed very similar views on avoiding primaries.

State party involvement in recruitment and nomination resembles that of the legislative party, although in several cases state party leaders were less likely to report engaging in particular recruitment or nomination activities than were legislative leaders (see fig. 3.3).[33] For example, the state party was more likely than the legislative party to report discouraging candidates from running, with only 18 percent of state party leaders responding that they never discourage candidates. The state party is less likely than the legislative party to help a challenged incumbent in the primary, take sides in the primary, or formally endorse in a primary. State party leaders are more likely than legislative leaders to report selecting candidates for targeted races in many seats and less likely to report that activity in some seats.

While one may traditionally think of the party organization as the local and state party, I find that the legislative party is as important—if not more important—for understanding the recruitment of state legislative candidates as the local and state party. Legislative leaders rate their activity in candidate recruitment more highly than state party leaders rate the state party's involvement (see table 3.6). This survey question asked, "In your view, how active was each group in recruiting House/Assembly candidates for your party in the last election, on a scale from 1 to 5?" About half of legislative leaders

---

33. There is also a statistically significant difference in the means by party for state party leaders on one measure: Democrats are more likely than Republicans to report helping a challenged incumbent.

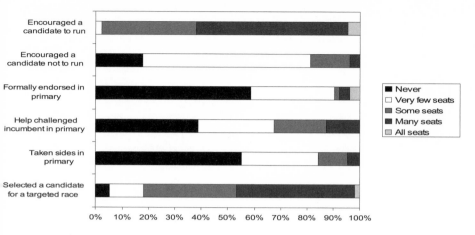

Fig. 3.3.   State party recruitment and nomination practices.
(Data from the State Party Leader Survey)

rated the legislative leadership at 5—the category for "very active" in candidate recruitment—compared to 39 percent of state party leaders who placed the state party in the same category.

Legislative leaders are perceived as the most active of the three groups in candidate recruitment. Table 3.7 compares the ratings of recruitment activity for the local, state, and legislative parties. In a total of forty-one cases, the state and legislative party leaders from the same state and party participated in their respective surveys. A direct comparison of these two sets of leaders reveals that perceptions of the legislative party's activities do not differ significantly across the two samples. Both sets of party leaders rate legislative leaders on average at about 4—fairly active—in candidate recruitment.

TABLE 3.6.   State and Legislative Parties Place Themselves on Candidate Recruitment Scale

	Not at all active 1	Not very active 2	Somewhat active 3	Fairly active 4	Very active 5
State Legislative Leaders (N = 71)	3%	4%	11%	32%	49%
State Party Leaders (N = 56)	4%	0%	21%	36%	39%

Source: State Legislative Leader Survey and State Party Leader Survey.

Note: Both groups (legislative leaders, state party leaders) rated their own recruitment activity.

Question wording: "In your view, how active was each group in recruiting House/Assembly candidates for your party in the last election, on a scale from 1 to 5? (Please check one box per row)."

TABLE 3.7. Party Leaders Place Local, State, and Legislative Parties on Candidate Recruitment Scale

	State Legislative Leaders	State Party Leaders
Placement of:		
Most local party leaders	2.85 (.96)*	3.34 (1.02)
The state party	2.95 (1.24)**	4.00 (1.05)
The legislative leadership	4.22 (1.06)	4.37 (.92)

Source: State Legislative Leader Survey and State Party Leader Survey. $N = 41$.

Note: This table is limited to states and parties where both the state party and legislative leadership participated in their respective surveys. Five-point scale from "Not at all active" to "Very active." Cell entries are means with standard deviations in parentheses. Asterisks indicate statistically significant differences between state legislative leaders and state party leaders.

$* p < .05; ** p < .01$

On the ratings of the state and local party, state party leaders rate these groups more highly than do the legislative leaders.[34] However, the two sets of leaders agreed that legislative leaders are more active than either the state or local party.

Thus, both state party and legislative leaders commonly recruit candidates for House races. Indeed, more than half of state legislative and state party leaders cited a full-time or part-time staff person who assists with recruitment; less than half said they had no staff assistance.

The Relationship between Recruitment and Nomination Practices

The surveys lend support to the distinction I outlined in chapter 2—that party activity with respect to candidate recruitment can be captured in two related dimensions: encouraging candidates to run (which I call recruitment) and seeking to influence the nomination (which I term gatekeeping).[35] Table 3.8 presents bivariate correlation coefficients of these measures for the state legislative leader sample. The statistically significant relationships are all in the positive direction.

34. These differences in means are statistically significant. State party leaders rate both the local party and state party higher than do legislative party leaders ($p < .05$).

35. I used principal components factor analysis to investigate the relationships among these seven variables. Among legislative party leaders, the variables loaded onto two factors, a recruitment factor and a nominations factor. The first factor included encouraging a candidate to run, selecting a candidate for a targeted race, and the five-point activity scale. The second factor included discouraging a candidate from running, taking sides in the primary, endorsing in the primary, and helping a challenged incumbent in the primary. The results of this analysis for state party leaders differed slightly, since discouraging candidates from running loaded onto a separate third factor.

BLE 3.8.   Bivariate Correlations: Legislative Party Recruitment and Nomination Activities

	Encourage candidates	Discourage candidates	Endorse candidates	Help incumbent	Take sides in primary	Select candidates
scourage candidates	−.11					
dorse candidates	.27*	.26*				
lp incumbent	.03	.15	.17			
ke sides in primary	−.004	.21[a]	.40**	.33**		
ect candidates	.42**	.03	.28*	.09	.27*	
cruitment activity (1–5)	.47**	−.07	.07	−.04	−.10	.45**

ource: State Legislative Leader Survey.
Note: Minimum N =70, Maximum N = 71.
$p \leq .10$; $* p \leq .05$; $** p \leq .01$

The strongest associations occur among encouraging candidates to run, selecting a candidate for a targeted race, and the five-point scale of recruitment activity. These items concern recruitment that entails encouraging candidates to enter the primary. Measures of attempts to influence the nomination are also positively related to one another. Helping a challenged incumbent, taking sides in the primary, and making formal endorsements in the primary are positively associated. Selecting a candidate for a targeted race is also positively related to some of these gatekeeping activities; selecting a candidate implies both recruiting a candidate to enter the primary and helping to prevent a primary or helping that handpicked candidate win the primary. Selecting a candidate entails both recruitment and gatekeeping, since it implies handpicking a candidate for important races.

I did not find that the recruitment activities of the legislative party and the state party are usually statistically related. I examined the correlations of legislative party activities with the activities of the state party for the forty-one cases where a legislative leader and a state party leader from the same state and party responded to the survey. However, two exceptions exist. Formal endorsements by the legislative leadership in the primary are positively related to the state party practice of taking sides in the primary (r = .39, $p < .05$). This suggests that where the legislative party is seeking to influence the primary outcome, the state party is likely to take sides as well. In addition, the legislative party practice of taking sides in the primary is negatively related to state party encouragement of candidates (r = −.39, $p < .05$). Where the legislative party is picking and choosing among primary candidates and taking sides in the primary, there is presumably a sufficient supply of candidates, and the state party is not active. If the candidate supply is sufficient, the state party may not need to become involved in recruiting state legislative candidates.

The Significance of Party Practices

Despite common claims that the parties are no longer relevant to candidacy, both legislative leaders and state party leaders believe that their role in recruiting state legislative candidates has increased in recent years. Among legislative party leaders, 57 percent thought activity had increased over the past eight years, with 65 percent of state party leaders taking that position. Forty-one percent of legislative party leaders and 26 percent of state party leaders believe that their recruitment activity has stayed the same. Only 1 percent of legislative party leaders and 9 percent of state party leaders said that their recruitment activity had decreased. This evidence confirms that the parties have become more active in recruitment (Aldrich 2000; Moncrief, Squire, and Jewell 2001; Jewell and Morehouse 2001).

Respondents also think that party recruitment of candidates explains why many candidates decide to run for the legislature, although this finding varies by state. Most party leaders believe that half of nonincumbent House candidates, if not more, run for the legislature because party leaders asked them to do so (see table 3.9). Significant variation occurs on this question, however, with less than half of states and parties reporting that candidates most commonly come forward on their own.[36]

In addition, most leaders believe that party efforts to influence the nomination can be important to the outcome of the primary. More than 40 percent of both sets of party leaders believe that if a House candidate is supported by most party leaders, his or her chances of winning the primary increase greatly; almost all remaining respondents think the candidate's chances of winning increase somewhat.

In sum, not only do party leaders widely report involvement in candidate recruitment as well as efforts to influence the nomination, but party leaders believe this activity is effective. Depending on the state, party leaders believe that party recruitment of candidates explains why most House candidates

---

36. State party and legislative leaders from the same state and party hold similar beliefs about the proportion of self-starters. These beliefs are positively correlated ($r = .41$, $p < .05$, $N = 41$). T-tests revealed no statistically significant difference between the two samples.

TABLE 3.9.   What Percentage of Nonincumbent Candidates Are Self-Starters?

	0–25%	25–50%	50–75%	75–100%
State Legislative Leaders (N = 66)	27%	30%	27%	15%
State Party Leaders (N = 56)	20%	34%	30%	16%

Source: State Legislative Leader Survey and State Party Leader Survey.

Note: Question wording: "About what percentage of nonincumbent House/Assembly candidates come forward on their own to run without being asked by the party?"

run for the legislature. Many party leaders also believe that a candidate with party backing is significantly advantaged in the primary.

My evidence of party activities in this chapter has primarily come from the perspective of party leaders. But this process can also be considered from the candidates' perspective. Though I have only discussed survey data from one state's candidates—Ohio—other scholars have conducted multistate candidate surveys. The decision to run for office is a complex one; it may unfold over time and it may be difficult to quantify how much of the decision to run is a function of self-recruitment versus external forces. But candidate surveys do provide a window into this decision-making process.

Some scholars believe that parties have negligible influence on the decision to run for the legislature. For example, the state legislative candidates in nine states surveyed by Frendreis and Gitelson (1999) rated the party's influence on their decision to run as less important than the influence of family and friends. The nonincumbent candidates in the Moncrief, Squire, and Jewell (2001) survey also were more likely to consult with their families than their parties when making the decision to run for the legislature.

However, whereas candidates from all states will want to take the views of their family members into account, the evidence from this chapter suggests that party leaders' influence on the decision to run is likely to depend on the state. Only 32 percent of candidates surveyed by Moncrief and his coauthors are pure "self-starters," and that study identified party leaders as frequent sources of the candidacy decision. Asked if they were approached and encouraged to run, candidates were most likely to report such recruitment by local party officials (46.1 percent), followed by local elected officials (33.5 percent), leaders in the state legislature (33.3 percent), and officials in the state party (32.9 percent). Thus, there is significant confirmation from the perspective of state legislative candidates that parties are quite active in recruitment. As I discuss later in the chapter, these surveys also demonstrate that candidates perceive the party role in recruitment as larger than the role of interest groups.

Interest Group Activity

The types of groups affiliated with the Democratic and Republican parties may have implications for which potential candidates are tapped to run for the legislature. As in the interviews, the types of interest groups that party leaders cite as helpful with respect to candidate recruitment vary somewhat across states (see table 3.10). The most common groups that legislative leaders cited were business associations, local/community groups, labor/union organizations, and teachers. These groups were also frequently mentioned in my interviews.

About 28 percent of legislative leaders cited women's groups as helpful to the party in recruiting candidates. State parties were much more likely than legislative parties to view women's groups as helpful to the party in recruiting candidates, with nearly half of state parties listing women's groups.

As in my interview data, important differences exist in the two parties' constituencies. Almost all Democratic leaders (86 percent) report that organized labor helps the party recruit candidates, compared to just 6 percent of Republican leaders. Republican leaders are more likely to report business

TABLE 3.10.   Recruitment and the Parties' Affiliated Interest Groups

	State Legislative Leaders (N = 71)	State Party Leaders (N = 56)
Business	55%	57%
Local/Community	52%	52%
Labor/Union	45%	48%
Teachers	44%	45%
Farmers	38%	38%
Pro-Life	35%	25%
Lawyers	31%	38%
Gun Owner	30%	21%
Women's Groups	28%	48%
Tax Relief	25%	18%
Christian Coalition	20%	18%
Environmentalists	17%	30%
Pro-Choice	17%	30%
Gun Control	7%	4%

Source: State Legislative Leader Survey and State Party Leader Survey.

Note: Question wording: "Which interest groups are helpful to your party in recruiting candidates for the House/Assembly? (Please check all that apply)."

groups (78 percent) than are Democratic leaders (31 percent). Democrats are aided by teachers (77 percent) and lawyers (51 percent), whereas only 11 percent of Republican leaders cite those groups. Republican leaders view pro-life groups (64 percent) and the Christian Coalition (31 percent) as helpful. A large partisan difference also exists on women's groups: about half of Democratic leaders but less than 10 percent of Republican leaders list women's groups. This difference is even greater in the state party leader sample, where 79 percent of Democratic leaders and only 18 percent of Republican leaders cite women's groups.

Interest groups were not usually perceived as very involved in recruiting candidates in general, although the parties often look to interest groups for suggestions of potential candidates. These perceptions resemble what I found in the case studies. The survey asked about general interest group activity in recruitment, as opposed to activity in conjunction with the party. About 45 percent of legislative leaders report that interest groups recruit candidates for the House in very few seats, with 45 percent saying that such groups do so for some seats. Only 9 percent reported that interest groups recruited candidates in many seats. State party leaders perceived somewhat greater interest group activity than did legislative leaders, with 51 percent of state party leaders responding that interest groups recruit for some seats and 13 percent for many seats.[37]

Party leader reports on this question about interest group involvement were not usually correlated with the party recruitment and nomination measures discussed previously. However, the statistically significant correlations run in opposite directions for the two groups of leaders. Legislative leaders' perceptions of interest group activity in recruitment are negatively related to the extent that leaders report encouraging candidates to run ($r = -.27, p < .05$). However, in the state party leader sample, the activity of the state party in recruiting candidates on the five-point scale is positively related to interest group activity ($r = .31, p < .05$). Legislative parties are less involved in candidate recruitment where interest groups are more involved, while the state parties are more involved in recruitment where interest groups

---

37. I also considered whether legislative and state party leaders from the same state and party rated interest group involvement similarly. I found that the difference between the two samples in the assessment of interest group activity was not statistically significant, although the assessments of interest group activity were also not significantly correlated ($r = .23, p = .16, N = 39$).

are more involved. Why the relationship between party and interest group activity is in the opposite direction for legislative and state party leaders is unclear. However, state parties may be more likely than the legislative party to work in conjunction with interest groups to recruit candidates.

Candidate surveys confirm that interest groups are less involved in recruitment than are the political parties. Only 13.6 percent of candidates in the Moncrief, Squire, and Jewell (2001) study reported being approached and encouraged to run by members of an interest group or association. This indicates that interest group recruitment is significantly lower than the rate of recruitment conducted by the parties, which I discussed previously. The Frendreis and Gitelson (1999) surveys of state legislative candidates confirm this trend: candidates rated the local and state parties and legislative campaign committees as more influential in their decision to run for office than labor, political action committees, or other groups.

In sum, almost all party leaders in my study perceive interest group involvement in recruitment to be limited to either very few or some seats. However, the parties commonly look to allied groups for names of potential candidates.

THE DETERMINANTS OF PARTY PRACTICES

What explains the likelihood that party leaders will recruit candidates or act as gatekeepers? In the case studies, where there is more concern with the outcome of the primary, party leaders tend to be more interested in shaping the nomination. Party leaders spoke of the significance of the race and the necessity of being involved in the nomination, arguing that some races are simply too important to leave selection of the nominee to chance. Party leaders are also more active in recruitment where competition is greater; even if the party is unwilling to take sides in the primary, the party can still try to induce other candidates to enter the race.

In addition to this case study evidence, a quantitative analysis can be used to predict party activities. Why are some parties more likely to engage in recruitment or gatekeeping than others? What explains the variation across states in these party activities? Are recruitment and gatekeeping more likely to occur where party competition is high? Are recruitment and gatekeeping more common where the office is more desirable?

I conducted a multivariate analysis using the parties' recruitment and gatekeeping practices as the dependent variables. I created an unweighted additive index of the three recruitment variables (the recruitment scale, encouraging candidates to run, and selecting candidates for a targeted race) and the three gatekeeping variables (discouraging candidates from running, endorsing in the primary, and taking sides in the primary).[38] Each index ranges from 0 to 3.

The key independent variables of interest are party competition and legislative professionalism. Party leaders should have a greater incentive to choose the nominee when the two parties are competitive in the state. In these cases, party leaders should be particularly invested in finding the strongest candidate to be the nominee (Jewell and Morehouse 2001). Party competition and party organization are thought to be closely related (C. Cotter et al. 1984; Aldrich 2000). Aldrich notes,

> Competition is likely to lead to greater efforts to organize to win in the face of that competition. And when that competition is itself organizing to seek to win and hold majorities in the electorate and in the government, then one way to compete is to try to out-organize to win those contests for majority allegiance. (2000: 661)

In addition, an office's attractiveness should shape party activities. If a sufficient pool of interested potential candidates is needed for party leaders to pick and choose among them, such a pool should be more likely in more professionalized settings. Given the higher salary and prestige, more professional legislatures should be that much more attractive to potential candidates (A. Rosenthal 1989). With a sufficient supply of candidates, party leaders should have more opportunities to play a role in candidate selection. Indeed, professionalism is associated with greater legislative efforts to shape the nomination (Gierzynski 1992; Jewell and Morehouse 2001). Interview subjects frequently observed that more than sufficient interest existed in seeking the nomination where the legislature was more professionalized. In Ohio and Massachusetts, for example, some respondents spoke about potential

---

38. Because the response options for all of these survey questions are ordered categories, but not necessarily equidistant categories, I recode each of these items into a dichotomous variable by dividing the categories at the median response. For legislative party activities, the Cronbach's alpha is .60 for the three recruitment measures and .49 for the three gatekeeping measures. For state party activities, the Cronbach's alpha is .60 for the recruitment measures and .74 for the gatekeeping measures.

candidates' high interest in seats, whereas party leaders elsewhere spoke of a dearth of potential candidates.

I consider the effects of two measures of party competition. I examine the difference between the two parties in House seats as a share of all seats. Therefore, positive values indicate that the party is in the majority, whereas negative values indicate the party is in the minority. I also examine a second measure to isolate the more competitive chambers. This alternative measure is a dummy variable for states where the seat difference between the two parties in the House consists of 10 percent or fewer seats.[39] This variable takes the value of 1 when the margin between the two parties is low and competition between the two parties is therefore high.

For legislative professionalism, I use a simple dummy variable coded 1 for those states with longer sessions and higher salaries, 0 otherwise (Hamm and Moncrief 1999). Based on past studies, I expect that party activities will depend partly on the state laws governing primaries (Key 1956; Tobin and Keynes 1975; Jewell and Morehouse 2001). To measure electoral rules, I use a series of dummy variables to account for the various types of primary systems from the completely open, blanket primary to more closed and restrictive primaries (Jewell and Morehouse 2001). These variables capture the extent to which the party restricts participation in the primary to voters registered with the party. I also include controls for region (South) and party (Democrat).

I begin with the models of recruitment (table 3.11). The dependent variable is the recruitment index composed of the three recruitment variables. I use an ordered probit model because the dependent variable is an ordered, categorical variable. For both the legislative and state parties, I examine the effect of professionalism and both measures of party competition. The results demonstrate that professionalism is unrelated to party involvement in recruitment. However, competition predicts legislative party involvement. The larger a party's seat advantage, the less likely the legislative leadership is to be engaged in candidate recruitment activities. Thus, where a party has more control over a chamber, less recruitment occurs.

In table 3.12, I examine the party gatekeeping index, which measures party involvement in the primary or discouraging candidate entrance in the primary. I find first that legislative parties are more likely to seek to influence

39. Data are from Council of State Governments (various years).

TABLE 3.11.　Determinants of Legislative and State Party Recruitment Activities

	Legislative Party	Legislative Party	State Party	State Party
Competitive chamber	.421	—	−.009	—
	(.419)		(.268)	
Party balance of seats	—	−.011**	—	−.004
		(.004)		(.007)
Professional legislature	−.021	−.050	−.376	−.360
	(.537)	(.537)	(.382)	(.390)
Open primary	.069	.344	.135	.166
	(.472)	(.474)	(.625)	(.612)
Closed primary	.460	.463	−1.127**	−1.127**
	(.426)	(.457)	(.355)	(.361)
Completely closed primary	.228	.273	−1.063*	−1.049*
	(.420)	(.428)	(.459)	(.451)
South	.255	.136	−.292	−.309
	(.397)	(.449)	(.510)	(.503)
Democrat	.413[a]	.418[a]	−.602	−.630
	(.257)	(.246)	(.407)	(.436)
Cutpoint 1	−.910	−1.071	−2.834	−2.849
	(.317)	(.314)	(.519)	(.542)
Cutpoint 2	.354	−.470	−1.656	−1.686
	(.332)	(.330)	(.437)	(.434)
Cutpoint 3	.467	.380	−1.119	−1.144
	(.382)	(.374)	(.398)	(.395)
N	70	70	53	53
Initial log-likelihood	−80.46	−80.46	−59.88	−59.88
Final log-likelihood	−77.65	−75.42	−53.11	−52.95
χ^2	5.22 (7df)	11.65 (7df)	17.29 (7df)*	16.34 (7df)*

Note: Cell entries are estimates from an ordered probit model. The dependent variable is the legislative party or state party recruitment index, which ranges from 0 to 3. The primary dummy variables examine the effect of completely closed primaries, closed primaries in which some voters may shift on election day, and open primaries wherein voters select a primary publicly (Jewell and Morehouse 2001: 103). The excluded primary category combines states with open, blanket primaries and completely open primaries. Party is coded 1 for Democrat, 0 for Republican. South is coded 1 for South, 0 for non-South.

[a] $p \leq .10$; * $p \leq .05$; ** $p \leq .01$

the nomination where the two parties are more competitive. In these chambers where only a small proportion of seats separates the majority from the minority, party leaders are more engaged in efforts to select the party nominee. Thus, precisely where party interest in the nomination is higher, the parties appear to be more involved in that process. In addition, in more professional legislatures, legislative leaders are more likely to act as gatekeepers.

Meanwhile, previous research suggests that party leaders are more influential in candidate selection when the electoral rules enable them to do so. In these states with more restrictive primaries, candidates are more likely to

TABLE 3.12.   Determinants of Legislative and State Party Gatekeeping Activities

	Legislative Party	Legislative Party	State Party	State Party
Competitive chamber	.701*	—	−.073	—
	(.342)		(.354)	
Party balance of seats	—	.001	—	.007
		(.004)		(.007)
Professional legislature	.707*	.795**	.158	.156
	(.278)	(.296)	(.380)	(.379)
Open primary	−.183	.162	−.614	−.566
	(.536)	(.409)	(.541)	(.530)
Closed primary	.180	.094	−.617	−.590
	(.335)	(.333)	(.394)	(.386)
Completely closed primary	.240	.234	−.831[a]	−.850[a]
	(.308)	(.326)	(.479)	(.479)
South	.368	.193	.581	.582
	(.617)	(.549)	(.471)	(.481)
Democrat	−.241	−.154	.404	.448
	(.277)	(.267)	(.355)	(.343)
Cutpoint 1	−.923	−.962	−1.15	−1.06
	(.277)	(.269)	(.411)	(.374)
Cutpoint 2	.244	.156	−.200	−.100
	(.277)	(.263)	(.393)	(.349)
Cutpoint 3	.929	.824	.218	.330
	(.285)	(.257)	(.384)	(.346)
N	70	70	52	52
Initial log-likelihood	−93.27	−93.27	−68.75	−68.75
Final log-likelihood	−88.28	−90.15	−65.85	−65.08
χ^2	19.99 (7df) **	13.67 (7df) [a]	5.63 (7df)	7.65 (7df)

Note: Cell entries are estimates from an ordered probit model. The dependent variable is the legislative party or state party gatekeeping index, which ranges from 0 to 3. The primary dummy variables examine the effect of completely closed primaries, closed primaries in which some voters may shift on election day, and open primaries wherein voters select a primary publicly (Jewell and Morehouse 2001: 103). The excluded primary category combines states with open, blanket primaries and completely open primaries. Party is coded 1 for Democrat, 0 for Republican. South is coded 1 for South, 0 for non-South.

[a] $p \le .10$; * $p \le .05$; ** $p \le .01$

seek the party nod and discuss their candidacies with party leaders (Tobin and Keynes 1975). However, I do not find evidence of this dynamic. The type of primary and the extent to which the primary is open are not related to gatekeeping activities at conventional levels of significance. For the state party only, more closed primaries are associated with fewer party attempts to influence the primary, which is in the opposite of the expected direction. Meanwhile, in table 3.12, more restrictive primaries are also associated with less recruitment activities.

CONCLUSION

Critics commonly argue that parties are no longer important institutions in today's era of candidate-centered elections. Parties no longer control the nomination. But they do identify candidates and encourage them to seek office. Moreover, parties continue to influence the nomination even though their ability to control the process has diminished. The decision to seek office is not limited to the influence of the party: for example, a candidate's family and friends arguably play a larger role in the decision to run than do party efforts (Frendreis and Gitelson 1999). However, the weight of the party as a factor in the decision to run should vary systematically across states.

The interviews revealed that the nature of recruitment depends on the state and party. North Carolina, Iowa, and Ohio have highly organized candidate recruitment efforts involving staff. Party officials in Iowa believe that the party's role in seeking out and encouraging candidates explains why many candidates decide to run for the legislature. Ohio parties actively support candidates in primaries. In other states such as North Carolina and Colorado and more commonly in the Democratic party than the Republican party, party leaders hope to avoid a primary, typically settling on a candidate to recruit beforehand. Even if there is already a candidate in the primary, party leaders may continue to recruit for the race to find the strongest candidate. As expected, party competition and a low supply of candidates largely explain party leader goals with respect to candidate recruitment.

The national surveys of state legislative and state party leaders confirm that the parties are actively recruiting candidates for House races, involvement that most party leaders view as being on the rise in recent years. Gatekeeping—formally endorsing a candidate or taking sides in the primary— is less common but clearly varies across states. Although few party leaders report that the legislative leadership or state party formally endorses a candidate prior to the primary, most leaders prefer to avoid primaries for competitive seats. In addition, party leaders commonly select a candidate for a targeted race, an activity that implies handpicking the party nominee.

Party officials perceive legislative parties as more actively engaged in candidate recruitment than either state or local parties. Both state party and legislative leaders agree that the legislative party is the most active of the three party groups. These leaders also see recruitment as substantively significant, although this finding depended on the state. From the vantage point of party leaders, half or more nonincumbent House candidates run because the party asked them to do so. Party leaders see their support of a particular candidate in the primary as influential, though more so in some states than others.

The party's efforts to nominate a preferred candidate are not limited to states with formal endorsement procedures. Party leaders may seek to influence which candidates run—or do not run, as the case may be—precisely because the party needs to remain neutral in the primary. When a dearth of candidates exists, gatekeeping may be irrelevant. Activities that involve attempts to influence candidate selection—by formally or informally taking sides in the primary—are less common than recruitment. However, most party leaders believe that for competitive general election races, primaries are best avoided.

Party and legislative leaders do not perceive interest groups as very active in candidate recruitment in most states. However, the parties look to interest groups to help identify candidates. Democratic leaders were more likely to look to teachers and lawyers; Republican leaders were more likely to look to business groups, pro-life groups, and the Christian Coalition. Democratic leaders were also much more likely to view women's groups as helpful to the party's recruitment efforts.

What shapes party involvement in the recruitment and nomination of candidates? The legislative party is less likely to recruit when it controls more seats in the legislature—no doubt because it has more incumbents seeking reelection. The legislative party is more likely to seek to influence the nomination where the two parties are more competitive. In addition, the legislative party is more likely to do so where the legislature is more professionalized. In these states, the office is more attractive, and the party can afford to be more selective.

In the next chapter, I examine party leader beliefs about women candidates and whether gender is a factor in the parties' recruitment strategies.

CHAPTER 4

Candidate Gender and Electoral Politics

The idea that women are less likely than men to win their races is arguably a myth that may erroneously lead women—and their potential supporters and donors—to believe that women are more difficult to elect (Seltzer, Newman, and Leighton 1997: 90). Any party leader bias against women or voter reluctance to support them is thought to be a relic of the past (Darcy, Welch, and Clark 1994). Voter willingness to elect women has been demonstrated through studies that show that women candidates have as much success as men do. Surprisingly, however, the conventional wisdom about political parties' receptivity to women state legislative candidates is not based on any direct evidence of party leader beliefs.

In the past, voters may have been more supportive than party leaders of women candidates. A national study from the 1970s showed that women officeholders thought that male party leaders posed a greater barrier to women's advancement than voters did: "Far larger proportions of women in every office perceive discrimination from men in political parties than perceive discrimination by voters. Between 68 percent and 86 percent agree or agree strongly that 'many men in party organizations try to keep women from attaining leadership positions'" (Johnson and Carroll 1978: 39A). These attitudes have no doubt changed since that time. However, if voters are more supportive of women candidates than party leaders are, women may be more likely to run for office where they do not need the approval of party leaders. For this reason, the direct primary may not hinder women's candidacies and may be more favorable than a situation of greater party control over the nomination.

The previous chapter demonstrated that the parties are quite active in encouraging individuals to run for the legislature. In this chapter, I investigate whether gender factors into these party recruitment strategies. I begin by providing background on women's representation in the legislature in the case-study states. I then turn to the party leader interviews regarding candidate gender.

I also use the mail surveys to analyze the beliefs of state and legislative party leaders. I find that about half of party leaders perceive an electoral advantage for one gender. State legislative leaders are slightly more likely to perceive a net advantage for men than for women, though state party leaders perceive the reverse. Moreover, party leaders do not agree that men and women are equally electable. Nearly half of party leaders believe that in a few districts in their states, it might be hard for a woman to win election to the legislature; indeed, some party leaders believe that many such districts exist. These party leader views about women candidates are quite unexpected given the conventional wisdom about women and elections and the idea that strengthening parties will lead to an increase in women officeholders.

WOMEN'S REPRESENTATION

How many women run for and hold state legislative office in the case-study states? Before turning to the interviews, I analyze women's representation (see table 4.1). In 2001—the year I conducted most of my interviews—Colorado ranked fourth in the nation for the percentage of women state legislators. Massachusetts ranked eighteenth, in the second quartile of all states. Iowa (twenty-seventh), North Carolina (thirty-third), and Ohio (twenty-eighth) were in the third quartile, with Alabama in the fourth quartile, ranked fiftieth among all states.

The presence of women within each party caucus in the state was generally similar across the two parties. However, while women comprised almost half of all Democratic legislators in Colorado and almost one-third in Ohio, they were less well-represented in those states in the Republican party. The raw numbers of women by state, party, and chamber appear in table 4.2.

TABLE 4.1.   Women State Legislators, 2001 (in percentages)

	AL	CO	IA	MA	NC	OH
Women state legislators	7.9	34	22	25.5	18.8	22
Democratic women state legislators	8.8	43.5	23.4	25.6	18.6	32
Republican women state legislators	6.1	25.9	20.9	28.6	19.2	16.3

Source: CAWP 2001a.

Note: The bottom two rows provide the percentage of women as a share of their party caucus.

TABLE 4.2.   Women State Legislators by Chamber, 2001

	AL	CO	IA	MA	NC	OH
House						
Democrats	6	13	12	32	14	13
Republicans	2	11	10	7	13	12
Senate						
Democrats	2	7	3	11	4	3
Republicans	1	3	8	1	1	1

Source: CAWP 2001a.

Note: Cell entries are raw numbers of women legislators by party.

In all six states, women's representation in the legislature has increased over time, although women's representation has declined in recent years in Ohio and leveled off in Colorado, Iowa, and Massachusetts (see figure 4.1).

The pattern of women's representation differs somewhat by party (see figures 4.2–4.7).[1] The share of Democratic women as a percentage of their caucus has outpaced that of Republican women in recent years in Colorado, Iowa, and Ohio, states where Republicans have usually controlled the House.

The presence of women state legislators reflects their presence as candidates. Table 4.3 examines the 2002 primary and general elections. Women constituted a greater share of candidates in Colorado than in the other states and were least well represented in Alabama. Consistent with past research on women's election to office, I find that the proportion of women general election winners is fairly similar to the proportion of women primary candidates. Women comprised 22 percent of primary candidates and 26 percent of general election winners in Massachusetts. In Colorado, women comprised 30 percent of primary candidates and 35 percent of general election winners.

The statistics on open-seat races tell a slightly different story. Open seats are of particular interest because incumbency constitutes a structural barrier to increasing women's representation. Because 2002 was a redistricting year, it should have been an important opportunity for an increase in women's representation through open seats. Yet the existence of opportunities does not automatically mean that women will run. Indeed, about 45 percent of open-seat races in these six states did not feature a woman candidate in either

1. The 25 percent statistic for Republican women's representation in Alabama in 1979 in figure 4.2 reflects the presence of one Republican woman who served in the House out of a total of four Republicans.

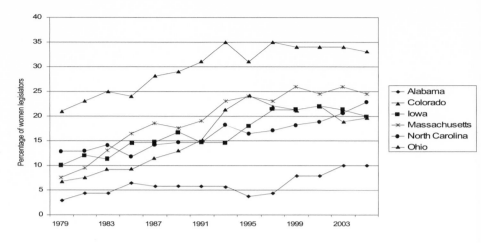

Fig. 4.1.   Women's representation, 1979–2005.
(Data from CAWP Fact Sheets, various years)

party's primary. At least one woman competed in 65 percent of open-seat races in Massachusetts and in just over 50 percent of open-seat races in Alabama and Iowa. Important differences exist across the two parties in this regard: while women comprised similar proportions of open-seat candidates in the two parties in Iowa, Democratic women were better represented than Republican women in open-seat primaries in the other five states. Women

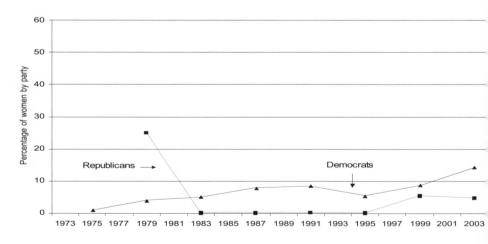

Fig. 4.2.   Alabama: women in house caucus.
(Data from Cox 1996; CAWP Fact Sheets, various years; Council of State Governments, various years; National Conference of State Legislatures, various years)

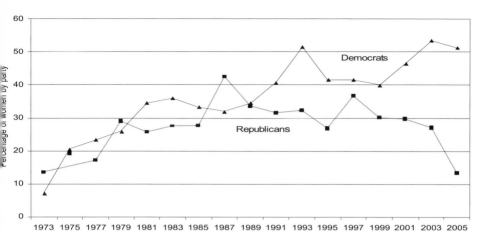

Fig. 4.3.   Colorado: women in house caucus.
(Data from Cox 1996; CAWP Fact Sheets, various years; Council of State Governments, various years;
National Conference of State Legislatures, various years)

constituted only 11 or 12 percent of Republican open-seat candidates in
Alabama, Colorado, and North Carolina, and Republican women won only
one open seat in Alabama and none in Colorado.

Although women made up 20 percent of open-seat primary candidates
in Alabama, they comprised only 6 percent of the eventual general election

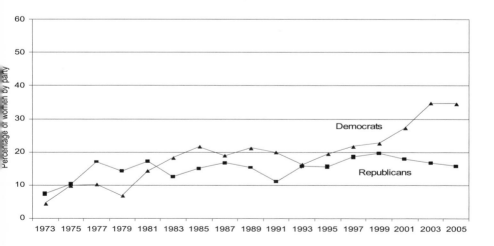

Fig. 4.4.   Iowa: women in house caucus.
(Data from Cox 1996; CAWP Fact Sheets, various years; Council of State Governments, various years;
National Conference of State Legislatures, various years)

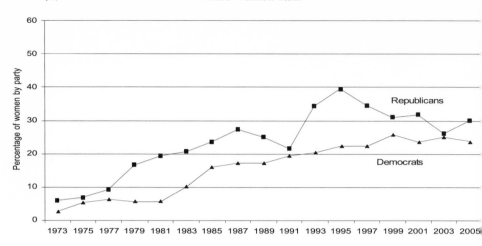

Fig. 4.5.   Massachusetts: women in house caucus.
(Data from Cox 1996; CAWP Fact Sheets, various years; Council of State Governments, various years;
National Conference of State Legislatures, various years)

winners of these open seats. Women amounted to 26 percent of Iowa's open-seat primary candidates; yet only 18 percent of open seats were eventually won by women. In the other states, women went on to win open seats at similar rates to men, and women in Massachusetts won at higher rates than men did.

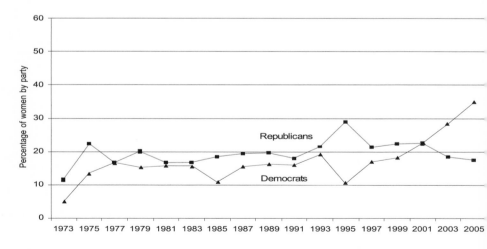

Fig. 4.6.   North Carolina: women in house caucus.
(Data from Cox 1996; CAWP Fact Sheets, various years; Council of State Governments, various years;
National Conference of State Legislatures, various years)

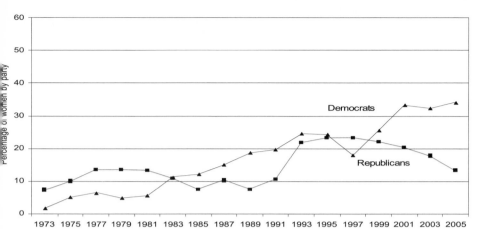

Fig. 4.7. Ohio: women in house caucus.
(Data from Cox 1996; CAWP Fact Sheets, various years; Council of State Governments, various years;
National Conference of State Legislatures, various years)

TABLE 4.3. Women's Presence as 2002 Candidates

	AL	CO	IA	MA	NC	OH
Primary Election						
Women candidates	12%	30%	25%	22%	19%	22%
Women winners	12%	32%	25%	23%	22%	23%
General Election						
Women candidates	12%	32%	26%	23%	22%	23%
Women winners	10%	35%	22%	26%	21%	22%
Open Seat, Primary Races						
Women candidates	20%	25%	26%	21%	21%	22%
Women Democratic candidates	35%	38%	27%	24%	30%	26%
Women Republican candidates	11%	12%	26%	13%	12%	18%
Open seat races without a	47%	43%	49%	35%	44%	41%
woman candidate	(8/17)	(10/23)	(24/49)	(6/17)	(16/36)	(9/22)
Open Seat, General Races						
Women winners	6%	22%	18%	35%	25%	23%
Women Democratic winners	0%	38%	21%	26%	38%	30%
	(0/3)	(5/13)	(5/24)	(5/14)	(6/16)	(3/10)
Women Republican winners	7%	0%	16%	33%	15%	17%
	(1/14)	(0/10)	(4/25)	(1/3)	(3/20)	(2/12)

Source: Calculations by the author of data from CAWP and state legislative election results.

In sum, although women generally fare well when they run, in some states women did not translate their open-seat candidacies into victories at the same rates as men did. Moreover, the existence of open seats does not guarantee an increase in women's representation. A large gender gap occurs in who runs for these openings: about half of open seats did not feature a woman in either party's primary. In all six states, women are much less likely than men to run for the legislature.

My analysis focuses on the political parties. But the presence of women as both state legislative candidates and state legislators is in part a function of women's representation in the social eligibility pool (Carroll 1994; Darcy, Welch, and Clark 1994). Table 4.4 provides data on how women's representation compares to other factors known to shape women's opportunities in the states. Women's progress in the field of law is typically correlated with the representation of women (Williams 1990). However, this does not appear to hold true in Alabama, where women are much better represented as lawyers than as legislators. On another, more distant measure of the social eligibility pool, women's labor force participation, Alabama also trails the other five states.

The percentage of women in local office arguably provides a more proximate measure of the pool of women with the informal requirements for the legislature. As expected, women tend to fare better at the local level than at

TABLE 4.4.   State Public Opinion and the Social Eligibility Pool

	AL	CO	IA	MA	NC	OH
Women state legislators, 2001	7.9%	34%	22%	25.5%	18.8%	22%
Women in local office, 1992	15.4%	19.9%	18.3%	31.5%	19.2%	23.1%
Women's labor force participation, 2001	55.8%	63.8%	67.1%	61.6%	62.6%	61.5%
Gender difference, labor force participation, 2001	15.1%	15.8%	10.5%	13.3%	11.5%	13.1%
Women lawyers, 1995	17.4%	24.9%	17.2%	27.1%	21.6%	19.8%
Ideology	−23.1	−8.6	−13.5	−0.8	−20.7	−10.1
Gender ideology	1.01	1.57	1.47	1.57	1.17	1.41

Source: Data on women state legislators are from CAWP. Data on ideology are from Erikson, Wright, and McIver 1993, based on data from CBS/NYT polls from 1976 to 1988. Gender ideology is from Brace et al. 2002, based on data from the General Social Surveys. Data on local elected officials are from the 1992 Census of Governments (U.S. Department of Commerce, Bureau of the Census 1994). Data on women's labor force participation in 2001 are from U.S. Department of Labor, Bureau of Labor Statistics 2002. Data on women lawyers in 1995 are from Carson 1999.

Note: Ideology is the relative difference between conservatives and liberals, with higher values indicating more liberal attitudes. Higher values on gender ideology indicate more liberal attitudes toward women's roles. Gender difference in labor force participation is the difference between men's labor force participation rate and women's labor force participation rate.

the state level: because local office can be a stepping-stone to state legislative office, inroads women make at the local level may take time to translate into gains at higher levels of office. For these reasons, the presence of women in local office is typically correlated with the presence of women in state legislative office. Data from the Census of Governments (U.S. Department of Commerce, Bureau of the Census 1994) indicates that among the six states, women fared best in local government in Massachusetts and Ohio. In 1992, women comprised 31.5 percent of local elected officials in Massachusetts and 23.1 percent in Ohio. Yet in Colorado, the presence of women in state legislative office has exceeded their presence in local office: in 1992, women comprised 19.9 percent of local officeholders and 31 percent of state legislators.[2]

As chapter 3 demonstrated, most state legislators lack prior officeholding experience. Elected experience at the local level is a useful credential for the legislature but is not a necessary qualification. Indeed, a 2003 study found that the percentage of women holding state legislative office exceeded the percentage of women holding municipal office in five of the six New England states, including Massachusetts (Hardy-Fanta 2003). Local elected officeholding experience is a common credential for Massachusetts and Ohio legislators, but not for those in Alabama, Colorado, Iowa, and North Carolina.[3]

Women's presence as candidates is also partly a function of state public opinion (Norrander and Wilcox 1998; Arceneaux 2001). Massachusetts and Colorado are the most liberal states according to polls of citizen ideology (see table 4.4). Alabama is the most conservative of the six states—and the state with the fewest women serving in the legislature. Given these differences in public opinion, party leader interest in fielding women candidates may depend on the state.[4]

2. Women's representation in 1992 in each state was as follows: Alabama, 5.7 percent; Colorado, 31 percent; Iowa, 14.7 percent; Massachusetts, 18.5 percent; North Carolina, 14.7 percent; Ohio, 15.2 percent (CAWP 1992).

3. See chapter 3.

4. A cursory analysis of all states indicates that citizen ideology and women's labor force participation are significant predictors of women's representation in the lower chambers of the legislature but only partially explain the variation across states in women's representation ($R^2 = .34$) (results not shown). I use multivariate analysis in chapter 6 to estimate the effect of party practices on women's representation when other state factors are taken into account.

Thus, studies have shown that state factors such as public opinion and the eligible pool of women shape the likelihood that women will be elected to the legislature. How the parties' recruitment and gatekeeping practices are related to women's representation has received much less attention. Most past studies have failed to consider how candidate gender may factor into the parties' candidate recruitment strategies. Thus, I turn next to the views of Democratic and Republican party leaders.

ELECTORAL STRATEGY AND CANDIDATE GENDER

Do party leaders think that women are viable candidates? Scholars have pointed to the presence of women candidates in competitive races to demonstrate that party leaders are not biased against women (Darcy, Welch, and Clark 1994). Party leaders may even believe that women have an electoral advantage. Yet given that women only began to seek public office in larger numbers fairly recently, women's electability may be uncertain. Party leaders who want to win elections may choose a man over a woman because they fear voter bias against women candidates—what can be called "imputed discrimination" (Norris and Lovenduski 1995: 14). Indeed, political experts in a recent national survey, the Candidate Emergence Study, thought that women potential candidates for Congress would be less likely to win than men potential candidates (Alan 1999).[5]

The view that voter bias no longer exists is bolstered by the statistic that women and men tend to win their races at similar rates. However, survey evidence and experimental research reveal that voters' gender stereotypes about politicians are widespread (Sapiro 1981–82; Sapiro 1983; Rosenwasser and Seale 1988; Leeper 1991; Huddy and Terkildsen 1993; Alexander and Andersen 1993; Kahn 1994; Matland 1994; Koch 2000; Matland and King 2002). These stereotypes help explain why many voters have a baseline preference—preferring to vote for either a male or a female candidate when other factors are equal (Sanbonmatsu 2002b). Some voter stereotypes disadvantage women. However, other stereotypes work to women's advantage. The electoral context may also be more favorable to women in

5. The Candidate Emergence Study surveyed political informants in two hundred U.S. House districts about potential candidates in their area. See Maisel and Stone 1997; Maestas, Maisel, and Stone 1999; Maisel, Stone, and Maestas 2001; Stone and Maisel 2003; Stone, Maisel, and Maestas 2004.

particular years, such as 1992, the "Year of the Woman," when women's status as outsiders appeared to give them an edge (Burrell 1994). However, other contexts have arguably been less favorable for women candidates (Fox 1997; Lawless 2004).

In this section, I use the interviews with party leaders to determine what, if any, role candidate gender plays in the parties' recruitment strategies. I find that many party leaders believe that women candidates have a more difficult time getting elected than men, either in the state as a whole or in certain parts of the state. Thus, to the extent that women perceive some states or districts to be more favorable environments for their candidacy than others, they are not alone in their thinking: women's electability remains a concern for many party leaders.

Party leaders also commonly reported that they do not consciously recruit candidates by gender: the party might be happy to find a woman candidate, but recruiting women is not a goal. Other leaders reported that they consciously seek out women candidates in the belief that women have an electoral advantage. In some places, this is a new belief; elsewhere, parties do not currently believe that women have an advantage, although such beliefs did exist during the 1990s.

Who Can Win?

A political party can recruit candidates as a strategy to win or maintain a majority. Across states, party leaders spoke of the need to recruit the candidate who can win. Central to that evaluation is finding the candidate who best fits the district. Any interest in increasing the presence of women in office is clearly secondary to winning elections. For example, I asked former North Carolina legislative leader Betsy Cochrane if she thought about gender strategically when recruiting candidates. While gender might matter in a particular race, she argued that winning is the most important goal:

> I think if there are not strong women—and I'm talking about assertive women as opposed to aggressive women, because aggressive women don't do as well in some districts in some areas. If there is not the right kind of woman candidate, there might be more of an effort to recruit a man who had those positive features. Because the winning is more important than the gender. The gender becomes important to the winning in many instances. But again, you need a candidate with the right characteristics. If someone cannot express themselves, if they do not meet people well . . . that's not what you're looking for.

Former Colorado House minority leader Peggy Kerns did not think that conscious efforts to recruit women occurred in her state, although she thought an awareness of the need to recruit more minority candidates existed. Nevertheless, this awareness did not change the party's focus on recruiting candidates who could win:

> But it comes right down to, it's the electability of the person, no matter what race, color, what creed, sex, or whatever they are. *That's* the overriding goal—it's to *win*. And so where the strategy comes in is, who can win this seat? And, what background does that person have? And are things a detriment or an advantage? . . .
>
> I would say that in Colorado, [in] recruitment, the main criterion is electability. And all these other factors are secondary. And if being a woman helps you get elected in a certain district, then they would recruit a woman. But there's not the overarching value or principle that says we need to have more women in the legislature or we need to have more African Americans or Latinos or Hispanics. There's not that overriding principle. It's who can best win the election.

Thus, interview subjects commonly mentioned the importance of winning. What varied across states, however, were beliefs about the relationship between gender and winning.

Colorado

As Kerns's statement indicates, Colorado's status as one of the leading states for women's representation does not appear to result from a belief that women have a net electoral advantage over men. The Democratic leaders I interviewed reported recruiting women candidates, but not because they were seeking out women in particular. Other Democratic leaders argued that the party thinks about everything when recruiting candidates—gender, race, ethnicity, and so on—trying to anticipate the type of candidate that would work best in a district and evaluating whether the district would be willing to elect a woman.

Most Republican leaders believe that voters do not care about gender and are accustomed to seeing women in leadership positions. House Majority Leader Lola Spradley, for example, believes voters are indifferent to candidate gender and explained that the party wants good candidates regardless of gender. However, the state Republican party expressed a specific interest in women candidates: chair Bob Beauprez and executive director Sean

Murphy argued that women help the party image and better communicate the party message.

In short, most party leaders said that gender does not factor into recruitment. The state Republican party believes that fielding women candidates is desirable, although the party has not been very active in candidate recruitment. At the same time, some Democratic leaders take gender into account in selecting state legislative candidates.

Massachusetts

"There's not a district in the state that can't be represented by a man or a woman," explained John Stefanini, chief counsel to the speaker of the House. The lack of concern about women's electability in both Massachusetts and Colorado is consistent with public opinion: of the six cases, the public is most liberal in these two states. For the most part, neither party in Massachusetts believes that women candidates have an electoral advantage or disadvantage compared to men. The Republican party is happy to find any candidate. When I asked if he had observed any conscious efforts in the state to identify women candidates, House minority leader Francis Marini responded,

> In my party, we'll take any good candidate where we can find them. I mean, our problem is *lack* of candidates, not choices among people to encourage to run. You know, I would love to have more women running. I would love to have more men running also. . . . In my party, I need people to participate. I can't afford to pick and choose among the genders. If somebody wants to run, I want them to run.

Marini believes that women candidates have a small advantage because voters perceive them as more trustworthy and because some voters want a more balanced political arena:

> I think women are by and large perceived to be—and this might even be true—more trustworthy, and I think the public views them as less susceptible to what the press is always trying to portray: public officials as making deals about everything. So I think they have an overall slightly better public perception, and I think there is a certain amount of the public who thinks that it ought to be more balanced between the genders, so that all things being equal, [they think,] "I will vote for the woman in order to have the larger political arena more balanced between the genders." So I think that provides them a little bit of an advantage. Again, all other things are hardly ever—in fact, never—equal, so there are a host of other things that play into this. But for some voters, where they don't

know either candidate particularly, they're not sure where they stand on the issues, they're not party driven—I think if you took those voters, they would tend to break a little more for the woman than the man. Not a huge amount, but a little.

Overall, however, Marini does not think voters care a lot about gender, instead making judgments about which person is best for the job.

North Carolina

Southern states typically trail the rest of the country in women's representation. Yet some North Carolina Republican party leaders consciously seek out women candidates. Representative Mia Morris, a member of the caucus recruitment committee, explained why she believes women currently have an advantage:

A female is hard to run against. Because more than 50 percent of our voters are women. And so people think automatically a woman candidate is going to be a tough opponent. And it's funny because guys are afraid to run against the women, and women are afraid to run against each other because that would be a really contentious race. . . .

I still believe it's a male-dominated world, and the number one rule of a campaign is contrast. And a male versus a female is a natural contrast there. And the woman is usually coming in as the underdog. Right there you've earned yourself a lot of media and a lot of attention that you don't have to pay for because you have a natural contest before you even open your mouth. Because the contrast is right there: you're female and you're running against a male. You're ahead out the door. . . . So it's a definite advantage.

Asked why women vote for women, Morris explained,

I guess they feel a certain, "Okay, my needs are going to be met if I vote for a woman because we understand each other." I think they feel a kinship or an understanding of, "Yeah, she's going to support women's issues." And for the most part that's true.

However, Republicans expressed some disagreement regarding whether the party had intentionally sought out women in 2000. Some members of the recruitment committee said that they looked for the best candidate and did not try to identify women in particular. Indeed, committee member and representative Rex Baker thought that women do not fare well in the state's mountain areas, a perspective that several other legislators echoed.

Senate Republicans also seek to recruit candidates but do so for what may be considered hopeless races. Joel Raupe explained, "We made an effort to recruit female candidates, not just because we have a dearth of them, but because we feel like they're easier winners." Senate Republicans lack the resources to buy television ads, and the Democrats have a significant advantage in most districts and a dramatic advantage in funds; consequently, Raupe explained, the Republicans have adopted a conscious strategy of recruiting women candidates to challenge Democratic incumbents:

> People generally tend to trust women who are running for office on sight. . . . We don't have much money. . . . So we thought this would be one of the ways of making up for our deficiencies, was to actively recruit women candidates. Plus we want more women here. But the primary reason is the marketing difficulties in this level of race.

Thus the Republicans have turned to women candidates as a marketing strategy, hoping that the trust that the public places in women candidates will yield votes.[6]

Some Democratic leaders argued that older voters are less willing to vote for women candidates; other leaders argued that women have a small net advantage overall. For the most part, however, Democratic leaders did not usually express a particular interest in women candidates. Wooten Johnson, the staff person for the House caucus campaign committee, said he takes gender into account to some extent, believing that women might vote for a woman candidate as a "default position" if they have no strong opinion about a race. He might want to field a woman against a Republican woman opponent or recruit a woman for an open-seat race.

Yet Johnson argued that the perception in the early and mid-1990s that women had an advantage was probably overstated. Voter preferences with regard to candidate gender seem extremely dependent on context:

> I probably need to go back and say—take that statement back, you know, that there is no voter preference. There sort of is, but it's got to be in a certain context. All things being equal, I don't think there are voter

---

6. The strategy did not yield any victories; however, their closest race in 2000 involved a woman candidate they recruited who lost by only six hundred votes. In the absence of other information, Raupe argued, women voters and some men will select a Republican Supreme Court candidate, and he thought a similar dynamic was at work with women candidates. He also argued that it is much more difficult to use negative campaigning with a female opponent.

[preferences]. But frankly most things aren't all things equal in a campaign. I mean, there's distinction, there's differences.

Thus, the Republican party currently has an interest in women candidates. Voter attitudes—either in terms of older voters or certain parts of the state—were cited as problematic for women's election to the legislature. Some Democratic and Republican leaders voiced the perspective that women candidates have less success than men and that women generally are not as thick-skinned or aggressive as men. Overall, more concern about voter support of women candidates was raised in North Carolina than in Colorado or Massachusetts.

Alabama

Subtle changes in the relationship between gender and legislative service in Alabama were evident in my visit to the Alabama Department of Archives and History in Montgomery. Scrapbooks documenting the activities of the Alabama Legislative Wives Club, first organized in 1971, eventually gave way to the scrapbooks of the Alabama Wives and Husbands Club during the 1980s and finally to the current Alabama Legislative Club. But despite a small increase in the presence of women in the Alabama Legislature, the state placed last among all states for women legislators at the time of my interviews.

Alabama Republican chair Marty Connors does not think about gender in his search for candidates, arguing that voters are "relatively indifferent" to candidate gender. Instead, he looks for the candidate who is most likely to run and most likely to win. As in North Carolina, some Alabama party leaders believe that gender matters to how voters respond to candidates. However, unlike North Carolina, neither state party believes that women candidates have an advantage in Alabama.

House majority leader Ken Guin consciously seeks to identify women candidates, although he said he had not been able to recruit as many women as he would have liked. Guin believes that women voters who would otherwise support a Republican candidate might cross over and vote for a Democratic woman. This strategy, as well as the role of the caucus in recruiting candidates, seemed to be new in 2002. He looked for women candidates in their late thirties to forties who might be able to appeal to Republican voters of the same age group because Republican growth has occured among young voters.

The Democratic state party expressed more reservations about voter support for women candidates. Alabama Democratic party executive director Marsha Folsom, for example, believes that a subset of voters is unwilling to vote for women candidates. The party's chair, Redding Pitt, argued that the impact of gender depends on the race, the year, and the area of the state. Pitt believes that some voters are probably more predisposed to vote for women candidates than others and that some bias probably exists both for and against women candidates. Some Republicans expressed similar views, with one respondent arguing that the question of whether women and men are equally likely to win their races depends entirely on the specific race, including the district and the candidates. Neither Folsom nor Pitt reported intentionally seeking out women candidates, with Pitt saying that party officials look for the strongest possible candidates.

Thus neither state party consciously recruits women, and neither perceives a net advantage for women. The House Democratic majority leader thinks women may be advantaged, a new and at the time of my interviews untested belief. For the most part, party leaders believe that some voters are more likely than others to support women and that candidate gender can be a very significant factor in particular elections.

Iowa

The Iowa Republican party no longer consciously recruits pro-choice women candidates, which had been its strategy in the early 1990s; most Republican party leaders and staff, including Senate president Mary Kramer and Senate majority leader Stewart Iverson Jr., said that candidate gender is not relevant to who is recruited or how candidates are slated. Party officials generally believe that women and men are equally likely to win their races. Marlys Popma, the Republican party's executive director, said that the party looks for the most qualified individuals and does not seek out candidates with specific issue positions, although she thought that additional interest or excitement arises when a good woman candidate is identified, given that women remain a minority in the legislature.

House speaker Brent Siegrist said that some observers believe that women have an advantage in swing districts because women might vote for a woman over a man, but he was not sure that this view is correct. Instead, he emphasized that attention to candidate gender is uncommon:

> You have people come out of the woodwork that want to run, and in some cases you'll look at a profile of a district and may decide you want to recruit

a woman. Some other places maybe, a man might fit the district better—whatever it may be. And so some of those things have come into play, but generally speaking, it's been a situation where whoever we can recruit, we're going to recruit. It's always been to a degree desirable to be able to say we recruited X amount of women or in some cases minorities and what have you. So it plays into the process, but it's difficult to get people to run at the legislative level, as I'm sure you know, in terms of the time away from family and the money, and so we take whoever comes up. And occasionally we'll continue to recruit after somebody surfaces, but by and large gender doesn't enter into it too much as long as we think we have a good candidate. . . .

We're looking for good candidates. We don't much care about the gender. If you have X amount of women running, that sounds good. We recruit people blindly, I guess. We're trying to get the best person, and so we'll go after a man or a woman, doesn't matter, just so long as we think they can do the job. So it's very challenging to get anybody to run.

Republican chair Chuck Larson Jr. argued that more women should serve in the legislature and said that he had made it a personal priority to try to recruit more women. He believes that women bring a different perspective to the legislative process and different life experiences. The party would go the "extra mile" to help a woman candidate get started, but Larson said he does not exclusively look to recruit women candidates. Majority whip Libby Jacobs said that the caucus consciously recruits women and is very cognizant that the caucus needs to be diverse and representative of the state.

Women appear to run better in some parts of Iowa than others. A number of leaders and staff from both parties thought that women tend to fare better in urban or suburban areas than in rural areas. Popma believes that women might have more difficulty winning in rural Iowa than in suburban or urban areas and that women who were not farmers would probably have more trouble getting elected than men in those rural areas. Larson said that national polls indicated that a Republican woman had an advantage of three to five points over a Democratic man in urban areas, but he pointed out that women in the caucus also come from rural areas.

Representative Bill Dix, the assistant majority leader and the designated legislative campaign chair, personally believes that women have an advantage with independents and new voters and that this advantage has developed in recent years. He may prefer a woman candidate if he is looking for a challenger to a Democratic incumbent or if he knows the opponent is going to be a woman candidate. Dix also thinks that some areas of the state would be more likely than others to elect a woman, although he did not think there is any area of the state where a woman could not get elected.

Democratic party leaders were more likely than Republican leaders to express concerns about voter attitudes. House minority leader Dick Myers, for example, was not sure that men and women are equally likely to win their races:

> I'd like to think so. I won't say that's always true. . . . There are too many parts of the state where that's not true, but it is changing. And it certainly has changed in the cities. Because there are more women of course that are active and out there. I think women are more open to criticism than men are. Because after all, they're expected to take care of the children, so to speak.

For the most part, however, party leaders think that women and men fare similarly when they run. Some respondents pointed out that women tend to be more likely to come from urban or suburban areas than rural areas.

Myers argued that more women and other members of underrepresented groups are needed in the House. However, one of his two assistant leaders in charge of recruitment, Polly Bukta, argued that recruiting women was not a top priority: she focuses on finding the best candidate to fit the particular district. Bukta was very happy to have a diverse group of candidates but said that it was a coincidence that House Democrats had recruited such a large number of women candidates in 2002.

A more concerted effort to field women occurred on the Senate side. Senate Minority Leader Mike Gronstal consciously sought out women candidates because he believes it is harder for men to run a negative campaign against a woman and because voters may see women as cooperative, a desirable trait in the current political atmosphere. Moreover, women senators were retiring that year, and the Democratic caucus did not want to be all male.[7]

In short, the Republican party is no longer identifying pro-choice women as it had in the 1990s. Some individual Republican leaders believe that women have an advantage, but most leaders reported that the party recruits without attention to gender. Democrats were more likely to express an interest

---

7. Gronstal's concerns were well founded: only one Democratic woman served in the Senate in 2003.

in recruiting women for the sake of diversity but also expressed more reservations than Republican leaders about women's electability.

Ohio

Both state parties in Ohio believe that women have a net advantage in state legislative races, all else equal, though this advantage is thought to be smaller than the advantage women have in judicial races. Many Republican leaders, including the state party chair, cited a female advantage. According to state Democratic party political director William DeMora, women tend to have a three- to four-point advantage in state legislative races because of the importance of the school funding issue in the state. He also argued that women fare well in suburban areas. Similarly, chair David Leland noted that women vote more than men and that women will vote for women candidates, all else equal; at worst, he thought that women and men candidates fare equally. Leland also argued that women's electability is unrelated to the area of the state. But other Democrats thought that women have a more difficult time winning election in some areas of Ohio, including rural areas.

Only limited support existed among Democratic legislative leaders for the idea of an advantage for women. Minority leader Jack Ford said that his preference, all else equal, was to recruit women; at the same time, he said that it was rare for all else to be equal. In particular, he sought a woman candidate in her mid-forties who was a professional, teacher, or lawyer or who had a built-in constituency, pointing out that the average voter in most districts is a woman. However, Antoinette Wilson, a Democratic House caucus consultant, did not think that women have an overall advantage and argued that women's electability depended on the candidate and the district's demographics. However, she said that she was committed to recruiting more women because she believes diversity is important. Democratic Senate leaders also do not perceive an advantage for women. Indeed, Senate assistant minority leader Greg DiDonato said that gender does not figure into the caucus' candidate recruitment decisions.

In sum, in Alabama, Iowa, North Carolina, and Ohio, some respondents thought it might be harder for a woman to get elected in some districts or parts of the state than others. Respondents were most likely to report voter indifference to candidate gender in Colorado and Massachusetts, where public opinion is more liberal. Most Republican leaders and some Democratic leaders in North Carolina and Ohio believed that women have an electoral advantage. In Alabama, several party leaders thought that candidate gender matters a great deal but that how it matters depends entirely on the race. In other parts of the interviews, it became clear that party leaders often look for a particular type of woman candidate, as I describe in the following section.

Women's Electoral Advantage: Finding the "Right" Woman Candidate

Regardless of party leader beliefs about the extent to which women are advantaged or disadvantaged, party leaders commonly believe that voters hold stereotypes about men and women candidates. Some of these stereotypes, including stereotypes about issue expertise, affect the conduct of campaigns. And some stereotypes are thought to advantage women candidates, whereas other stereotypes are thought to advantage men.

Voters' gender stereotypes were often the reason that some party leaders prefer a woman candidate in a particular race and the reason that women candidates are thought to have an advantage. Across states, some party leaders argued that it is harder to "go negative" if the candidate is a woman. Some party leaders pointed to the stereotype that women are more trustworthy or honest. In Ohio, one respondent said that polling data revealed the existence of an advantage but not an explanation for it. Across states, interview subjects sometimes cited the belief that women might cross party lines to vote for women as the mechanism behind women's perceived electoral advantage.

Some respondents who said that candidate gender does not figure into recruitment nevertheless expressed views on what kinds of women candidates are more competitive. North Carolina's Cochrane argued that the Republican Party did not think about candidate gender when she was in leadership, but she also mentioned the need for the "right kind of woman candidate."[8]

In some cases, party leader beliefs about women's electability and the existence of a net advantage for women candidates depend on other conditions. Raupe, the assistant to the Senate minority leader in North Carolina, prefers a woman candidate to challenge incumbents from the majority party—that is, all seats for which he recruits candidates. However, he is not sure that this advantage extends to other types of races. In Alabama, several party leaders argued that candidate gender is an important factor but that whether it is a

---

8. This is reminiscent of the Fowler and McClure (1989) study of New York's Thirtieth Congressional District, where interview subjects speculated that the "right woman" could win the seat.

net negative or net positive for women depended entirely on the race. In some instances where party leaders expressed a particular interest in recruiting women candidates, party leaders have an ideal profile of a woman candidate in mind. Both House minority leader Ford in Ohio and majority leader Ken Guin in Alabama believe a specific type of woman candidate has an advantage in an open seat.

The limitations of the perceived advantage for Ohio women state legislative candidates is evident in the negative stereotypes that women are believed to face both inside and outside the legislature. One Republican male respondent believes that women have a net advantage over men; however, he explained that women face different challenges as candidates than men face:

> The downside that I think women face in a job like this, and if I can be blunt, is that they've got a *really* fine line to walk in terms of how they come off to voters, and then, once they're here, how they interact with other members. . . . They've got a lot to prove when they get here, more so than men do. And of course it's not fair. But you want to be a—you want to be strong, and you want to be looked to as a leader and a decision maker. But the danger is for women that men don't face is that you don't want to be considered a bitch, you know? Because if you're hard to work with, it's chalked up, "Oh, she's just a high-strung woman." And it's very easy to fall into that category. Right or wrong, women have to work a *lot* harder on their presentation and how they mold their persona here inside the legislature in order to be effective. It's too easy for a woman in the legislature to be labeled dingy, or you know, bitchy, or tough to work with. . . .
>
> Men don't have that problem. Men don't have that issue. We can be as jerky as we want to be and nobody's going to care in the little club, you know.

These obstacles do not mean that women can never succeed in the legislature, and he pointed to a number of women who have succeeded.

He also argued that women have more to prove with voters than men do: "They've got to establish their credibility. They've got to show that they're tough, depending on what they're running for. And they have to show that they're intelligent, more so than men seem to have to." In the end, the "fine line" women candidates need to walk cannot help but factor into recruitment decisions:

> I think it's one of the things that we gauge when we recruit candidates and how they would come off with voters and if we think someone's got

a perceptual problem. We do that for both men and women. But I can see where we might hold women to a different standard even in that process. . . . When you're recruiting a candidate, when you're working on the campaign side of things, your business is to put the strongest possible person out there to win the election, and you have to think like voters think.

Thus, in some cases, women are perceived to be particularly desirable candidates. Such a perception can create tremendous opportunities for women candidates. Yet whether the party recruits a woman may depend on finding a particular kind of woman candidate. In addition, even in those states where women are thought to have an advantage, many party leaders believe that voter support for women candidates depends on the area of the state.

Party Contagion

The presence of women candidates in the opposing party may also affect the electoral incentives of nominating a woman. In a recent study of industrialized democracies, Caul (2001) demonstrates that the adoption of a quota for women candidates by one party can generate further quotas within the party system. Parties may adopt quotas because of electoral competition; they may nominate women candidates "to demonstrate their commitment to equal rights" out of the fear of losing votes (Matland and Studlar 1996: 712).

I expected that party interest in women candidates resulting from this contagion effect would be significant. Yet I found very little evidence that the parties perceive themselves to be in competition with one another with regard to nominating women candidates. Very limited evidence of this dynamic existed in Iowa, where both parties were aware of the two parties' records on women candidates. Both Senate minority leader Gronstal and Senate majority leader Iverson knew that the Republicans had fielded more women for the Senate in 2002, though Iverson said he had not consciously sought to recruit women.[9] Meanwhile, speaker Siegrist said that the Republicans had apparently fielded slightly fewer women for the House than the Democrats, though he personally did not know the numbers. However, he noted that in 1996, Republicans had more women committee chairs than the Democrats did in 1992, a situation that may have been driven by

9. Iverson had issued a March 2002 press release stating that eleven of thirty-five Republican candidates filing for the Senate were women, compared to only three of thirty Democratic candidates.

seniority.[10] Thus, leaders from both parties in Iowa knew the numbers on
women candidates, possibly as a result of the spotlight a new women's organization put on the number of women candidates running in 2002, as the
next chapter discusses. However, because most of the state's party leaders
argued that they did not recruit candidates on the basis of gender, the importance of this knowledge about women candidates in the other party is
not clear.

The Party Reputations

The opportunity structure facing women may differ by party because of
majority party status and the extent of competition within the party for
nominations (Sanbonmatsu 2002c). Because different social groups constitute each party's base, the relevant eligibility pool for women candidates
may differ somewhat for each party (Sanbonmatsu 2002c). In cross-national
studies, left parties have typically been more sympathetic to the election of
women to office (e.g., Norris 1993; Matland and Studlar 1996; Caul 1999).
Thus the Democratic party may be more interested than the Republican
party in increasing the presence of women in office. Nationally, Democratic
women outnumber Republican women in the state legislatures: in 2005,
1,044 Democratic women served as state legislators, compared to 604 Republican women (CAWP 2005d). Democratic women state representatives
outnumber Republican women state representatives (see figure 4.8), and
Democratic women also constitute a larger share of all Democratic representatives than Republican women constitute of their party (see figure 4.9).

To some extent, Democratic party leaders were more likely than Republicans to express an interest in a more diverse government. Some Republican leaders pointed to the gender question as a dividing line between the
two parties' ideologies: for example, Massachusetts House minority leader
Marini said,

> There's a certain segment of [Democrats] at least that won't be happy un-
> til the legislature, everything is fifty-fifty, or whatever the differentiation

10. Siegrist issued a 1999 press release that compared the two parties' records on committee chairs under Democratic versus Republican control of the House. He responded to
a candidate recruiting event that had apparently taken place at the governor's mansion,
arguing, "I'm glad the Democrats have finally seen the light on this one. We've not only
been recruiting highly qualified women to run for State Representative, but we've also put
them in positions of leadership once they get elected."

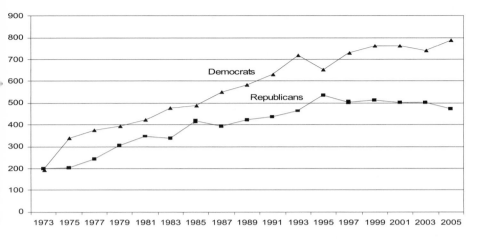

Fig. 4.8.   Number of women state representatives by party.
(Data from CAWP Fact Sheets, various years)

in the population is, I don't know what it is, but if it's fifty-one to forty-nine, [they think] something's wrong and something's rotten in Denmark unless the legislature is exactly the same as the population, and the work-force is exactly the same. And we'll make rules to make sure. Now, that doesn't apply just to gender, but to ethnicity, skin color—a whole host of things. So those people—obviously since the legislature is not fifty-fifty,

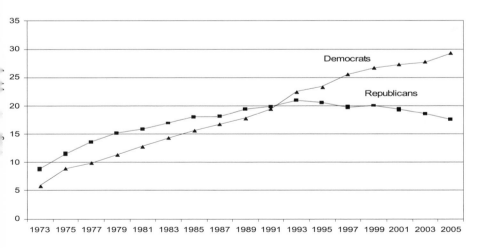

Fig. 4.9.   Percentage of women in house caucus by party.
(Data from CAWP Fact Sheets, various years; Council of State Governments, various years;
National Conference of State Legislatures, various years)

they would perceive, I'm guessing, that there are all kinds of stumbling blocks with women, that there's probably some gender bias out there and all these people are voting against them because they're women. That's ideologically driven trash, in my judgment.

Attention to group membership marks a fundamental difference between the parties, Marini argued,

> At least in the Republican party, everybody is welcome and can rise as far as their own abilities will take them, and that's what I think we should all be after in the end. That we all get treated based on who we are, what is the content of our character, as Martin Luther King said. And how qualified are we for whatever position or job we're seeking, not carry with us the burden of some group identity. Democrats seem to love that. I think that's one of the fundamental differences between the parties. They tend to love people's groups—ethnic, color, gender, disability, slice it up as many ways as you can. They tend to look at groups. I think we tend to look at individual human beings and treat them accordingly, and that's the way I prefer it.

Indeed, the Democratic party mandates equal representation of women on its state party committees, which is not true of all state Republican parties (J. Freeman, forthcoming).

Democratic rather than Republican leaders also more commonly believed that women have more opportunities to become candidates within their party, though Republican leaders often disputed this notion. Iowa Democratic party chair Dr. Sheila McGuire Riggs argued that the Democratic party offers more leadership opportunities for women and cited her path within the party as an example:

> I'd like to think that the Iowa Democratic Party has some fundamental things in place that build leadership skills that then *make* it more open to women running. For instance, we have rules that say our delegation to national conventions has to be gender neutral. Our state central committee needs to be gender neutral. You know, all these different things that give women equal footing in that leadership training. That really makes a difference. Because the Democratic party had equal genders going to the national convention in 1984, I went on the track to running for Congress and being chair of the Iowa Democratic Party.

Most party leaders and staff I interviewed in Iowa believe that the two parties' records are comparable. Even Riggs reflected on women who had recently won statewide office from each party as well as the presence of a Republican woman as Senate president and argued that the numbers are fairly well balanced.

However, the case studies usually lacked a conventional wisdom about which party provides more opportunities for women to become candidates. To some extent, each party was inclined to claim that it offered women more opportunities. But Democrats often expressed surprise about the extent to which Republican women had achieved success in electoral politics in their state. In Ohio, Republican women were serving as lieutenant governor and attorney general at the time of my interviews, and a Republican woman had just served as House speaker. Ohio State Senator Rhine McLin's view was not uncommon: "The thing that's so interesting though, even though the philosophies are so different, the Republicans as a whole have outshined, I think, the Democratic party, even if it's tokenism." Some Colorado Democrats also expressed surprise at how well Republican women have fared in the state.

The status of women in party politics also did not conform to expected ideological lines in Alabama. At the time of my interviews, plans were under way to charter the Alabama Federation of Democratic Women.[11] Republican chair Marty Connors expressed amusement at this new Democratic initiative for women; after all, the Alabama Federation of Republican Women was chartered in 1962 and has more than twenty women's clubs across the state. Connors argued, "If we're talking women, the assumption is, 'Well, Democrats are the party of women, of course.' . . . Apparently not in Alabama. So, we're proud of that."

Meanwhile, Massachusetts Democratic chair Philip Johnston believed that his party was more open to both women and minorities. In contrast, most Republican party leaders and staff in the state thought that the two parties have similar reputations regarding women candidates, pointing to the role of women in legislative leadership and the state party within both parties. Kerry Murphy Healey, elected as Republican party chair shortly

---

11. By nurturing women and encouraging their political involvement, the state party hopes to court women voters, which eventually will lead more women to run for office. Because women appear to be less partisan and less committed to the parties' stances on racial issues, they represent an opportunity to break out of the traditional issue cleavage between the two parties. In addition to the Alabama Federation of Democratic Women, the party's executive director is working to create a political action committee, WIN PAC, that will give to both men and women candidates who agree with the issues supported by the federation.

after I interviewed her, thought that her party was very welcoming to women, citing her position as the likely party chair as well as Governor Jane Swift to support the argument that women had equal or better opportunities to become candidates in the Republican party.

Many Massachusetts respondents argued that women have more opportunities in the Republican party because of its minority status. Stefanini, in the speaker's office, commented that the Republican party offers more opportunities for everyone simply because the state is overwhelmingly Democratic: "The pool within the Democratic side tends to be much more finite and exclusive, whether you're male or female. On the Republican side, it tends to be much more infinite or open-ended." The Republican party's executive director concurred, arguing that his party offers everyone, including women, better opportunities to move up the ladder.

In short, party leaders held a wide range of views about women candidates. Some party leaders said that they attach no weight to candidate gender, while others believe women have a net advantage and consequently like to recruit women candidates. Gender may also figure into slating decisions. For example, some party leaders believe that a woman candidate is a good contrast to a male opponent; others believe a woman candidate is preferred if the opponent is a woman. Meanwhile, those interviewed commonly believed that women are more difficult to elect in some districts or among some subgroups of voters.

Social desirability bias, or the possibility that party leaders provided answers that conform to social norms, is a potential problem for interview questions such as these, which deal with attitudes toward women candidates. Therefore, the extent to which the parties are interested in recruiting women candidates may be overstated. At the same time, party leader doubts about women's electability may be understated. Some party leaders were careful about the ways in which they characterized voter bias because they did not want to sound critical of voters in their states.

To the greatest extent possible, I probed the party leaders I interviewed about how many women they had recruited in cases where they thought such recruitment was advantageous to the party. I also sought further details in those cases where leaders identified voter bias as a problem. By doing so and by comparing across party leaders in the same state, I believe that these interview data reveal important insights about party leader beliefs. Some leaders I interviewed believe that women are advantaged; others believe that some voters are reluctant to support women. Whether party leaders attach significance to candidate gender clearly depends on the state and party. But the interview data may on balance overstate party leader interest in women candidates. I consider this possibility when I turn to the responses of other interview subjects in the next chapter.

PARTY LEADER BELIEFS ABOUT CANDIDATE GENDER: NATIONAL SURVEYS

Scholars commonly argue that women candidates have their parties' full support (Burrell 1994; Darcy, Welch, and Clark 1994). Yet the party leader surveys echo my interviews: whether women are believed to be viable for state legislative seats remains an unsettled question and depends very much on the state. I find that party leaders frequently think that one gender has an electoral advantage. Slightly more state legislative leaders cite an advantage for men than women, whereas the opposite is true for state party leaders. Beliefs about the relevance of candidate gender thus do not necessarily put female candidates at a disadvantage. However, party leader views on women's electability depend on the district: a majority of party leaders believe that it might be hard to elect a woman in at least a few districts in their state. These findings about party leader beliefs provide an important corrective to past studies.

Both the State Legislative Leader Survey and the State Party Leader Survey asked if one gender group has an electoral advantage in races for the House, other factors being equal (see table 4.5). Almost half of legislative leaders and nearly 40 percent of state party leaders reported that neither gender has an advantage. However, 20 percent of legislative leaders and 34

TABLE 4.5. Party Leader Beliefs about Candidate Gender and Electoral Advantage

	State Legislative Leaders (N = 71)	State Party Leaders (N = 56)
Women have some advantage	20%	34%
Men have some advantage	24%	29%
Neither has an advantage	44%	38%
Don't know	8%	0%
Depends (volunteered)	4%	—

Source: State Legislative Leader Survey and State Party Leader Survey.

Note: Question wording: "In races for the House/Assembly, other factors being equal, do you think that women candidates usually have an electoral advantage over men candidates, that men have an electoral advantage over women, or that neither has an advantage?"

percent of state party leaders saw an advantage for women, whereas 24 percent of legislative leaders and 29 percent of state party leaders saw an advantage for men.

These data depart somewhat from the case-study evidence. The party leaders I interviewed typically argued either that men and women are about equally likely to win their races or that women have a slight advantage. In the surveys, however, respondents who saw a net advantage for women were matched by respondents who saw an advantage for men.

The survey evidence contradicts the conventional wisdom that women's electability is no longer an issue: party leaders quite commonly believe that women's electability depends on the area of the state. Party leaders were asked, "Are there districts in your state where it might be hard for a woman to win election to the House/Assembly?" As table 4.6 shows, legislative leaders and state party leaders gave similar overall responses. Response options were "Yes, many," "Yes, a few," "No," and "Don't know." Almost half of state party leaders and about 40 percent of legislative leaders said that their states had no districts where it might be hard for a woman to win election to the House. Yet about 45 percent of both groups reported that a few districts existed where women might have difficulty being elected. Indeed, about 10 percent of both groups reported many such districts in their states.

These results echo the findings from the interview data. Precisely because of the belief that some voters remain reluctant to elect a woman, party leaders may take gender into account when they recruit candidates. The party leaders I interviewed frequently spoke of wanting to find a candidate who fits the district. Whether that district will elect a woman is one aspect of this calculation.

Note that the perception of a net electoral advantage for women candidates does not preclude the view that some state legislative districts may be

TABLE 4.6.   Party Leader Beliefs about Women's Electability

	State Legislative Leaders (N = 71)	State Party Leaders (N = 56)
Yes, many	10%	9%
Yes, a few	46%	45%
No	38%	46%
Don't know	6%	0%

Source: State Legislative Leader Survey and State Party Leader Survey.

Note: Question wording: "Are there districts in your state where it might be hard for a woman to win election to the House/Assembly?"

problematic for women candidates. Of those legislative leaders who believed women had an advantage in House races, half did not believe there are districts where it might be hard for women to be elected, but 7 percent believed that many such districts existed and 36 percent believed that a few such districts existed. Therefore, in states where women are generally perceived to have an electoral advantage, women still might have trouble winning election in some parts of the state. One of the factors in the "other factors being equal" part of the question about gender and electoral advantage may be the district.

To the extent that party leaders actively recruit candidates and influence the nomination, these beliefs about women's electability and electoral advantage may have important implications for women's representation. Recall that about 58 percent of legislative leaders encouraged candidates to run in many seats, and 44 percent of leaders selected candidates for targeted races in some seats. In addition, about 10 percent of state and legislative leaders thought that women might have difficulty being elected in many districts, and nearly half thought that such was the case in a few districts. Whether party leaders recruit and help to nominate women candidates is likely to be influenced by these beliefs about voter behavior.

Democrats and Republicans differ somewhat on these candidate gender questions. Both Democratic legislative leaders and state party leaders were more likely than Republican leaders to think that *men* have an advantage. For example, 19 percent of Republican legislative leaders saw an advantage for women, 19 percent an advantage for men, and 53 percent no advantage. Among Democratic legislative leaders, 20 percent saw an advantage for women, 29 percent an advantage for men, and 34 percent no advantage.

Democratic leaders were also much more likely than Republican leaders to believe that women might have trouble winning in a few districts. Among legislative leaders, about 60 percent of Democrats and only 33 percent of Republicans believed that a few such districts existed, with 26 percent of Democrats and 50 percent of Republicans reporting none. In sum, Republican leaders reported fewer concerns about women's electability than did Democratic leaders. This relationship may seem counterintuitive because Democratic women outnumber Republican women in the state legislatures. However, in the case studies, some leaders from both the Republican and Democratic parties thought that women candidates could appeal to swing voters. In addition, at the national level, the Republican party has sought to recruit women candidates to close the gender gap (Burrell 1994).

To summarize, about half of party leaders believe that one gender has an advantage with voters, other factors being equal. Moreover, a majority of party leaders believe that women might have difficulty winning election in at least a few state legislative districts. Leaders do not commonly think that "many" such districts exist: only 10 percent of party leaders selected that option. Nevertheless, this proportion is much higher than I had anticipated.

CONCLUSION

Whether party leaders perceive men and women as equally viable for the legislature very much remains an open question. The interviews clearly demonstrated that party leader views about candidate gender depended on the state. Gender is a minor consideration in candidate recruitment, according to many party leaders; these leaders spoke of their desire to find the best candidate or the candidate who best fits the district, regardless of gender. In other cases, however, finding the best candidate for the district means that party leaders take gender into account as one aspect of a potential candidate's profile. In some states, leaders think that women candidates have an electoral advantage, increasing the party's interest in recruiting a woman. Yet the strategy of running a woman often depends on a particular type of woman candidate.

Moreover, party leaders in the case-study states commonly believe that women are more likely to be elected in some parts of the state or in some types of districts than others because of district demographics. The belief that women's electability depends on the district was more commonly expressed in North Carolina, Iowa, Ohio, and Alabama than in Colorado or Massachusetts. Thus, candidate gender factors into recruitment because party leaders anticipate voter reaction to candidates.

Some party leaders expressed interest in increasing women's representation as a means of bringing more perspectives into the legislature. Yet this interest was typically secondary to finding a candidate who can win; more often than not, party leaders welcomed women candidates when they were identified but did not pursue a conscious strategy of recruiting women.

Whether voters are equally supportive of men and women candidates also remains an open question among the party leaders I surveyed. Most party leaders believe that women might have difficulty winning election to the legislature in at least a few districts in their states; in a small number of cases, party leaders see many such districts in their states. About half of party leaders believe that one gender has an electoral advantage when other factors are equal. Of these leaders, about half believe that women have an advantage, whereas about half believe that men have an advantage. The advantage that women candidates have in some areas is likely to be canceled out in the aggregate by the advantage that men candidates may have in other areas; some environments seem more favorable to women candidates, while others seem more favorable to men candidates, on average. Yet none of the party leaders I interviewed thought twice about whether men could win election in all districts in their state—a question often asked about women candidates. Even in states where women candidates are thought to have a net advantage, a substantial share of party leaders thought it might be hard for a woman to win election in some districts.

In the next chapter, I analyze perceptions of barriers and opportunities facing women in each of the case-study states, drawing primarily on the interviews with state legislators. I seek to understand respondents' views on whether and how party recruitment and nomination practices affect women's opportunities to become candidates in each state.

CHAPTER 5

Barriers, Opportunities, and the Gendered Path to Office

Do perceptions of women's opportunities as candidates vary across states? In this chapter, I compare the results of the interviews across the case-study states to determine if the party practices outlined in chapter 3 are related to perceptions about women's status as state legislative candidates. How do interview subjects perceive women's opportunities for the legislature? Do respondents believe that women are differentially likely to be recruited or nominated because of gender? Or is the recruitment and nomination process perceived to be gender neutral?

To some extent, respondents believe that women face similar barriers and opportunities across the six states. However, in important respects, perceptions of women's status in electoral politics depend on the state. In particular, interview subjects perceive party practices as having implications for women's representation. The interviews suggest that party efforts to restrict candidate entry in the primary or to support candidates in the primary put women at a disadvantage. Moreover, rather than viewing the recruitment process as a mechanism that can increase women's representation—the relationship I have hypothesized—interview subjects identified the recruitment process itself as a barrier to women's candidacies in some states.

I begin by discussing the methodology used in this chapter. I then analyze the barriers and opportunities identified by interview subjects, supplementing these interviews with the survey of Ohio candidates.

STUDYING PERCEPTIONS

The difficulty of studying the informal dynamics of the candidate selection process has led some scholars to study the success rates of women candidates

(Darcy, Welch, and Clark 1994). However, a focus on women candidates presents a possible selection problem: by studying the electoral fates of women who seek office, we do not learn why other women do not seek office. And this gender gap in who runs for office lies at the heart of women's underrepresentation. Analyzing the state-level correlates of women's candidacies can provide insight into the contextual factors shaping women's representation. However, this approach does not specify the causal mechanisms that link state-level factors to women's decisions about seeking office. I have therefore turned to case studies as a way to help to identify these causal mechanisms (Gerring 2004).

As Carroll and Liebowitz have recently argued, some of the most compelling questions in the study of women and politics call for more diverse methodological approaches:

> Finding answers to many of the most pressing substantive questions in the field of women and politics requires the use of less frequently employed methods such as in-depth interviews, participant observation, focus groups, case studies, content analysis, or some combination of these approaches.
>
> In fact, whenever possible, multiple methods (for example, a combination of surveys, quantitative data analysis, in-depth interviewing, and participant observation) should be used. Relying on any one particular method, no matter what the approach, constrains both the questions that can be asked and the findings that are generated. Utilizing quantitative and qualitative methods as complementary research tools will strengthen women and politics scholarship. (2003: 11)

Looking inside parties and at what happens prior to the primary can provide insights into why more women do not run (Carroll 1993; Baer 1993; Norris 1993; Niven 1998). By studying perceptions and informal selection practices within states, I seek to leverage the comparative framework of the states to understand women's representation. Perceptions can be critical to candidate emergence. Indeed, the subjective probability of winning is central to ambition models (G. Black 1972; Rohde 1979; Jacobson and Kernell 1983; Brace 1984; Abramson, Aldrich, and Rohde 1987; Maisel et al. 1990). Scholars of women and politics have also argued that if women do not perceive the electoral process as open to them, they are unlikely to run (Darcy, Welch, and Clark 1994).

Do parties factor into these perceptions? Parties' receptivity to women's candidacies may shape where women run for office because potential candidates may be less likely to run if they lack party support. Whether women are encouraged to become candidates may also depend on the state and party. By looking within states, I hope to shed light on the interplay between individual decision making and institutions. As Fowler has argued, research is needed to link individual-level models of potential candidates' decision making with the context in which they make their decisions:

> What should a more comprehensive theory of candidacy look like? First, it should identify the eligible contestants within the population at large and explain why those prospective candidates who eventually run are different from those who do not. Second, it should account for the interactions among candidates and political elites as they occur within varying local and national contexts. Third, it should be dynamic to allow for changing expectations and circumstances that move politicians in and out of the candidate pool. The task of the theorist, then, is to reconcile the goal-seeking behavior of prospective candidates with the relevant socioeconomic and institutional constraints that govern their emergence and determine their success. (1993: 42)

I treat the state legislators, candidates, party officials, and political activists I interviewed in each state as informants about women's status as candidates and potential candidates for the legislature. These respondents constitute a sample of experts in each state. These in-depth interviews enable me to make comparisons across states about the informal practices of candidate emergence and recruitment for the legislature and to identify mechanisms by which party activities are thought to matter to women's candidacies. Knowledge of these informal practices has been missing from past research on women and elections.

I use a qualitative approach to analyze the informal ways in which individuals become candidates within specific states. The interview evidence is not without limitations. The interviews are semistructured rather than structured, and I lack a random sample of respondents. By relying on a sample of elite informants in each state, I am using a somewhat indirect strategy to assess the barriers facing women potential candidates. However, by using the same interview procedures in all six states and by interviewing a similar sample of respondents in each state, comparing interviews across states can reveal important insights about the electoral process.

The semistructured interviews allow women an opportunity to describe the electoral environment in their own words. A standard, open-ended question in the interviews was whether the respondent perceived any barriers or opportunities facing women as candidates or potential candidates for the legislature in their state.

Do respondents perceive parties as important agents of recruitment with regard to women in particular? Or do these observers believe that the parties recruit candidates regardless of gender? What are the perceived obstacles to women's candidacies? Are any of the barriers or opportunities to women's representation that respondents identify related to the political parties? If parties are unrelated to women's representation, then respondent perceptions should not vary in meaningful ways according to the party practices I established in chapter 3. Alternatively, if the situation women face as women differs across states and these informant perceptions vary according to party activities, this comparison would suggest that parties are related to women's representation.

In this chapter, I primarily analyze areas of disagreement across the states, rather than areas of agreement. In particular, I focus on the perceptions about barriers and opportunities that varied across the cases. Most of the respondents are state legislators or candidates and therefore have firsthand experience with the decision to run for the legislature. In addition, many respondents are active in candidate recruitment and are therefore familiar with women who chose not to seek office. Most interview subjects were active in their parties and were familiar with their recruitment and nomination practices. If their responses are biased, it is likely that the obstacles identified may underrepresent the problems facing women; most interview subjects are legislators and party leaders who have successfully run for and won office.

CROSS-CASE COMMONALITIES

I will not devote significant attention to perceptions about barriers and opportunities facing women that did not vary in obvious ways across states. Instead, I will briefly highlight the many commonalities across states. For example, respondents—particularly women active in politics for many years —commonly cited the significant progress women have made in politics over the past several decades. Many respondents argued that changes over time in women's opportunities for the legislature had improved and that women are now accepted as candidates more than ever before. Former Ohio Women's Political Caucus president Joyce Garver Keller observed that the number of women in office has increased. In years past, women were not recruited and did not think of themselves as candidates. But women's opportunities have changed dramatically: "Women in their twenties, if you talk about this, they think they're reading an ancient history book. The thought that a woman wouldn't be considered to run for something is just not on their radar screen."

Many respondents, including Representative Edward Jerse of Ohio, pointed to the unique advantages of women candidates: "It's fresh, it's different. I still think that it's probably more likely that women will vote for a woman than men will vote for men, on that basis alone." He explained,

> There seems to be societal premium on looking like America and being open-minded and being diverse. There's a real plus to that. So if you find a talented candidate who falls into an unusual category, genderwise, whatever, that is a plus. I mean, it just makes you look better if you've got a diverse ship, to the public. They say, "Well, those people are inclusive."

A few male legislators in Colorado and Massachusetts spoke of intimidation they experienced running against women candidates with women's networks and activists behind them. Representative Andrew Dedmon, a Democrat from North Carolina, routinely runs against a Republican woman, Debbie Clary, in his multimember district and believes that women cross party lines to support her:

> Going against a woman is tough. I don't care what anybody says. It is tough. Women bond to another female. They will support them. That's how it is. My district is skewed where it is a majority female district. And they vote that way. And I have sat in Democrat women meetings, and they will sit there and say, "I just don't understand how Debbie Clary gets elected." And I just about guarantee you half of them voted for her because she's a woman and they wanted a female representative.

Representative Jean Preston, a Republican North Carolina state legislator, defeated a Democratic incumbent in a multimember district in 1992. She explained that her district, which has more registered Democrats than Republicans, is 52 percent female. She believes that her success results from courting crossover votes: "You wouldn't believe how many women have come up to me and said, 'You know, you're the only Republican I've ever voted for.'" In each of her campaigns, she has written a letter to all of the women in her district: "But I truly have always written women—unaffiliated, Democrats, and Republicans, to tell them what I stand for. And what my voting record is on issues. And so that's—I guess if there's success, that's why, and that's how I got started." Thus, some respondents believe that women have an advantage in drawing female support and perhaps in courting crossover voting.

Some obstacles facing women were also common across all six states. More women would seek office, many respondents argued, were it not for family responsibilities. This factor was easily the most commonly mentioned barrier to women's representation. Interview respondents acknowledged change in gender roles but perceive that gender roles remain an extremely significant and structural barrier to women's candidacies. In addition to the burden this places on women's time, cultural stereotypes about women persist. One implication of these beliefs is that a woman candidate with young children might encounter skepticism because voters prefer that she make her family the priority. Alternatively, some respondents argued that the public is not completely comfortable with women in political leadership roles.

Many respondents believe that fund-raising is no longer a problem for women, but other respondents disagreed, arguing that funding issues discourage women from seeking office. Many interview subjects contended that money is simply less forthcoming for women candidates than for men candidates, even from the same donors. Women lack men's access to networks for fund-raising. For example, this comment from Ohio was not unusual: "I think fund-raising is a major, major barrier, and I think a lot of women just haven't had the life, business, or professional experience that can give them the credibility and stature and the aggressiveness to successfully fund-raise."

The interview subjects also thought that the absence of role models slows the pace at which women seek office. Women of color have even fewer role models, according to Representative Beverly Earle from North Carolina.

> I think that probably, men don't really need any support. I mean, it's automatic for them. They consider themselves as being leaders, and this is something that they want to do. I mean, from childhood, you know, they've got role models like their fathers or other relatives or whatever. . . . Some of us women, especially minorities, I mean, we don't have anybody to identify with that was in this type of position, you know what I'm saying? So, there's no immediate role model to look to.

In addition, across states, some respondents—including party leaders sympathetic to recruiting more women—expressed the view that women are harder to recruit than men, in part because women do not perceive themselves as qualified even when they have the requisite qualifications. North Carolina Representative Mia Morris argued,

One of the most difficult things is convincing women to run or getting women to run. And I've spoken to women's leadership courses and women's professional development and training groups. And oftentimes what I hear is, you know, "I could never do that," "I don't know how," "I don't know enough," "I'm not smart enough," or "I've never been involved in politics." . . . I think that's the biggest stumbling block to get over.

Similarly, Assistant House minority leader Jennifer Veiga from Colorado stated,

Men are much more willing to jump into it than women. You need to push women a lot harder to do it, and for whatever reason, they feel like they're not as qualified or they're not as ready. I don't know who's sending them that message necessarily, but it certainly seems to be one that's fairly universal from the folks I've talked to. And you know, it's changing a little bit. We're having more and more women candidates run. But certainly still not in the numbers that we see men.

More women than men tell Veiga, "I need to be more qualified," regardless of their actual qualifications.

Women frequently argued that they must work harder than men candidates and must prove that they are capable of doing the job. In addition, some women legislators argued that women are more likely to feel that they need to seek additional qualifications before running for the legislature, whereas young men will run directly out of college or law school. Representative Mary Jarrell from North Carolina noted that more women need to join the pool by running for local office. But she also thought that more recruitment of women was necessary: "I think we're going to have to recruit women. I think we're going to have to say to them, 'Why don't you run for higher office?' Women are a little bit timid about doing it, and they have to be overly qualified." Women's concerns about their qualifications may stem from lack of self-confidence or from the fact that others lack confidence in them, according to Jarrell.

To give them the confidence to run or maybe to be accepted. They just have to be a little better qualified than men. Men can just decide, "I think I'd like to go to Washington," and they run for the Congress. And they've never been [in] state, local government. And they don't have as much trouble raising money as women candidates do, for whatever reason.

Women are also less likely to plan political careers. Echoing past studies about gender differences in potential candidates' decision-making processes, a Republican woman in Ohio noted,

> I think men start out with the idea of running for office, being candidates at an earlier age—they see themselves that way, or at least in the past. I mean, times change and are changing. But I don't think most women start out seeing themselves as the candidate. You know, they may start out on a variety of other volunteer—they may work on campaigns, become involved that way. But I don't think they start out with the idea that "I'd like to be governor some day." I don't think that's the experience—with talking to people, that doesn't seem to be the way they get there.

Similarly, Representative Edward Jerse of Ohio said,

> I guess I see, and this is thinking off the top of my head, I see more men in the legislature that I think were like me, where they said, "I'm going to be a politician someday." You see a few women like that. But I think you see more women who said, "I'm going to be a lawyer and I'm going to have a family," and then they get recruited into politics. Or they said "I'm going to do something differently."

Some interview subjects argued that women no longer face barriers in politics. Keller, the former president of the Ohio Women's Political Caucus, argued,

> Women are serious candidates. I mean, no one says, "A woman can't run for this." There isn't any office in the state that people would look at and say that it isn't appropriate or would be peculiar. Even though we've never had a woman governor, I don't think that you'd even poll on the question, "Can a woman become governor of the state?" I don't think it's a question. People would look at you as being strange for even asking them. What? What's the question? This is what we wanted to accomplish. We wanted to accomplish that women would be able to succeed in the political arena on an equal footing with men, to be considered seriously, to be able to be elected and to be able to serve, because they bring—sometimes, they bring a different perspective. And then you can make the decisions.

Women's groups have worked to change the party's views on qualifications as well as women's views of themselves, according to Keller: "I think while we were working to change the parties' vision of what a candidate looked like in the state legislature or on a statewide basis, I think we were also working to have women change their vision of themselves in moving up."

In sum, these perspectives about women's opportunities for state legislative office were common to some extent in all six states. While important, these points of view were not obviously present or absent in particular states. Respondents often cited the progress of women officeholders. In addition, some barriers, such as women's ability to balance a political career with family responsibilities, were mentioned across the case-study states and appear to be fairly universal problems for women candidates.

THE CONSEQUENCES OF PARTY PRACTICES FOR WOMEN CANDIDATES

Other barriers and opportunities identified by interview subjects varied a great deal across the cases. Because women remain underrepresented in politics and because running for elective office is not a typical career path for women, I expected that greater party activity in recruitment would further women's representation. However, the interview data suggest that the recruitment process itself can disadvantage women. While many scholars have assumed that recruitment is gender neutral, many interview respondents identified the party's recruitment of candidates as an obstacle. In addition, some respondents perceived the gatekeeping process as creating barriers to women's candidacies. Where recruitment and gatekeeping by the party are closely related, informal political and social networks are particularly important to the process of becoming the party's preferred candidate.

Ohio and North Carolina respondents were much more likely to identify the parties' recruitment practices as a barrier to women's representation than were respondents in Alabama, Colorado, Iowa, and Massachusetts. At the time of my interviews, the level of women's representation in both Ohio and North Carolina resembled the national average: women comprised 22 percent of legislators in Ohio and 18.8 percent in North Carolina, compared to a national average of 22 percent. For this reason, the barriers that respondents identified in these two states were somewhat surprising. In addition, of the six case-study states, Ohio is known to have the strongest party organizations. Therefore, Ohio should have demonstrated the ways in which stronger parties can enhance women's representation.

This is not to say that all respondents in Ohio and North Carolina were agreed that the parties' recruitment and nomination practices put women at a disadvantage. Many respondents in both states argued that no barriers are unique to women's candidacies. However, in comparison to the other four states, many more respondents—and particularly women respondents—in North Carolina and Ohio identified recruitment as an obstacle.

Gender and Party in North Carolina and Ohio

Precisely how respondents thought party practices disadvantaged women differed to some extent across the two states as well as the two parties within each state. In Ohio, where the party much more actively seeks to influence the nomination and make formal and informal endorsements, the problem of recruitment and gatekeeping appear to be one and the same. Meanwhile, more North Carolina respondents emphasized the recruitment stage. Some interview subjects believe that women are disadvantaged because of the attitudes and conscious behavior of male party leaders. But respondents more commonly believed that these practices disadvantage women as a result of unconscious and unintentional processes.

Why does perception hold that the political parties' involvement in the recruitment process poses an obstacle to women's candidacies? Ohio and North Carolina respondents taking this point of view typically articulated one of four perspectives, although they are not necessarily mutually exclusive and overlap to some extent. First, respondents argued that the recruitment patterns of party leaders, who are usually men, tend to favor male candidates, though not as a result of the intentional exclusion of women. Second, respondents believed that the recruitment process favors men through a more conscious dynamic. Third, respondents had either observed that party leaders viewed women as less viable candidates or surmised that party leaders held such views. Fourth, some respondents argued that a gradual, over time process of grooming and networking accrues an advantage to men. I discuss each of these mechanisms in turn.

The glue that typically undergirded these observations was spontaneous respondent use of the term "old boys' network" or "good old boys' network," with more respondents in North Carolina than Ohio using this term. Beliefs about how parties mattered to women in particular were usually connected to the existence of this old boys' network. Reference to this network was also common in Alabama but was much less common in Iowa, Massachusetts, and Colorado.

In North Carolina, respondents thought that the informal processes of recruitment have a negative effect on women's representation in the legislature because of the old boys' network, although not all respondents who mentioned the network thought that it disadvantages women. Most of the respondents taking this view—almost all of them women—argued that women tend to be overlooked as potential candidates. Representative Verla Insko, for example, discussed the old boys' network in the context of my question about whether anyone in particular is known for consciously identifying women state legislative candidates in North Carolina.

> I think [Representative] Ruth Easterling does, that she talks to women about running. I think that probably a lot of us do it informally, like when we're speaking to a women's organization—that we will almost always say, "It's very important for us to have more. I hope that you will consider running for office," and that when we speak especially to young women, that we say, "It's very important for you to consider doing this and to go ahead and get experience and learn how to raise money," because that's an important part of having a successful campaign, is being able to raise money. I think that informal and general support is there. But we don't have an organized effort to identify women. I think the Democratic party is still the party of the good old boys here in North Carolina, to a large extent.

A key feature of the good old boys' network is informal social contact, according to Insko, a Democrat.

> A lot of the decisions are made informally, through informal conversations that take place in the hallways, on the golf course, out to dinner at night after session. And those groups that go out to dinner are not—at the leadership level—they're not especially integrated groups. So I think a lot of the informal contact, the informal social contact, is still segregated by gender. So it promotes the good old boy network where the men just have more contact with each other. The women are not part of that group. The women have a lot of contact with each other too, but we're not in leadership positions by and large. So there's no decision to make.

Insko argued that men in leadership positions tend to recruit men because their contacts happen to be men. This type of recruitment process is not necessarily intended to exclude women but instead results from the fact that men tend to know other men:

> I don't think it's conscious. I think that they would pick whoever they thought could win. I think if they had a man and a woman who were—it wouldn't even make any difference if they were equally qualified. If the woman looked like she was the better winner and could win more easily, I think they'd support the woman. They want candidates who can win. I don't think they really care whether they're men or women. I think it's just that they have more contacts with men, and that there are more men

in leadership positions back in the community—in those important, visible, power positions back in the community.

Thus, these gender-based contacts are exacerbated by a social eligibility pool that is more likely to be male. Representative Mia Morris, a Republican, echoed the belief that men unconsciously identify men as candidates:

> Oh I don't think men would consciously look for a female candidate. I don't think it would dawn on a man, unless they were *told* to do so. I guarantee any man who was told to find a female candidate could find one. Right away, I'm sure a bunch of men could think of right off the top of their bat, "She would be a great." . . . And I don't think it's anything conscious of men versus women. It's just—I don't know—women know where *we* are, and we know each other.

Morris argued that men tend to look to whom they know: "Where they work, or who they do business with, or who they play golf with or socialize with." Jan Pueschel, a former vice chair of the Wake County Republican party, also argued that men automatically think of other men as candidates. But she also believed that they are happy to support a woman candidate if one is suggested.

> It's just like, "Okay, let's sit down and think. Who could we get to do this?" And all of a sudden, five names pop out of their minds and they're all boys—they're all men. And later you say, "Well, what about, you know, Carol? Or what about Jan? Or what about—" And they go, "Oh, you know, she would be good." But it never occurred to them when they were first making their list or deciding who they were going to ask.

Democratic women in North Carolina echoed these views. House Majority Whip Beverly Earle argued that men do not necessarily think of women:

> They tend to recommend other men for almost everything. . . . It's almost like we're not the first to pop into their minds, as good as we may be at whatever it is we're doing. We're not the automatic person that jumps out there unless it's a task involved. Then, "Oh, Beverly can do this good. She would be excellent at doing this, seeing to it that it gets done." But when they're promoting somebody or awarding somebody, it's almost like it's automatic. I just think that's just the way it is. I don't think things have changed an awful lot.

Thus, the gender composition of the social networks of party leaders is one set of obstacles facing women in North Carolina: the old boys' network is believed to play a consequential role in recruitment. As I discuss later in the chapter, turning to potential candidates who are personally known can arguably constitute an efficient way to conduct candidate recruitment.

Another obstacle interview subjects identified is concern about women's electability and overall competence as candidates. Some male respondents expressed the view that women are not well suited for the rough-and-tumble of politics. A number of women respondents also attributed this viewpoint to male party leaders. Others interviewed believed that support for women candidates depended very much on the area of North Carolina and the willingness of voters and party leaders to take women seriously.

These doubts about women candidates may affect women who put themselves forward to run, not just women who are recruited. Whether through party leaders or other important local community leaders, early reactions to a potential candidacy can be definitive. For example, North Carolina Secretary of State Elaine Marshall, a former state senator, identified informal reactions to a potential candidacy as one of the leading barriers women face in running for the General Assembly:

> Being taken seriously as a candidate—part of that is reflected in the contribution. The other part of it is reflected in when women want to float their name, a lot of them get derailed. They try to find another job for them to do or pat them on the head, tell them they're not ready for it, and this kind of stuff. The kind of things that I don't think are going on when men say, "Gee, I'd like to run for the State House." You know, all of these made-up barriers, make-do obstacles that really aren't obstacles, but they try to plant seeds of doubt in people's minds and try to make the challenge exaggerated—make it worse than it really is. So those are all barriers here. . . .

> You know, every savvy candidate will sit down with the leaders, whoever they might be, and say, "I'm interested in this office. I'd like to have your support. Tell me what you think the challenges are"—you know, whatever kind of list of questions you ask. I always ask, "Who else do you think I ought to be seeing?"—make sure you're getting all of the community leaders and what have you. And those community leaders, they see each other, whether it's at coffees at Hardee's or at church or at the Rotary Club meeting, or what have you. And they talk. And that's where political careers, in my opinion, are made or broken. . . .

> And if a bunch of people think, "She can't do it, she can't do it. . . . She's not strong enough," those kind of little things, that sets the tone for the campaign. If you have that going on against you out there, then you

have to be a tremendous campaigner to convince those people differently —if it's possible.

In North Carolina, the parties wield less influence over the nomination than in Ohio. However, both North Carolina parties have become increasingly involved in recruitment for the legislature over the past decade. And many respondents believe that the recruitment process tends to exclude women because of gender differences in social networks and a failure to perceive women as candidates and to take women seriously.

Chapter 3 demonstrated that having party support or receiving the party nod is much more common in Ohio than in North Carolina. In Ohio, therefore, any gender differential in the recruitment process is amplified by the party's status as both recruiter and gatekeeper. The recruitment process is more tightly linked to the nomination in Ohio and is usually very selective. As in North Carolina, Ohio respondents argued that women's lack of exposure to the old boys' network means that women are less likely to be recruited for the legislature.

Some Ohio respondents taking this view did not identify conscious bias against women; instead, they argued that because women have not traditionally been active in politics, it is easier for men to recruit men because men travel in the right circles to become candidates. Although these respondents see this network as an obstacle to women's candidacies they did not believe that women are consciously excluded. Men in the old boys' network simply tend to look to people they know and are comfortable with, and women lack exposure to the old boys' network.

Others believed that women are less likely to be recruited, are less encouraged, or have less access to the party structure because of bias against women and outdated views of women's roles, and/or the misperception that women cannot win in certain parts of the state. As in North Carolina, some Ohio respondents argued that men did not necessarily view women as candidates. Such attitudes at the local level can matter a great deal. Jo Ann Davidson, the first woman to serve as speaker of the Ohio House, argued that some of the barriers women face lie within the party:

> I still think we have a lot of stumbling blocks ahead of us. . . . Some of them are within the political party, that the party perhaps doesn't reach out—particularly on the county level—doesn't reach out as strongly to encourage women candidates. I think the women in many county organizations have typically been the people who bake the cookies and stuff the

envelopes, which is what I did for a number of years. I'm well versed in doing both of those. But at some particular point in time you have to step, you know, over and above that.

She argued that in some counties, women and men are not equally tapped to run for the legislature:

As much as we tried to say the old boys' network doesn't exist, it still does exist. There's no question in my mind about that. And you have to be a little aggressive in putting yourself in the right position and not take it for granted that you are going to be given the opportunity if you think you're well placed and well qualified for doing it.

The old boys' network means that women may not get the party nod even when they should, meaning that more men are recruited. According to Davidson,

Because of the associations that they may have. It may be through fraternities at college. It may be golfing buddies. They may shoot baskets together or whatever. So they tend to build those kind of relationships. And generally, men tend to be more involved in the political system. It's been part of what they view as career opportunities and increasing their potential, even résumé building. So they're pretty supportive of each other out there. And we haven't yet—we've been a little more slow at refining our ability to be as equally supportive. We've got a lot of little unofficial groups. The attorney general and I periodically host functions that we invite all of the women directors and all of the women legislators. We try to build those support networks and let them know there are people out there who want to help and are willing to help. And when they ask for help, we try to stand behind what we told them that we will do.

Attorney General Betty Montgomery, a former state senator, expressed a similar point of view. Although she believes that the state and legislative parties are aware that polls indicate women have a slight advantage, she believes that the situation differs somewhat at the local level:

I still think that at the local level, however, and through your party process and through your grassroots process, you probably still have a lot of impediments for women to be considered possible candidates. The caucuses may go out and recruit a woman. But the grassroots people may not. They may not because . . . the woman may not naturally come forward to propose herself because the party structure's not friendly to women. It's still good old boy, or it's antiquated, it's not easily accessible for women because it's cliquish. Or there may be in some of the areas, still a sort of unexpressed, maybe sometimes expressed, but probably at this point less expressed antagonism toward, a little prejudice against, that women belong in the home. . . .

At the local level, I suspect it's a less accessible process for women. I think in some of these small counties, it's a creaky, older structure, and so it's less accessible. These folks may be entrenched and used to doing business the old way, which didn't include women. And again, not necessarily in an antagonistic way, but in a sort of last generation view of what women's roles were or could be.

Lack of encouragement makes it much less likely that women will become candidates, according to a Republican woman legislator:

There are more men in the pipeline. There are more men out there doing it. There are more men ready to take over term-limited seats. I think one of the concerns that a lot of women have had about the impact of term limits is that it's harder to get women to run for office in the first place. I mean, by nature they're less inclined to stick their neck out. I mean, it's different. And so there are fewer women in the pipeline, and there are not going to be as many ready to go into an open seat. There are more men, I think, who have run for office at every level and who progress through the system. Because frankly, the system is not real conducive, I think, to encouraging women to actually run and succeed. . . .

I think [women] haven't been encouraged by the men who generally run the party and run the operation. And I'm not saying just Republicans. The same thing is true on the Democratic side.

Concern about the attitudes of some local party leaders is not limited to the Republican party. House Democratic Leader Jack Ford, for example, alluded to the difficulties women face in the local party:

There's still bias that women run against both within their counties and certain other institutions within the Democratic party. But women are doing well. Women have an edge both in voting registration and I think voters see them as being better candidates. But there's still—like there is throughout all of society—a certain amount of sexism.

When pressed to elaborate, Ford continued, "As I got around to different areas [of the state] and I saw how women were treated as opposed to men, there was a little more ease in the male candidates' being accepted. And like I said, in some areas, a household votes based on how the man says they're going to vote."

Men potential candidates were argued to be better positioned to become the party's preferred candidate because of the importance of the old boys' network and the cumulative advantage this gives to men. One Republican woman in Ohio stated, "If I hear the phrase *bright young man* one more time I think I'll drop out of my seat and scream"; "I think it's an attitude within the Republican party. I don't know about the Democratic party, but I think it's attitudinal in terms of seeing long-term political careers in terms of growth of young men and not of women, with some exceptions." Other Republican women also spoke of the consequences for women's opportunities when people invested early in the political careers of young men. These Republican women argued that women were much less likely to be groomed and mentored than men. As a result, women were thought to be at a disadvantage when seats become open.

This viewpoint was less common on the Democratic side, perhaps because the Republican party, which controls Ohio's legislature and all statewide offices, is much stronger organizationally in the state than the Democratic party. Yet Democratic women also expressed the sentiment that men tend to mentor other men. For example, Democratic House minority whip Erin Sullivan explained,

I think when elected officials are mentoring candidates, they tend to look for people who remind them of themselves, and in the case of women, it's going to be other women; in the case of men, it's going to be other young men. Traditionally, mentoring doesn't, I don't think, cross gender lines because people want to mentor people that they see themselves in, and I think that's why. So the more women you have in elected office, the more chances there are to mentor other women.

She also argued that "golden boys" are much more common than "golden girls" or "golden women": "Women, I see, have to work harder to get that golden girl status than men do." She argued that women have to work twice as hard as men to earn the same amount of respect. Asked if she meant that women had to work harder to earn the respect of voters or of other elected officials, she indicated the latter.

But more so with other leaders, other elected officials, leaders of the community who tend to give male candidates more respect initially than they do female candidates and you have to work hard to earn that respect, and I think it's worth it—working hard to earn their respect—because when you do, you know you worked hard to earn it.

Sullivan hoped that needing to work harder would not discourage women from running for office.

The idea that voters might be more open than party leaders to women candidates was also voiced on the Republican side. One Republican woman argued, "There's still some reluctance in the political system, hierarchy in some instances, in some geographic areas, particularly in some of the more rural counties, it's still hard to convince them that a woman candidate can win." However, this respondent was not convinced that such is the case:

> I think the younger women candidates that we're recruiting are much more self-confident. I think that the same obstacles are there. They're just maybe a little bit more under the surface and a little less intense. But they haven't gone away. The one thing that has made the difference is the fact that the voters' willingness to accept a woman candidate has shifted tremendously, and that shift is to the advantage of the woman candidate. And the fact that men are very nervous about running against women, and they need to be.

Other respondents argued that party leaders tend to recruit candidates with whom they are comfortable and make assumptions about whether voters will be likely to support women candidates and candidates of color.

Thus, respondents in both Ohio and North Carolina frequently cited gendered social networks and doubts about women's competence or viability as candidates as barriers facing women as candidates and potential candidates. However, not all respondents were skeptical about how women fared in terms of recruitment.

It was more common for men respondents rather than women respondents and party leaders rather than activists, candidates, or legislators to argue that the problem of women's underrepresentation will be resolved as a matter of course—that as the pool of women in local office grows and generational change continues, women's representation will necessarily increase. In Ohio, for example, both state party chairs expressed this view, arguing that women's underrepresentation is essentially a mathematical problem; women will first fill lower offices, and it is only a matter of time before the presence of women in the legislature increases.

It was not unusual to hear this perspective—that increases in the pool will inevitably yield more women in the state legislature—across the case-study states. For example, House minority leader Francis Marini of Massachusetts explained that women's family responsibilities provide one explanation for their underrepresentation; he also cited generational change:

> This transition from completely male-dominated government to a completely integrated one in terms of gender takes probably a generation or more to accomplish, not because people are biased, because I don't believe they are, but because people in positions in local decision-making authorities, their tenure tends to extend for years. And we all tend to associate with people more like ourselves, so you get a little bit of a male-dominated hierarchy that takes time for it to change. But I think clearly it's in the process of changing. And, you know, I would say that—my guess is that ten years from now, there will be no reason, other than reasons maybe we don't fully understand, but there'll be no direct impediment or bias that is keeping women from being 50 percent or maybe more.

Yet some North Carolina and Ohio interview subjects—particularly women—strongly believe that the presence of women candidates and legislators will not increase as long as the normal recruitment process continues. Dissatisfaction with the typical recruitment process and its failure to yield a sufficient number of women candidates is much more widespread in Ohio, North Carolina, and Alabama than in Colorado, Massachusetts, or Iowa. New women's organizations had recently been created for precisely this reason. In North Carolina, for example, some of the founders of Lillian's List, a pro-choice Democratic political action committee modeled after EMILY's List, were motivated in part by a belief that the typical party mechanisms were not generating many women candidates for the legislature and that more could be done to recruit women. Republican women legislators, meanwhile, have formed a group called the Committee to Elect Republican Women as a way to increase their numbers in the legislature.

Davidson's Ohio efforts to create support groups for Republican women to address barriers that women face began in the 1970s. In 1984, she organized the Republican Women's Campaign Fund, which supports candidates for local and state office. Davidson recently created a leadership institute to train Republican women for government and politics, as is reflected in one of its stated objectives: "To place at least 15 of the program's participants in either elective or appointive positions in politics or public service within five years of their completion of the program."[1] Davidson explained that the in-

---

1. <http://www.jadleadershipinstitute.com/>

stitute encourages women to seek party leadership roles in addition to public office:

> Sometimes it's encouragement into political party leadership roles. That's important too. Because if there aren't women in political party leadership roles who are willing to reach out and help women, then you've still got the same obstacles that you had before. Some of the really good county chairmen understand that women candidates now are very marketable and so they do more recruitment of women candidates.

In sum, women have consciously developed alternative networks to support women candidates.

Evidence from Ohio Candidates: Beliefs about Gender and Recruitment

Ohio interview respondents, particularly women, frequently argued that women were overlooked as candidates in the recruitment process, which, in Ohio, is strongly related to who wins party support in the primary. The survey responses of women Ohio candidates confirm these perceptions about obstacles. In addition, the survey data indicate that on questions related to gender, the views of men and women candidates differ dramatically.

Most women candidates believe that the party is more likely to encourage men than women to run for the legislature (see table 5.1). While 78 percent of men candidates believe that the party equally encourages men and women to run for the legislature, only 34 percent of women believe that such is the case. Instead, about 29 percent of women responded that men are sometimes more encouraged to run for the legislature, with 26 percent responding that men are often more encouraged. Thus, more than half the women believe that their party is more likely to encourage men to become candidates than women. Although the number of women respondents is small (N = 35), this group represents more than half of the universe of

TABLE 5.1.   Ohio Candidates: Perceptions of Gender and the Recruitment Process

	Women are often more encouraged	Women are sometimes more encouraged	Men and women are equally encouraged	Men are sometimes more encouraged	Men are often more encouraged	Don't know
Men (N = 118)	3%	3%	78%	3%	2%	12%
Women (N = 35)	3%	3%	34%	29%	26%	6%

Source: State Legislative Candidate Survey, Ohio. Rows may not sum to 100 percent due to rounding.

Note: Question wording: *"In your view,* are men and women equally likely to be encouraged by your party to become candidates for the Ohio House and Senate?"

women who ran for the legislature in 2002 (the response rate was about 61 percent); women comprised only 22 percent of 2002 Ohio state legislative candidates.

Candidates may observe the dearth of women candidates in the state and assume that women are less likely to be recruited. Such a dynamic would indicate that respondents are making inferences about recruitment by extrapolating from the presence of women candidates rather than answering based on knowledge of the recruitment process. This does not seem to be the case, however. Instead, the large gender gap suggests that men and women perceive the recruitment process differently. Women candidates believe the party is much more likely to encourage men than women to seek state legislative office.[2]

Comparisons across States

These concerns identified in North Carolina and Ohio about how the recruitment process affects women generally did not surface in Massachusetts and Colorado, where the parties are less involved in candidate recruitment. I argued in chapter 3 that candidates in Massachusetts do not need the party's approval to seek state legislative seats and that respondents did not think that the political parties' efforts explain how most candidates decide to run for the legislature. Massachusetts respondents indicated that no shortage existed of candidates on the Democratic side. While the two parties have become increasingly competitive in North Carolina, the Democratic party's control of the legislature in Massachusetts is overwhelming.

Interview subjects also did not usually identify recruitment as a barrier facing women in Iowa, where both parties have sophisticated recruitment operations but neither party takes sides in the primary. In Alabama, where most candidates come forward on their own, respondents did not necessarily consider the parties either a help or a hindrance to women's candidacies.

MASSACHUSETTS AND COLORADO

Some Massachusetts and Colorado respondents identified the recruitment process as an obstacle to women's representation. For example, one Massachusetts legislator argued that the Democratic party has become more re-

---

2. This sentiment resembles the findings of Niven's (1998) study of four states, including Ohio, in which most women in local office argued that party leaders discouraged women from running.

ceptive to women candidates but that for many years women have faced (and continue to face) bias within the party because it has historically been dominated by Irish Catholic men. Another respondent argued that women from outside the Democratic party structure do not seem to get the same reception as men who are new to the party: party leaders do not seem to hold a woman candidate without party connections in as high a regard as they would an equivalent man. In addition, the party's lesser role in nominations in Massachusetts than in other states does not preclude formation of a line for elected office. For example, male legislators reprimanded one female state senator for her ignorance when she entered a race for an open congressional seat: Did she not realize that they had been waiting in line for years for that position?

Respondents do not perceive voter attitudes as a problem for state legislative races. However, many of those interviewed pointed to the criticism of Governor Jane Swift, arguing that women faced significant barriers in reaching statewide office in Massachusetts. Respondents also pointed to the absence of a woman in the state's congressional delegation.

Some Colorado respondents believe that women candidates do not always receive the support they merit at party nominating conventions. In addition, dissatisfaction with the normal recruitment process has led to new efforts to improve women's networking opportunities. One Democratic county chair began the Democratic Women's Mentoring Group, a program for young women in her local party. In addition, former state senator Gloria Tanner created a leadership institute for African American women aimed not only at the legislature but at serving on boards and commissions. Senator Tanner's Institute of Future Black Women Leaders of Colorado is intended as a support group for women.

In sum, some Massachusetts and Colorado interview subjects argued that the typical networking and recruitment processes work to men's advantage. These perspectives are not unimportant and suggest that even in states where the term *old boys' network* is not widely used in discussions of women's status, barriers may still exist in recruitment. However, unlike in North Carolina and Ohio, these types of perceptions were quite infrequent.

As chapter 3 discussed, respondents generally believed that the party's role in candidate recruitment is less consequential in Massachusetts and Colorado than in North Carolina and Ohio. It is the province of primary voters rather than party leaders to select the nominee in Massachusetts; for the most part, candidates decide to seek office independent of the wishes of party leaders. The parties are more active in recruiting candidates in Colorado than Massachusetts, but the relatively open process and the absence of a strong, informal candidate selection process arguably explains why women do so well in the state, according to majority leader Lola Spradley. The absence of gatekeeping on the Republican side is evident in primaries that are known to be quite contentious affairs between the moderate and conservative wings of the party.

To the extent that the parties do act as gatekeepers for competitive races in Colorado, this process does not appear to disadvantage women. Democratic chair Tim Knaus explained, "There's never been a fear of fielding women candidates." Women candidates stood for three of the Senate seats that the Democrats targeted in 2000: according to Knaus, "We went with three women candidates. There was no hesitation about doing that—because of who they were individually."

Party practices are not the only factors that differentiate these four states. For example, public opinion is more liberal in Massachusetts and Colorado than Ohio and North Carolina. In Colorado, which ranked fourth in the nation in women's representation at the time of my interviews, I expected to find strong women's organizations that recruited women. However, I found little evidence of conscious recruitment of women candidates by the parties or by women's groups. Women's success in representation in Colorado arguably derives from the electorate, not from the presence of women's groups or a conscious effort on the part of the parties to recruit women. Former House minority leader Peggy Kerns, a Democrat, argued, "But I think it has more to do with the electorate accepting women candidates and less to do with the parties or other entities recruiting women candidates."

IOWA AND ALABAMA

Unlike North Carolina and Ohio, Iowa respondents did not usually identify the recruitment process as a barrier to women's candidacies. The parties are very actively looking for candidates, though not necessarily for women in particular. However, both parties have welcomed a new women's organization intent on increasing the presence of women in the legislature, Iowa's Women in Public Policy (WIPP).[3] Both the Republican and Democratic state party

3. Brunnette began the group in the fall of 2001 as a way of creating a network of women who affect public policy across the spectrum, including elected officials, staff, lobbyists, and business and community leaders. WIPP soon decided to take advantage of open

chairs in Iowa serve on the board of directors of WIPP. Leeann Brunnette, the lobbyist who began the group, argued that WIPP had elevated the search for women candidates and had helped the parties recruit women.

Women in Iowa did not identify the recruitment process as a source of women's underrepresentation. As I argued in chapter 4, the Iowa party leader interviews showed some limited support for the idea that women candidates have a slight electoral advantage. However, most party leaders I interviewed in the state did not believe that such an advantage exists, and most believed that women are more electable in some districts than others. Respondents also pointed to the fact that Iowa has never elected a woman to Congress as evidence that voter support for women candidates remains problematic. Opportunities exist in Iowa, as in any state, for doubts about women's viability to enter into the recruitment process. And respondents in Iowa raised many more concerns about voter attitudes than did those interviewed in Colorado or Massachusetts.

Recruitment in Iowa is selective. For example, Marlys Popma, executive director of the Republican party, argued that local gatekeepers matter more at the recruitment stage than at the primary stage: "Because if you have someone who is tremendously influential, and you're discussing who should run for that office, and that very influential person says, 'No, that's not the right person,' the likelihood that that recruitment process stops with that person is great." As chapter 3 demonstrated, neither party takes sides in Iowa's primaries, and many party leaders believe that supporting candidates in the primary can backfire. But informal evaluations of potential candidates mean that some potential candidates are recruited rather than others.

In Alabama, Representative Jeanette Greene, a Republican, had a simple answer to my question about what barriers or opportunities women faced in running for the legislature:

> The problem is that this *is* Alabama and that it is a male-dominated—in the political realm—it is still male-dominated. Eight women out of 105

---

seats. Incorporated as a 501(c)3, WIPP does not offer financial help to women candidates but instead seeks to educate and create an awareness about the need for women to get involved, to identify women to run for office, and to support women who run. Recruitment is an important component of WIPP's agenda. The awareness created by WIPP and the campaign training the group held in the fall of 2001 seemed to have paid off: Brunnette looked over her list of sixty-nine candidates who had filed to run in the primary, including thirty-one women running in twenty-six open races, and attributed both direct and indirect effects to WIPP.

in the House—that tells you something. Three out of the 35 in the Senate. That's the main problem. Getting them to see that a woman is going to stand up, she needs to stand up and do the things that need to be done. . . . But that's the main thing: they just think men should be in politics.

Greene argued that women do not think about running for office because the political realm is male dominated. At the time of my interviews, Alabama ranked last among the fifty states in women's representation, with women constituting less than 10 percent of the legislature. Moreover, the state parties were not looking to increase women's representation: neither Alabama's Democrats nor its Republicans consciously sought to field women candidates. As I described in chapter 4, the Democratic House majority leader suspects that women candidates may attract crossover Republican votes, but the state party, which has more responsibility for recruitment, did not share this viewpoint.

Signs of change are becoming apparent, however. A statewide, bipartisan political action committee, Alabama Solution, started in 1992 to fund women's candidacies. A new effort, the Alabama Women's Initiative, may signal the beginnings of a more organized political network of women in Alabama. The group held a press conference at the legislature in the spring of 2002 to promote a policy agenda. The Alabama Women's Initiative seeks to educate women and the state about women's status in Alabama and to encourage women to play leadership roles. Its 2002 *Report on the Status of Women in Leadership in Alabama* rejected the notion that the pool of candidates for elective office contains insufficient numbers of qualified women:

> There are plenty of qualified women in Alabama at all levels. If the most qualified person had been chosen in each election, Alabama would not still be in last place in the number of women officeholders. What women have been denied is a fair opportunity in our present system. (Alabama Women's Initiative 2002: 40)

In my interviews in Alabama, women often used the term "old boys' network." However, the parties were not necessarily cited as an obstacle to women's representation because most state legislative candidates are thought to be self-starters. When I asked if men and women have equal opportunities to seek office if they choose to do so, as one respondent argued, no one will stop them: no party nod is needed in Alabama. Indeed, House speaker pro tempore Demetrius Newton said that the Democratic party rarely recruits candidates. In response to my question about whether women had more opportunities to become candidates in the Democratic or Republican party, Newton explained that the Republicans

> do more soliciting candidates to run for certain spots. And if in their numbers, they don't get a lot of women, I have to assume it's because they don't choose the women. But we don't pick them over here. In the Democratic party, if they decide to run, they run under our banner. And if they win, they are our candidates.

Both parties were more interested in women's candidacies today than in the past, but those interviewed thought that this more receptive climate to women candidates was a very recent development.

Alabama's recruitment and nomination process differs significantly from that in the other case-study states because of the major role that interest groups play in primaries, providing funds and critical endorsements. The role of interest groups in primaries is "huge," in the words of one respondent. Some interview subjects thought that interest groups would support a woman candidate if the candidate were brought to their attention. However, other respondents identified interest groups as a barrier to women's candidacies. Skepticism on the part of interest groups about women candidates discourages women from seeking office. This lack of support can be a formidable barrier given that winning interest group support is critical to surviving the primary.

Thus, a combination of factors seems to explain the dearth of women legislators in Alabama: the absence until recently of party involvement in candidate recruitment; the recency of party receptivity to women candidates; the newness of a movement to elect women; the reluctance of interest groups to support women candidates; and voter attitudes.

In Alabama, then, the party is not regarded as the problem. But it is also not regarded as the solution. The Alabama case demonstrates that a weak party environment provides no guarantee that women will be better represented in office. Unlike Massachusetts, where women's groups and networks are strong and the public liberal, neither is the case in Alabama. Women in Alabama appear to be in the early stages of forming a political network for women in the state. In contrast, the group most active in Massachusetts in helping women achieve office, the Massachusetts Women's Political Caucus (MWPC), was founded in 1971. The MWPC has a large network, holds annual campaign training for women candidates, and alerts women to open-seat opportunities.[4]

Women have not come forward to run in Alabama on their own. Yet they also have not been recruited. In Massachusetts, John Stefanini, chief counsel to the speaker of the House, observed that women state legislators are more likely to come from suburban districts because the salience of education issues creates a natural fit for women candidates in those areas. In short, he argued that political campaigns tend to be "self-selecting": "To the extent that a candidate sees themselves as viable or not, increases the likelihood that they will in fact be a candidate." Presumably, women do not see good opportunities to become candidates in Alabama. Former state senator Ann Bedsole, the first woman to serve in the state Senate and the first Republican woman to serve in the House, argued that it is very difficult for women to win in state legislative races in Alabama. When I asked if the problem is that more women need to run for the legislature, she replied that women probably know better than to try. Thus, women may not enter if they think they will lose.

The Promise of Recruitment

The typical party recruitment and nomination process in North Carolina and Ohio is believed to put women candidates at a disadvantage. However, the interviews also revealed two factors that appear to disrupt the typical process: women party leaders and party leaders interested in increasing women's representation, and the belief that women candidates have a net advantage over men.

First, as the Ohio and North Carolina interviews clearly illustrated, a potential problem with the candidate recruitment process is that respondents believe party leaders do not personally know women and do not necessarily think of women as candidates. These attitudes about the old boys' network imply that party leaders who do know women are likely to identify them as

---

4. MWPC announces open seats on its email listserv that includes nine hundred recipients. In addition, in October 2001 its political action committee held an event, Political Musical Chairs, Massachusetts Style, that focused primarily on expected open seats for the state legislature in 2002. The state boasts other women's groups as well, including Women In, which is a project of the progressive Commonwealth Coalition, which includes labor, environmental, citizen action, and women's groups and endorses candidates for the state legislature. Women In began in 1996 and helps progressive women win office. It has not been very involved in recruiting candidates but hopes to do so in the future.

candidates. In cross-national research, the presence of women in high positions within the party helps to explain the presence of women in office (e.g., Caul 1999).

As part of the interview, I asked respondents if they knew of any individual or group making a conscious effort to recruit women candidates in particular for the legislature. At this point in the interview, individuals usually mentioned women's groups in the state, including women's political action committees and other groups. Depending on the organization, respondents usually thought that these groups assisted declared candidates rather than recruited candidates. In North Carolina and Ohio, the same party leaders or individuals were identified as making an effort to recruit women across interviews, although this phenomenon occurred much more commonly in Ohio than in North Carolina. In most but not all cases, these individuals were women. Interview subjects in Alabama, Iowa, Colorado, and Massachusetts did not identify a few well-known individuals active in recruiting women for office.

By most accounts, more important than any women's group in Ohio were several key party leaders and staff within both parties. For example, several Republican women I interviewed had been recruited by speaker Jo Ann Davidson; they had not thought about running for the legislature and would not have run were it not for Davidson's suggestion. Some critics may contend that Davidson recruited women ahead of men; however, Davidson argues that she recruited the best candidates, who in some cases happened to be women.

Senator Rhine McLin, a Democrat, echoed the view that women leaders make a difference to women's representation in Ohio.

> It's one of those things where, when you do the statistics that show the voting populace trust women more so than they do the men. Women are generally more straight shooters. But women—unless you have women in leadership who make a concerted effort, it won't happen. And sometimes if the woman comes up and says she wants to do that, they'll say okay, but they'll keep looking.

The presence of women legislators and legislative leaders in Iowa in both parties had implications for the recruitment of women candidates. For example, Senate President Mary Kramer frequently mentors women about becoming candidates. In addition, women in the caucus query the leadership about the number of women who have been recruited and suggest names of potential candidates.

Having at least one woman in state legislative leadership has become more common across the country. As Ohio Representative Edward Jerse explained,

> There is a real effort to look like America among the leadership—whether it's real or just window dressing—to try to put people in offices, so that leadership will always have a woman [leader] on both sides [of the aisle], whether that woman would have been elected on their merits or not.

However, even when pressure exists to diversify the caucus, that pressure may not extend beyond token status. Some evidence from the judicial arena indicates that women may be more likely to receive judicial appointments if a state court is all male; however, when a woman serves on the court, it is less likely that another woman will be appointed (Bratton and Spill 2002).

Relatively few women have achieved state legislative leadership positions. Women comprised 11.2 percent of state legislative leaders in 1999, 12.6 percent of leaders in 2001, and 13.6 percent of leaders in 2003 (CAWP 1999, 2001b, 2003).[5] In 2003, three women served as Senate presidents and five women served as speakers of the House. In all of U.S. history, only nine women (three Democrats and six Republicans) have ever served as Senate presidents and twenty women (six Democrats and fourteen Republicans) have served as speakers of the House. Most local and state party leaders are men as well (Handlin 1998; Baer 2003; J. Freeman, forthcoming). In 2002, only thirteen Democratic women and eight Republican women served as chairs of the fifty state parties. Fewer than 15 percent of all Republican county chairs in Ohio in 2004 were women, as were just over one-quarter of Democratic county chairs.[6] The Party Transformation Study conducted in 1979 and 1980 found that 19.1 percent of Democratic county chairs and 24.2 percent of Republican county chairs were women.[7]

Women commonly perceive barriers to their influence within the legislature, including access to leadership positions. A recent survey of state legislators by the Center for American Women and Politics found that 58 percent of women and 79 percent of men agreed that leaders in their legislature are as likely to consult with women in the legislature as men when making important decisions; however, 40 percent of women and 17 percent of men

---

5. These statistics include Senate presidents and presidents pro tempore, House speakers and speakers pro tempore, and majority and minority leaders.

6. I compiled these data from party Web sites.

7. Women comprised about one-quarter of county party chairs in the Party Elite Studies conducted in 1980 and 1984 (Baer and Bositis 1988).

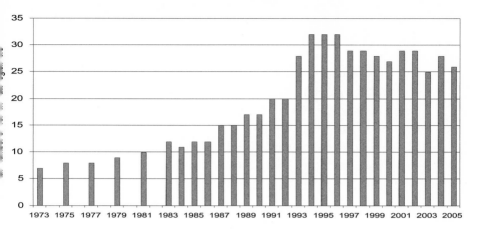

Fig. 5.1.   Ohio women state legislators.
(Data from Cox 1996; CAWP Fact Sheets, various years)

disagreed (CAWP 2001c). Moreover, 56 percent of women and 80 percent of men agreed that most men in their legislatures supported moving women into leadership positions, but 42 percent of women and 15 percent of men disagreed.

Furthermore, because those key leaders and staff who identified women candidates are no longer in the Ohio legislature, a number of interview subjects observed that an impetus for the recruitment of women no longer exists within either party. Many Ohio respondents believe that women's representation is unlikely to increase in the near future. Indeed, the number of women in the Ohio legislature has declined in recent years (see figure 5.1).

Thus, party leaders who have a particular interest in recruiting women (who tend to be women) and women party leaders (who tend to know other women) may mitigate the negative effect of gatekeeping. Second, the perception that women are *not* disadvantaged electorally may be a necessary—though insufficient—condition for recruitment to aid women, including selective recruitment for competitive seats. In Colorado, for example, women are not perceived as advantaged, but they are also not perceived as disadvantaged. Thus, the selection of women in Colorado for key Senate races took place in a setting where women are generally believed to be as viable as men. In contrast, Republican interest in women candidates in North Carolina centered on women as women and the belief that women candidates have an advantage. This belief has increased the party's interest in women candidates and represents a departure from the typical process whereby women are thought to be overlooked as candidates in North Carolina.

As chapter 4 demonstrated, polls indicate that women have an electoral advantage in Ohio. The view that women have a net advantage appears to be more prevalent among state party and caucus leaders than local leaders. Attorney general Betty Montgomery explained that the caucus may seek out a woman candidate intentionally because of this perceived advantage: "Now they may go out and deliberately recruit a woman. But at the local level, you are still going to have—depending on who is in control of the party framework—you may still have an impediment." Later in the interview she summarized, "I guess the party can be an impediment. It can also help, but it can be an impediment." Other respondents echoed this view. For example, one respondent explained: "I really think that the recruiting machinery in the [Republican] party right now is very geared towards women. I think they're very sensitive to the positives of women candidates, especially in certain [swing] areas."

Given the sum of the perceived obstacles facing women, the idea that women may have a small advantage appears to generate more interest within the parties in women candidates than would otherwise be the case. In addition, a number of women legislators I interviewed had not thought about running for the legislature until they were recruited.

Evidence from Ohio Candidates: Political Parties and the Decision to Run

The importance of recruitment for women's representation is evident in the Ohio candidate survey. Table 5.2 demonstrates that the difference between women's and men's decisions to run for the legislature is striking: women are more likely to run because they were recruited by the party. This confirms past research that women are more likely than men to report that they ran for the legislature because they were recruited (Moncrief, Squire, and Jewell 2001; Squire and Moncrief 2004).

Men and women candidates in Ohio also differed significantly in their beliefs about voters. Candidate beliefs about whether men or women candidates for the Ohio House have an electoral advantage depended on the gender of the respondent (see table 5.3). Similar proportions of women and men agreed that women have an electoral advantage when other factors are equal. This finding comports with the party leader interviews in chapter 4, which demonstrated that many Ohio party leaders believe that women have a net advantage. However, a gender gap exists among candidates on the ques-

TABLE 5.2.   The Decision to Run for the Legislature (in percentages)

	All (N = 143)	Men (N = 114)	Women (N = 29)
It was entirely my idea to run	37	39	28
I had already thought seriously about running when someone else suggested it	23	25	17
I had not seriously thought about running until it was suggested by			
friends, family, co-workers, and/or acquaintances	9	9	10
members of an association or organization	3	3	3
party officials and/or legislative leaders	27	23	41
local elected officials	1	2	0

Source: State Legislative Candidate Survey, Ohio.

Note: Question wording: "In thinking about your initial decision to run for the legislature, which of the following statements most accurately describes your decision?"

tion of whether men have an advantage. Women candidates are much more likely than men to believe that men have an advantage; men are much more likely to believe that neither gender is advantaged.

Whether candidates believe that party leaders perceive an advantage for one gender also depends a great deal on the gender of the respondent (see table 5.4). Many candidates reported that they did not know the views of party leaders on this question. However, women were much more likely than men to believe that party leaders see an advantage for men, while men were much more likely to believe that party leaders see no gender advantage. Men were more likely than women to believe party leaders see an advantage for women.

Thus, both men and women candidates in Ohio perceive an electoral advantage for women candidates. Yet a plurality of women perceive an advantage for men, a perception men candidates do not share. The candidate data

TABLE 5.3.   Ohio Candidates: Perceptions of Gender and Electoral Advantage (in percentages)

	Women advantaged	Men advantaged	Neither advantaged	Don't know
Men (N = 119)	34	8	44	14
Women (N = 34)	38	41	15	6

Source: State Legislative Candidate Survey, Ohio.

Note: Question wording: "In races for the House/Assembly, other factors being equal, do you think that women candidates usually have an electoral advantage over men candidates, that men have an electoral advantage over women, or that neither has an advantage?"

TABLE 5.4.   Perceptions of Party Leader Beliefs about Gender and Electoral Advantage
(in percentages)

	Women advantaged	Men advantaged	Neither advantaged	Don't know
Men (N = 118)	39	8	28	25
Women (N = 35)	26	31	9	34

Source: State Legislative Candidate Survey, Ohio.

Note: Question wording: "What about *most party leaders?* Do you think that most party leaders think women candidates usually have an electoral advantage over men candidates, that men have an electoral advantage over women, or that neither has an advantage?"

confirm the perspective of many women I interviewed: women believe that women overall are disadvantaged by the recruitment process. The idea that women have an advantage has increased the parties' interest in fielding women. However, women still believe that men are less likely to recruit women and that the party poses an obstacle to women's representation. Men are more likely than women to believe that women have an advantage with voters and much less likely than women to believe that women face barriers in the recruitment process.

GENDER, CANDIDACY, AND POLITICAL PARTICIPATION

The interview evidence suggests that the recruitment of candidates for public office is structured by gender and reflects gender differences in social networks. My interview subjects' insights are consistent with state legislative candidate and state legislator surveys that have identified gender differences in the path to office. On average, men and women are involved in different types of organizations and come from different types of occupational backgrounds. In a process that resembles the patterns of which citizens are recruited to participate in politics, these various gender differences have implications for who is asked to run for office.

Women's political activities continue to depart from the traditional male candidate profile. There are important gender differences in the types of backgrounds and qualifications that individuals bring to office (Carroll and Strimling 1983; Burrell 1994; Thomas 1994). The nature of occupational sex segregation means that women are more likely to pursue some types of professions and networks than others (Costello and Stone 2001). In a 2001 Center for American Women and Politics study, for example, 22 percent of female and 7 percent of male state legislators came from education fields;

10 percent of women and 19 percent of men worked as attorneys (CAWP 2001c).

Gender also shapes social networks. Squire and Moncrief (2004) found gender differences in the types of organizations that motivated the activism of nonincumbent state legislative candidates. Women candidates were much more likely than men to report being active in parent-teacher associations, the League of Women Voters, the Junior League, and community cultural groups. Women were also more likely to work in charitable organizations. Thus, important differences exist in where men and women gain experience and the contacts they are likely to develop.

Burns, Schlozman, and Verba (2001) have identified gender differences in their national study of citizen participation, finding that men and women commonly join gender-segregated political organizations: while about 60 percent of men and women work in mixed-gender organizations, 17 percent of women and 13 percent of men work in organizations made up entirely of their gender group, and 17 percent of women and 26 percent of men work in organizations made up mostly of members of their gender group (76). Similar gender differences characterize men's and women's experiences in nonpolitical organizations. Moreover, in mixed organizations, women earn less organizational experience than men. Meanwhile, single-sex organizations yield more participatory benefits for both men and women than do mixed organizations, but this is particularly the case for women. Women's organizations boost women's political activity, putting "them on a level with or at an advantage when compared with men in organizations of men" (230). The authors conclude,

> In short, in crucial ways, organizations of women provide the kinds of experiences that have been attributed to them: providing opportunities for leadership, facilitating the exercise of voice in organizational matters and the development of civic skills, and generating requests for political activity. But this formulation leaves out half the picture. Organizations dominated by men—which actually constitute a larger share of the organizations that male respondents designated as their most important—have some of the same effects for men. (230–31)

Thus, women and men work to some extent in sex-segregated organizations and reap different political skills as a result.

Studies of citizen participation also demonstrate that requests to participate in politics are not random. In their study of mobilization, Rosenstone and Hansen (1993: 31) observe that "politicians, parties, and other activists are most likely to mobilize the people they already know. For one thing, they are close at hand, easy to contact, and responsive to requests—because they are friends or associates." Brady, Schlozman, and Verba (1999: 155) also argue that recruiting acquaintances is efficient: "Focusing on targets to whom they are close is an efficient strategy for rational prospectors. They should find it easier to locate, connect with, and get the message across to people with whom they have close relationships." These studies of recruitment and citizen participation find that mobilization activities reproduce participatory inequalities.

The case studies revealed a similar dynamic at work in recruitment for the legislature. Party leaders, who are typically men, commonly turn to their contacts around the state when looking for a candidate. At the same time, women and men often work in different types of occupations and volunteer in different organizations. Because women are much less likely than men to be party leaders, party leaders will, on average, be less likely to come into contact with women potential candidates than men potential candidates. This gender differential in whom people know, combined with the rational strategy of recruiting personal acquaintances, reduces the likelihood that women will be recruited to run for public office.

CONCLUSION

Beliefs about the barriers and opportunities facing women as state legislative candidates or potential candidates were to some extent similar across the six case-study states. Many interview subjects believe that women have made significant progress in their candidacies for the legislature. Women voters and gender stereotypes that benefit women provide important opportunities for women candidates. The obstacles identified were familiar ones, such as family responsibilities, lack of self-confidence, and fund-raising.

However, important differences existed across states in perceptions of women's opportunities for the legislature. Respondents in Ohio and North Carolina identified party recruitment of candidates as a barrier to women's representation. The problem with the recruitment process, according to interview subjects, is that informal processes allow for social networks and subjective beliefs about women candidates—including their competence and viability—to enter into party decisions about who should be recruited. Respondents in both North Carolina and Ohio believe that party leaders do not always think of women as candidates. In addition, Ohio candidates may not succeed without the party's backing in the primary. Because political careers unfold over time, respondents think that gender differences in personal networks have a cumulative effect, with more support accruing to men's political careers. In short, those interviewed identified informal selection processes as significant obstacles to women's opportunities for state legislative office in these two states. Where the parties have more influence in restricting the nomination, these processes become that much more important.

The interviews also suggested two conditions in which gatekeeping does not negatively affect women's opportunities: the presence of women in leadership positions or of male leaders sympathetic to women's candidacies, and a perception that women have a net electoral advantage over men candidates. For example, a number of individuals in Ohio and to a lesser extent in North Carolina have reputations for fielding women. These individuals make a significant contribution, given that party involvement in the recruitment process is so consequential in these states. In addition, as chapter 4 demonstrated, the idea that women have a net advantage can create an incentive for party leaders to recruit women candidates. The parties wield less influence over candidate recruitment and nominations in the other four case-study states. And where the parties do restrict the nomination, such as in Colorado, the electability of women is not usually a matter of debate.

In the next chapter, I return to the perspective of the fifty states. I use a quantitative analysis to determine if party recruitment and nomination practices are related to where women run for and hold state legislative office.

CHAPTER 6

The Pattern of Women's Representation across States

W omen comprise 22.5 percent of all state legislators, but their presence varies across states from a low of 9 percent to a high of 34 percent (CAWP 2005a). Thus, the fifty states are not equal with respect to women's representation: some parts of the country appear to provide a more favorable environment than others for women candidates. This pattern in women's representation is not simply a matter of chance. Instead, a number of state characteristics predict the presence of women officeholders—for example, where the public is more liberal, more women typically serve in the legislature.

What about political parties? Previous chapters demonstrated that nearly all state and legislative parties actively recruit state legislative candidates and that many also seek to influence the nomination. Thus, parties are an important feature of the political opportunity structure facing potential candidates. Chapter 5 provided qualitative evidence from the case-study states of how parties are related to women's representation. In this chapter, I return to the party leader surveys to investigate whether party activities are systematically related to the pattern of women's representation across the country.

I do not find support for the view that strengthening party organizations will lead to an increase in women's representation. Scholars typically view both recruitment and gatekeeping activities as components of party organizational strength and both are thought to enhance women's opportunities for office. However, I find that a stronger party role in candidate selection is not positively related to the presence of women general election candidates or women state legislators. Instead, more party involvement in candidate selection has a negative effect: where the party more actively seeks to influence the nomination, fewer women run for and hold seats in the legislature.

I do not find a relationship between greater party efforts to recruit candidates and the level of women's representation. Thus, there is no simple connection between candidate recruitment by the party and the election of women to public office.

To shed light on these results, I return to the interview evidence. The interviews suggested that recruitment is not necessarily gender neutral. The interview subjects believe that whether the party recruits women depends on who is in charge of recruitment. In addition, respondents in some states argued that more selective processes may put women at a disadvantage because of gender-based networks and concerns about the competitiveness of women candidates. In sum, the evidence from this chapter challenges the conventional wisdom that strong political parties facilitate women's representation.

THE PATTERN OF WOMEN'S REPRESENTATION

The state settings in which candidates seek office do not appear to be gender neutral.[1] Not surprisingly, incumbency is one factor that is related to where women hold state legislative office: states with higher turnover have a greater percentage of women state legislators. The presence of women in the eligibility pool—for example, the percentage of women in the labor force or earning law degrees—is also positively related to women's representation. Scholars consider these two factors—incumbency and the social eligibility pool—to be the main obstacles to increasing women's representation.

Scholars have also used a number of other state characteristics to predict where women hold office. Public opinion, as measured by ideology and gender role ideology, helps explain the pattern of women's representation across states, with women more likely to hold state legislative office where state public opinion is more liberal. Southern states and states with traditional political cultures are likely to have fewer women and moralistic states more women. The strength of women's interest groups has also been linked to the level of women's officeholding.

Legislative salary, length of session, size of legislative staff, and the ratio of legislative seats to state population have also been found to have a negative

1. See E. Werner 1968; Diamond 1977; Welch 1978; Hill 1981; Rule 1981; Nechemias 1985; Volgy, Schwarz, and Gottlieb 1986; Nechemias 1987; Rule 1990; Williams 1990; Nelson 1991; Matland and Brown 1992; Squire 1992; Carroll 1994; Darcy, Welch, and Clark 1994; B. Werner 1997; Norrander and Wilcox 1998; Darcy, Hadley, and Kirksey 1997; Arceneaux 2001; Hogan 2001; Sanbonmatsu 2002c.

effect. In general, the more prestige associated with serving in the legislature, the more competitive it is and the fewer women who will be found there. Finally, women tend to fare better in multimember districts that elect more than one representative than in single-member districts.

Political parties are yet another feature of the state setting. I have hypothesized that where the parties are more engaged in candidate recruitment, more women will seek office. The conscious efforts of recruitment agents such as parties may be particularly beneficial to furthering women's candidacies because of women's historic underrepresentation, and running for office remains a male-dominated enterprise. Because parties may encourage individuals to run who might not have otherwise considered becoming candidates, party activities may be helpful in convincing women to seek public office.

At first glance, the idea that women fare better in settings where the political parties recruit more candidates finds some support. The survey asked party leaders to estimate the share of state legislative candidates who are self-starters—that is, who come forward to run on their own without party encouragement. State legislative leaders' assessments on this subject are negatively related to women's representation: fewer women are general election candidates ($r = -.33, p < .01$) and state representatives ($r = -.31, p < .01$) in states where there are thought to be more self-starters.[2] Assessments by state party leaders about the percentage of candidates who are self-starters do not bear a statistical relationship to the pattern of women's representation.

Thus, at least preliminary evidence indicates that where more candidates come forward on their own, fewer women run for and hold office. This correlation suggests that recruitment has a positive effect on women's representation: women are better represented where candidates are more likely to be recruited by the party. Whether specific party recruitment activities are related to women's representation merits further attention.

Women Candidates

To investigate these questions, I conducted a multivariate analysis of the effects of party practices on women's representation.[3] The dependent variable

---

2. Legislative party reports of self-starters are not related to women's representation in a multivariate analysis (results not shown).

3. The appendix to this chapter discusses a number of alternative specifications of these models. Those robustness checks confirm the main results presented here.

in the analyses is the percentage of 2002 major party nominees for the lower chamber of the legislature who were women.[4] I use the terms *women candidates, women general election candidates,* and *women party nominees* interchangeably. Past research on women's representation has focused on women's presence in the legislature, which I also examine. But I go beyond past research by analyzing women's candidacies at the general election stage. The Center for American Women and Politics tracks women candidates in the general election. I supplement these data with information compiled from the various states on the total number of general election candidates. In preliminary analysis, I find that the percentage of the party's general election candidates who are women is highly correlated with the percentage of primary candidates who are women ($r = .94, p < .01$). The presence of women general election candidates is also correlated with the percentage of the party's primary contests in which at least one woman candidate entered the race ($r = .76, p < .01$).[5]

I use a least squares regression model because the dependent variable— the percentage of each party's general election candidates who were women— is a continuous variable theoretically bounded by 0 and 1. I calculate robust standard errors clustering on state because the same state can appear in the data set twice (once for each party), thereby violating the assumption of independence across observations. Thus the unit of analysis is the Democratic or Republican party in a given state.

The key independent variables of interest are the parties' recruitment and nomination practices. I created an unweighted additive index of the three recruitment variables: the recruitment scale, encouraging candidates to run, and selecting candidates for a targeted race. I also created an index of the three gatekeeping variables: discouraging candidates from running,

---

4. For states with off-year elections, the data are taken from the most recent election.

5. Data on candidate gender at the primary stage are not currently collected. I therefore assembled a data set of primary election candidates and calculated the percentage of the party's primary contests in which at least one woman entered the primary, excluding those contests where I could not verify a candidate's gender. I also exclude Louisiana because of its nonpartisan primary system; I exclude New Hampshire because candidates can appear in both primaries. Preliminary results I have obtained with these data on the percentage of primary contests in which at least one woman entered the primary resemble the main conclusions I reach in this chapter about party activities with respect to women candidates in the general election.

endorsing in the primary, and taking sides in the primary.[6] Each index ranges from 0 to 3.[7]

Because most incumbent state legislators seek reelection, the pattern of where women were holding office prior to the 2002 election should be correlated with where women sought office. Therefore, I include a control for the previous level of women's representation. With this control, I am essentially estimating the effect of the parties' practices on any change in where women sought state legislative office in 2002.[8] Including this variable enables me to take into account the level of women's representation and the state-level contextual factors that other studies have found to be related to the pattern of women's representation.[9]

I control for turnover in the chamber because women's representation should be facilitated where there are more open seats.[10] Because incumbency poses a significant structural barrier to increasing women's representation, women are expected to increase their numbers by running for open seats; differences across states in the extent of turnover may explain any change in where women run. I include a dummy variable for party (Democrat) to determine if women's presence as candidates differs by party. I add a control for region (South) because legislative leaders from outside the South were more likely to participate in the mail survey; controlling for region enables me to take into account this difference in the response rate.[11] Republican

6. Because the response options for all of these survey questions are ordered categories, but not necessarily equidistant categories, I recode each of these items into a dichotomous variable by dividing the categories at the median response. Thus, the variable equals 1 if the response is equal to the sample median or above and 0 otherwise. In one case, the median response was 0, so the responses of 1 or above are coded as 1. For legislative party activities, the Cronbach's alpha is .60 for the three recruitment measures and .49 for the three gatekeeping measures. For state party activities, the Cronbach's alpha is .60 for the recruitment measures and .74 for the gatekeeping measures.

7. For the legislative party, the mean for the recruitment measures is 2.24 and 1.69 for the gatekeeping measures. For the state party, the mean is 2.20 for the recruitment measures and 1.70 for the gatekeeping measures.

8. Not surprisingly, the presence of women as House candidates in 2002 is highly correlated with the percentage of women serving in the House in 2002 ($r = .77, p < .01$) as well as the percentage of women serving in the House in 2003 ($r = .86, p < .01$).

9. Doing so enables me to preserve degrees of freedom, which is particularly useful given the small size of the sample.

10. This measure of turnover is at the chamber rather than caucus level. This measure of turnover is from the National Conference of State Legislatures and is preelection turnover (<www.ncsl.org>).

11. The results are unchanged if I exclude the South variable (see chapter appendix).

leaders were also more likely to respond to the survey where Republicans held a larger share of seats. Therefore, I control for party composition in the House in the previous session as measured by the seat difference between the two parties as a share of all seats. Positive values indicate that the party is in the majority, whereas negative values indicate the party is in the minority.

I have hypothesized that recruitment is positively related to women's representation. Women arguably stand to gain as parties increasingly seek out candidates: recruitment may entail identifying new candidates who had not thought about running. However, I do not find a systematic relationship. Where the legislative party more actively recruits candidates, women are not necessarily more likely to run in the general election. The first column of table 6.1 analyzes the effects of the activities of the legislative party; the second column examines the activities of the state party. The coefficient on recruitment is not statistically significant, meaning that we cannot be sure that the effect of the parties' recruitment practices differs significantly from

TABLE 6.1.   Effect of Party Practices on Women's Presence as Candidates

	Legislative Party	State Party
Party Variables		
Recruitment activities	−.0002	.004
	(.006)	(.010)
Gatekeeping activities	−.013*	.008
	(.005)	(.008)
Control Variables		
Democrat	.050**	.067**
	(.014)	(.021)
Women's representation$_{(t-1)}$	.605**	.517**
	(.063)	(.097)
Turnover	.061	.029
	(.045)	(.072)
Party balance of seats$_{(t-1)}$	−.006	−.009
	(.027)	(.037)
South	−.030**	−.025
	(.010)	(.019)
Intercept	.075**	.049[a]
	(.024)	(.030)
N	70	53
R^2	.78	.67

Note: Cell entries are parameter estimates from a least squares regression model with robust standard errors in parentheses. The dependent variable is the percentage of all 2002 general election candidates for state representative who are women, by party. Both recruitment and gatekeeping range from 0 to 3. Party is coded 1 for Democrat, 0 for Republican. Turnover is the percentage of seats in the chamber that were vacant prior to the general election. Party balance of seats is the difference between the two parties in House seats as a share of all seats. South is coded 1 for South, 0 for non-South.

[a] $p \leq .10$; * $p \leq .05$; ** $p \leq .01$

zero. Thus, women candidates in particular do not appear to benefit when the parties engage more actively in candidate recruitment.

Legislative party gatekeeping has a negative and statistically significant effect on women candidates: where the parties more actively seek to influence the nomination, fewer women are nominated. Thus, stronger parties, as measured by party leader efforts to shape the nomination, reduce the likelihood that women will constitute a larger share of party nominees—an effect in the opposite direction than would be expected if stronger parties were a solution to women's underrepresentation.[12]

Turning to the control variables, women constitute a larger share of Democratic nominees than Republican nominees. Therefore, women's presence within the Democratic party continues to outpace that of women in the Republican party. As expected, women comprise a larger share of general election candidates where women held office in larger numbers prior to the election. Neither turnover in the legislative chamber nor the balance of seats between the two parties is related to women's representation; however, region is statistically significant and negative, indicating that women are less likely to run in the South.

In the analysis of the state party, neither recruitment nor gatekeeping predicts the presence of women as general election candidates (see table 6.1, column 2). Thus, while I find that the more the legislative party seeks to influence the nomination, the less likely the party's nominees include women, I do not find a similar effect for the state party. Why legislative party but not state party activities are related to women's representation is unclear. How state parties shape women's opportunities for office may be idiosyncratic to individual states, leaving no pattern. However, finding a significant result is also less likely because of the smaller size of the sample: more states are represented in the legislative leader sample than in the state party sample. Given this possibility, I analyze a larger number of states later in the chapter by using existing measures of party activities for additional tests of whether stronger parties are related to women's representation.[13]

12. The effect of recruitment and nomination practices do not differ significantly by party (results not shown).

13. I also combined the two sets of analyses—for legislative and state parties—for those states and parties where I have data for both the legislative and state parties ($N = 40$). The results are similar for the separate analyses of legislative and state parties: gatekeeping by the legislative party has a negative effect, while recruitment has no effect, and the state

Women Legislators

The previous analysis examined the impact of parties on women's presence as candidates. Here I consider the impact of parties on where women hold office: Are parties related to where women win? This analysis is identical to that of women candidates, but the dependent variable is the percentage of women state representatives by party. I analyze the effect of party activities on the percentage of women as a share of the House caucus in 2003 for each state and party.

The results for women state representatives resemble those for women general election candidates: neither recruitment nor gatekeeping has a positive effect on where women hold state legislative office (see table 6.2). Instead, legislative party gatekeeping activity is negatively related to women's representation. The more the legislative party seeks to influence the outcome of the primary, the fewer women can be found in the legislature. Gatekeeping by the state party is also negatively related to women's representation, though the effect on women legislators is not statistically significant ($p = .14$). Thus, in states and parties where the legislative party is more actively involved in shaping the nomination, fewer women run for and hold state legislative office.

Recruitment

Why did recruitment by the party fail to have the positive effect on women's representation that I anticipated? As an indicator of party organizational strength, party recruitment activity should have been associated with greater representation. As discussed earlier, women candidates are less likely to be self-starters than men—indeed, a greater proportion of women candidates than men candidates reports running because they were recruited by the party (Moncrief, Squire, and Jewell 2001; Squire and Moncrief 2004). In a number of my interviews, women reported that they had not thought about running for the legislature before being approached by party leaders and asked to run. In addition, more women than men in the Ohio candidate survey had not seriously considered running for the legislature before being recruited by the party. As Leann Brunnette, the leader of Iowa's Women in Public Policy, explained, women need to be asked and encouraged to run for office:

---

party data also bear no relationship to women's representation as candidates or legislators (see chapter appendix).

TABLE 6.2.   Effect of Party Practices on Women's Presence as Legislators

	Legislative Party	State Party
Party Variables		
Recruitment activities	−.003	.005
	(.006)	(.007)
Gatekeeping activities	−.013*	−.008
	(.006)	(.005)
Control Variables		
Democrat	.030*	.029*
	(.014)	(.013)
Women's representation$_{(t-1)}$	.874**	.869**
	(.086)	(.073)
Turnover	−.027	−.079
	(.047)	(.062)
Party balance of seats$_{(t-1)}$	−.018	−.029
	(.020)	(.025)
South	−.010	.001
	(.011)	(.013)
Intercept	.053*	.045*
	(.026)	(.022)
N	70	53
R^2	.83	.84

Note: Cell entries are parameter estimates from a least squares regression model with robust standard errors in parentheses. The dependent variable is the percentage of 2003 state representatives who are women, by party. Both recruitment and gatekeeping range from 0 to 3. Party is coded 1 for Democrat, 0 for Republican. Turnover is the percentage of seats in the chamber that were vacant prior to the general election. Party balance of seats is the difference between the two parties in House seats as a share of all seats. South is coded 1 for South, 0 for non-South.
[a] $p \leq .10$; * $p \leq .05$; ** $p \leq .01$

"You just need to continually build them up and let them know they would do a great job."

Evidence from the case studies sheds light on why recruitment failed to have the positive effect that I had anticipated. Candidate recruitment by the parties may not be related systematically to women's representation precisely because recruitment is not necessarily a gender-neutral process. According to the interviews in chapter 5, recruitment by the party does appear to be fairly gender neutral in some states. This characterizes Colorado, where party leaders believe that women and men are equally viable as candidates. However, in other states—notably Ohio and North Carolina—respondents generally believed that the typical recruitment process put women at a disadvantage. Thus, how those surveyed believed that recruitment affected women's representation depended on the specific state and party.

Party involvement in candidate recruitment means that informal social networks, which are often segregated by gender, as well as party leader beliefs about the viability of women candidates can shape that process. These networks may make it much less likely that women potential candidates will be tapped to run for office or less likely that women potential candidates will receive informal party support when they express an interest in running. In chapter 3, for example, party leaders commonly explained that they turn to their friends around the state for names as well as evaluations of potential candidates. What names are provided by these personal contacts and how they rank potential candidates are quite important to the recruitment process. More recruitment activity may not have had an effect on women's presence in either direction—positive or negative—because the effect depends on who is in charge of recruitment as well as the content of party leader beliefs about women candidates.

Other studies corroborate the importance of who is in charge of recruitment. For example, in a national study of political experts, the Candidate Emergence Study, women political informants were more likely than men political informants to name women as potential candidates for open congressional seats (Alan 1999). In addition, Niven's (1998) study of local party leaders revealed that women party leaders were more likely than men party leaders to name women potential candidates for the legislature.

Thus, more recruitment by the parties does not necessarily lead to more women candidates and more women in office. I return to this point in chapter 7.

Gatekeeping

Formal preprimary endorsements as well as the informal support that party leaders confer on or withhold from particular candidates can have important consequences for who successfully captures the nomination. Party leaders may even discourage potential aspirants from entering races. According to the analyses in this chapter, these activities have important implications for women: where party leaders are more likely to take steps to try to influence the nomination, women are less likely to be candidates and legislators, other factors being equal.

Why is gatekeeping negatively related to women's representation, particularly given that scholars frequently view stronger parties as a solution to the problem of women's underrepresentation? The case studies provided many examples of female candidates who had been recruited by the parties, indicating that such a process of handpicking candidates does not necessarily yield only male candidates.

As I argued in chapter 2, party leaders can be more selective if they can pick and choose among a field of potential candidates. Moreover, for important races, we would expect that uncertainty about a candidate's competitiveness would diminish that candidate's chances of winning formal or informal party support in the primary. Meanwhile, chapter 4 demonstrated that many party leaders believe that women's electability depends on the district. Together, these dynamics suggest that where the party cares enough about the race to become involved in the nomination, a woman candidate is less likely to be the nominee.

According to the evidence in chapter 3, party leaders seek out candidates who they think can win. For example, the Iowa and North Carolina parties' concerted recruitment efforts to field candidates involves vetting the names of potential candidates and trying to persuade the strongest candidate to enter the race. Party leaders and staff devote significant effort to finding the best candidate—not just any candidate. Democratic leaders in the North Carolina House, for example, look to former legislators, their personal contacts, or the party chair in the area, conveying a list of desired candidate criteria. The leaders begin their contacts in the district with the question "Who can win?" Above all else, party leaders seek to nominate candidates who can win.

Given women's relatively recent entry into electoral politics, doubts remain about the quality and competitiveness of women candidates, as chapter 4 illustrated. At the same time, the belief that women are advantaged can mitigate what would otherwise be a negative effect of gatekeeping on women's representation, as has been the case to some extent in Ohio. However, even when women candidates are perceived to have an advantage, this belief does not guarantee that women will be recruited: the interviews suggested that the likelihood of recruiting a woman candidate may depend on locating a particular type of woman candidate.

Chapter 3 demonstrated that gatekeeping by the party is more likely to occur where the party can afford to be more selective—in more professionalized settings, for example, where the office may be more attractive to potential candidates than in other states. In addition, I found that party leaders are more active in candidate selection where the two parties are more competitive. Therefore, party competition appears to indirectly affect women's representation. Where there is more competition, party leader interest in the nomination is likely to increase. Competition ultimately spurs more party leader interest in restricting the candidate selection process, with negative implications for women's representation. This finding may seem counterintuitive; competition might be expected to increase women's representation by increasing turnover and therefore open legislative seats (Darcy and Beckwith 1991). Some of my interviews supported the notion that competition can create an opening for women candidates, particularly on the part of the minority party. The minority party seeks a new formula for winning elections in its pursuit of the majority, and that formula could very well entail turning to women candidates. However, to the extent that greater party competition increases the perceived stakes in selecting the nominee, such a dynamic appears to work against an increase in women's representation.

LOCAL AND STATE PARTY ORGANIZATIONAL STRENGTH: ADDITIONAL EVIDENCE

Additional analyses of party activities confirm that stronger party organizations are typically negatively related to where women hold office. For another test of how party organizations matter to women's representation, I take advantage of existing measures of party organizational strength. Across different types of data, time periods, and conceptualizations of party organizational strength, I do not find support for the view that strong parties facilitate women's representation.

I use three measures of party organizational strength from past studies to analyze the relationship between parties and women's presence in the legislature, pooling data from the past thirty years. The dependent variable is women's representation in the House caucus. The model resembles the analyses I conducted of legislative and state party activities: I include a control for the previous level of women's representation as well as region, party, turnover in the chamber, and the balance of seats between the two parties. The measures of state and local party organizational strength come from the Party Transformation Study based on mail surveys of state and local party chairs (C. Cotter et al. 1984).[14] One dimension of party organizational strength is candidate recruitment, measured with questions about state and local party recruitment of candidates and party endorsements. I also consider the effect of the traditional party organization measure devised by Mayhew

14. The authors also conducted interviews with state party chairs and executive directors. Data on party organizational strength are available for ninety parties in forty-nine states. The local party organization data are from mail surveys sent to all states.

TABLE 6.3. Party Organizational Strength and Women's Presence as Legislators

	Model 1	Model 2	Model 3
Party Variables			
State party organizations	−1.845[a]	—	—
	(.958)		
Local party organizations	—	−.104	—
		(.436)	
Traditional party organizations	—	—	−.248[a]
			(.135)
Control Variables			
Democrat	.680*	.852**	.862**
	(.308)	(.245)	(.248)
Women's representation$_{(t-1)}$	.845**	.837**	.831**
	(.016)	(.020)	(.021)
Turnover	.017	.013	.008
	(.011)	(.011)	(.011)
Party balance of seats$_{(t-1)}$	−.613	−.620	.369
	(.559)	(.547)	(.540)
South	−1.300**	−1.190*	−1.316**
	(.429)	(.503)	(.414)
Intercept	4.542**	3.642**	4.379**
	(.807)	(.640)	(.770)
N	1,245	1,370	1,370
R^2	.78	.75	.75
States	48	49	49

Note: Cell entries are parameter estimates from a least squares regression model with robust standard errors in parentheses. The dependent variable is the percentage of women state representatives, by party, from 1973 to 2003. The state and local party organization variables are from C. Cotter et al. 1984 and the traditional party organization measure is from Mayhew 1986.

** $p < .01$; * $p < .05$; [a] $p < .10$

(1986). Mayhew's measure ranks states according to whether parties in the state historically had more influence over the nomination.[15]

These measures of party organizations tend to be negatively related to women's representation (see table 6.3). State party organizational strength is negatively related to women's presence in the legislature, though this effect is only marginally statistically significant ($p = .06$). Traditional party organization states, in which parties have historically exercised more influence over the nomination, are also less likely to have women in the legislature;

15. Though this measure is arguably somewhat dated and party organizations have declined since the late 1960s, the end point of his study, the pattern Mayhew identified has largely persisted. For example, Mayhew's organization states, including Illinois, New Jersey, New York, and Pennsylvania, are the same states where parties would continue to be expected to have more influence than in the rest of the nation.

this effect is also marginally statistically significant ($p = .07$). Local party organizational strength is not related to the pattern of women's representation.

Thus, party organizational strength is typically negatively related to women's representation, consistent with the results of the mail surveys I conducted of legislative and state party leaders. I do not find support for the view that strong parties lead to an increase in women's representation.

CANDIDATE QUALIFICATIONS

Perhaps political leaders are more likely to recruit men than women because of gender differences in the paths that men and women take to office. Do the types of backgrounds and occupations for which leaders look in state legislative candidates explain women's representation? Views on the desirability of particular candidate characteristics vary across states, with legislative and state party leaders expressing similar views (see table 6.4). The survey asked leaders to rate the importance that a House candidate have particular qualifications in order to win election. The characteristic most highly rated by party leaders is "community activist/volunteer," followed by holding local office and being active in the party.

Respondents considered being independently wealthy, being a teacher, or serving as a local appointed officeholder as less important qualifications. Of course, some parties may value particular qualifications. About one-third of legislative parties rate local elected office as not at all important or not too important, but nearly half of the parties consider such experience somewhat

TABLE 6.4.   Perceived Importance of Candidate Qualifications

	State Legislative Leaders ($N = 71$)	State Party Leaders ($N = 56$)
Has held local elected office	2.85 (.87)	2.68 (.88)
Has held local appointed office	2.41 (.92)	2.27 (.88)
Has been active in the party	2.82 (.90)	3.15 (.95)
Is a businessperson	2.73 (.83)	2.66 (.84)
Is a teacher	2.21 (.74)	2.36 (.90)
Is independently wealthy	2.20 (.97)	2.34 (.92)
Is a community activist/volunteer	3.28 (.91)	3.66 (.79)

Source: State Legislative Leader Survey and State Party Leader Survey.

Note: Cell entries are means with standard deviation in parentheses.

Question wording: "In your opinion, how important is it that a candidate from your party have the following qualifications in order to win election to the House/Assembly? (Please check one per row)." Respondents are asked to rate each qualification on a five-point scale from "Not important at all" to "Extremely important."

important, and a quarter consider it very important. The parties perceive being independently wealthy as not too important or not important at all; however, more than a quarter view wealth as somewhat important. More state party leaders than legislative party leaders consider experience in the party to be very important (22 percent) or extremely important (9 percent). State party leaders also perceive being a teacher as a useful qualification, with 38 percent rating teaching experience as somewhat important and 9 percent as very important.[16]

Are these party leader beliefs about candidate qualifications related to where women run for and hold office? I replicated the earlier models of recruitment and gatekeeping, adding these qualification measures. Few of these qualifications explain the pattern of where women run for and win general elections. Table 6.5 summarizes the results. The findings provide only very limited support for the idea that these informal criteria explain the pattern of women's representation. Perhaps not surprisingly, where legislative leaders perceive that being a teacher is desirable, more women serve in the legislature. Being independently wealthy is also a factor positively associated with where women run. Meanwhile, where the state party sees businesspeople as desirable candidates, fewer women serve.

The effects of teaching and business credentials are perhaps not unexpected: teaching is a predominantly female field, while business has been a male one. The effect of the wealth qualification is less intuitive. The time commitment and therefore opportunity costs of legislative service should mean that independent wealth makes service possible for both men and women. Overall, however, most of these qualifications have no effect or are not consistently related to women's representation. Thus, it does not appear that differences across states in party leader perceptions of the requisite qualifications for the legislature explain the pattern of where women run and hold office.

16. Democratic and Republican leaders rate qualifications similarly. However, Republican legislative leaders give higher ratings to the importance of being a businessperson. In addition, some differences exist between the majority party and the minority party. Legislative leaders from the minority party are more likely than those from the majority party to rate local elected office as important. However, leaders from the majority party rate party activity more highly than do leaders of the minority party. In addition, wealth is more important to the minority party than the majority party, presumably because the minority party lacks the financial resources of the majority party and may hope that candidates can self-finance their campaigns. A comparison of means reveals that these differences by majority party status are statistically significant at $p < .10$. The party experience and independent wealth measures are significant at $p < .05$.

TABLE 6.5.   Summary of the Effects of Perceived Qualifications on Women's
Representation

	Women Candidates		Women Legislators	
	Legislative Party	State Party	Legislative Party	State Party
Local elected office	.006	.007	.007	−.006
	(.007)	(.009)	(.006)	(.005)
Local appointed office	.007	.002	.005	−.008
	(.006)	(.011)	(.005)	(.006)
Active in the party	−.0004	−.009	.004	−.008
	(.006)	(.008)	(.006)	(.006)
Is a businessperson	−.001	−.016	.001	−.021*
	(.009)	(.011)	(.008)	(.007)
Is a teacher	.011	.004	.015*	−.010
	(.009)	(.011)	(.006)	(.009)
Is independently wealthy	.007	.019*	.006	.004
	(.006)	(.009)	(.005)	(.008)
Is a community activist/volunteer	−.007	.001	−.001	.002
	(.006)	(.011)	(.006)	(.009)

Note: The dependent variable in the first two columns is the percentage of all 2002 general election candidates for state representative who are women, by party. The dependent variable in the last two columns is the percentage of all 2003 state representatives who are women, by party. Each cell entry represents a different model. Included in each model are controls for party recruitment, party gatekeeping, party (Democrat), women's representation last time, turnover, party balance of seats, and region.

[a] $p < .10$; * $p < .05$; ** $p < .01$

Studies of mass political participation find persistent gender differences (Burns, Schlozman, and Verba 2001): men tend to participate more than women. However, gender differences in activities such as working informally in the community or serving on a local governing board are fairly narrow. In addition, longitudinal data on participation also demonstrate that gender differences in political or organizational work are quite small. If being a "community activist/volunteer" is the single most common qualification for which leaders look in state legislative candidates, it is perhaps not unexpected that party leader beliefs about qualifications do not explain the pattern of women's representation in the states. The pool of women working in their communities appears to be sufficient.

WOMEN'S ORGANIZATIONS

Before concluding that the party's recruitment of candidates bears no relationship to women's representation, I conduct one additional analysis. We might expect that women candidates would be more likely to be recruited where women's groups are closely allied with the party organization. The case studies indicated that women's groups may bring the names of potential women candidates to the attention of party leaders. Many interview subjects believe that party leaders do not necessarily think of women as candidates: the names of women potential candidates may not readily leap to the minds of party leaders looking for candidates. Therefore, ties between women's interest groups and party leaders may make it more likely that women potential candidates will come to party leaders' attention.

The legislative and state party data provide an opportunity to investigate this possibility. The surveys asked party leaders which interest groups help the party with candidate recruitment. I conducted a multivariate analysis similar to the previous models in this chapter. The key independent variable is the party's affiliation with women's groups—more precisely, whether the party looks to women's groups for help with recruitment. Table 6.6 examines whether these ties affect the pattern of where women run in the general election.

I find only limited support for the idea that the recruitment assistance of women's groups yields more women candidates. For the legislative party activities only, recruitment that involves working with women's groups has a positive effect on where women run in the general election as well as where women hold office (see table 6.7). However, the coefficients are only marginally statistically significant, indicating that we have less certainty about these effects. In both tables, women's groups' ties to the state party are not related to the presence of women party nominees or legislators.

To the extent that women's groups have a positive effect, the relationship may be a straightforward, causal one: where parties look to women's groups, those ties yield more women candidates because women's groups link women to the party and therefore to recruitment. However, the connection between women's groups and the parties raises the possibility of endogeneity or mutual causality. The causal direction may not lead from recruitment to women's candidacies; instead, where legislative leaders are open to women's groups, parties may also be more open to women's candidacies—willing and able to field women candidates and perhaps ideologically interested in doing so as well. Alternatively, the relationship may indicate that where women's groups are strong, more women run for and hold office. A correlation with parties may be spurious: party leaders may be more likely to list women's groups because women's groups are more active in their state. With only one

TABLE 6.6. Effect of Women's Groups on Women's Presence as Candidates

	Legislative Party	State Party
Women's interest groups	.025[a]	.011
	(.013)	(.023)
Party Variables		
Recruitment activities	−.001	.005
	(.006)	(.009)
Gatekeeping activities	−.010*	.008
	(.005)	(.008)
Control Variables		
Democrat	.042**	.061*
	(.014)	(.026)
Women's representation$_{(t-1)}$	.596**	.516**
	(.062)	(.096)
Turnover	.046	.022
	(.045)	(.074)
Party balance of seats$_{(t-1)}$	−.007	−.011
	(.028)	(.039)
South	−.027**	−.023
	(.009)	(.018)
Intercept	.074**	.046[a]
	(.024)	(.027)
N	70	53
R^2	.79	.68

Note: Cell entries are parameter estimates from a least squares regression model with robust standard errors in parentheses. The dependent variable is the percentage of all 2002 general election candidates for state representative who are women, by party. Women's interest groups is a dummy variable coded 1 if the party is assisted by women's groups in recruiting candidates, 0 otherwise. Both recruitment and gatekeeping range from 0 to 3. Party is coded 1 for Democrat, 0 for Republican. Turnover is the percentage of seats in the chamber that were vacant prior to the general election. Party balance of seats is the difference between the two parties in House seats as a share of all seats. South is coded 1 for South, 0 for non-South.

[a] $p \leq .10$; * $p \leq .05$; ** $p \leq .01$

survey item to measure the party's relationships with women's groups, it is difficult to unpack the nature of the relationship.

Women candidates and legislators are more likely than men to be assisted by women's groups. Not all women have ties to women's organizations, but such ties are common. For example, in a recent survey of state legislators by the Center for American Women and Politics, 25 percent of women and only 14 percent of men reported support from the National Organization for Women in the last election, 26 percent of women and 11 percent of men from the Women's Political Caucus, and 56 percent of women and 36 percent of men from "any other women's organizations" (CAWP 2001c). In another survey, 73 percent of women legislators and only 30 percent of men

TABLE 6.7.   Effect of Women's Groups on Women's Presence as Legislators

	Legislative Party	State Party
Women's interest groups	.020[a]	.019
	(.011)	(.011)
Party Variables		
Recruitment activities	−.004	.007
	(.006)	(.007)
Gatekeeping activities	−.011*	−.007
	(.006)	(.005)
Control Variables		
Democrat	.023[a]	.019
	(.014)	(.013)
Women's representation$_{(t-1)}$	.866**	.868**
	(.088)	(.073)
Turnover	−.039	−.091
	(.045)	(.060)
Party balance of seats$_{(t-1)}$	−.018	−.033
	(.020)	(.026)
South	−.008	.003
	(.010)	(.013)
Intercept	.052*	.038[a]
	(.026)	(.021)
N	70	53
R^2	.83	.85

Note: Cell entries are parameter estimates from a least squares regression model with robust standard errors in parentheses. The dependent variable is the percentage of all 2003 state representatives who are women, by party. Women's interest groups is a dummy variable coded 1 if the party is assisted by women's groups in recruiting candidates, 0 otherwise. Both recruitment and gatekeeping range from 0 to 3. Party is coded 1 for Democrat, 0 for Republican. Turnover is the percentage of seats in the chamber that were vacant prior to the general election. Party balance of seats is the difference between the two parties in House seats as a share of all seats. South is coded 1 for South, 0 for non-South.

[a] $p \leq .10$; * $p \leq .05$; ** $p \leq .01$

reported women's groups among their strongest supporters in the last election (Carey, Niemi, and Powell 1998).

The door remains open for parties to provide an avenue for increasing women's representation through their ties to women's groups. However, in none of the case-study states did party leaders identify women's groups as the major interest groups providing help with candidate identification.

CONCLUSION

As Gimpel and Schuknecht (2003) note, state settings may be consequential because of the demographic and attitudinal characteristics of state populations. Some scholars have pointed to state demographics and ideology to explain women's representation. In Gimpel and Schuknecht's framework, these explanations about the characteristics of voters residing in a state offer a compositional account for why states matter to women's representation. By arguing that parties shape women's representation, I have forwarded a contextual account that emphasizes the importance of a state's political institutions, rather than a state's composition.

Parties are one feature of the environment facing potential candidates. By encouraging individuals to consider candidacy for the legislature and by seeking to influence the primary, party leaders can play an important role in elections. Yet where parties more actively seek to influence the nomination, fewer women are party nominees and state legislators. And more party recruitment of candidates failed to yield a positive effect on women's representation. Many scholars have suggested that more party influence over the nomination would benefit women as a group, but the analyses in this chapter do not support this contention.

More party recruitment of candidates should theoretically benefit women. Yet no guarantee exists that recruitment will have this positive effect. The case studies pointed to the importance of who is in charge of recruitment as well as to party leader beliefs about the competitiveness of women candidates. Gatekeeping appears to be negative for reasons rooted in the importance of those races and in party leaders' reasons for wanting to influence the nomination. More selective, restrictive processes appear to put women—a relatively new group of candidates—at a disadvantage.

Appendix

A number of alternative specifications confirm the main results of the analyses presented in this chapter. This chapter appendix presents the details of these robustness checks. The results of the main models that examine the effects of legislative and state party practices on women's presence as candidates and legislators are largely similar if I exclude the dummy variable for region (see table 6.A1). I included a dummy variable for the South because legislative leaders from outside that region were more likely to return the mail survey. Whether the model includes this control does not affect the results. Legislative party gatekeeping remains negatively related to women's representation. The state party's gatekeeping activities are not statistically significant, and recruitment remains unrelated to women's representation.

Throughout the analyses in the chapter, I control for the previous level of women's representation in the legislature. The results are basically unchanged

TABLE 6.A1.   Effect of Legislative and State Party Practices on Women's Presence as Candidates and Legislators without Controlling for Region

	Women Candidates		Women Legislators	
	Legislative Party	State Party	Legislative Party	State Party
Recruitment activities	−.001	.003	−.004	.005
	(.006)	(.010)	(.006)	(.006)
Gatekeeping activities	−.013*	.007	−.013*	−.008
	(.005)	(.008)	(.006)	(.005)
Democrat	.048**	.067**	.030*	.029*
	(.013)	(.021)	(.014)	(.013)
Women's representation$_{(t-1)}$	.640**	.558**	.886**	.868**
	(.061)	(.084)	(.083)	(.068)
Turnover	.037	.011	−.035	−.079
	(.044)	(.071)	(.045)	(.060)
Party balance of seats$_{(t-1)}$	−.004	−.002	−.017	−.029
	(.027)	(.036)	(.020)	(.024)
Intercept	.069**	.042	.051*	.045*
	(.025)	(.028)	(.025)	(.021)
N	70	53	70	53
R^2	.77	.66	.83	.84

Note: Cell entries are parameter estimates with robust standard errors in parentheses. The dependent variable in the first major column is the percentage of all 2002 general election candidates for state representative who are women, by party; the second major column is the percentage of 2003 state representatives who are women, by party.
[a] $p \leq .10$; * $p \leq .05$; ** $p \leq .01$

if I also include a host of state-level contextual factors in the model. For example, table 6.A2 presents these results for women's representation as state legislative candidates. The table presents only the coefficients on recruitment and gatekeeping for both the legislative party and the state party. The model is identical to the main models from the chapter, which include women's previous representation, party (Democrat), turnover, party balance of seats, and region (South). Each row in the table presents the results for the legislative and state party activities with the inclusion of a new state contextual variable. I examine the key factors from past research that are thought to explain women's representation: the social eligibility pool, moralistic political culture, legislative professionalism, multimember districts, term limits, and ideology.[17]

17. The social eligibility pool is measured with data on women's labor force participation and the presence of women among local elected officials, using data from the U.S. Bureau of Labor Statistics and the U.S. Department of Commerce, Bureau of the Census (1994). Political culture is from Elazar 1984. Data on professionalism, measured with length of

TABLE 6.A2. Summary of Legislative and State Party Practices with State Contextual Controls on Women's Presence as Candidates

	Legislative Party		State Party	
	Recruitment	Gatekeeping	Recruitment	Gatekeeping
Model 1	.0004	−.012*	.001	.007
	(.006)	(.006)	(.011)	(.008)
Model 2	.000	−.013*	.003	.008
	(.006)	(.006)	(.010)	(.008)
Model 3	−.001	−.012*	.004	.009
	(.006)	(.006)	(.010)	(.008)
Model 4	.0005	−.009[a]	.004	.005
	(.006)	(.005)	(.010)	(.008)
Model 5	.004	−.009	−.005	−.0002
	(.006)	(.006)	(.009)	(.008)
Model 6	−.0001	−.013*	.003	.008
	(.006)	(.005)	(.010)	(.008)

Note: N ranges from 47 to 70. Each row and each major column (legislative or state party) represents a separate analysis. Cell entries are parameter estimates with robust standard errors in parentheses. The dependent variable is the percentage of all 2002 general election candidates for state representative who are women, by party. All models include controls for party, women's representation last time, turnover, party balance of seats, and region. In addition, the following controls are added to specific models:

Model 1: social eligibility pool (working women) and political culture (moralistic)
Model 2: legislative professionalism (length of session, base salary), and multimember districts
Model 3: term limits
Model 4: ideology (Erikson, Wright, and McIver 1993)
Model 5: gender role ideology (Brace et al. 2002)
Model 6: 1992 women local elected officials (U.S. Department of Commerce, Bureau of the Census 1994)
[a] $p \leq .10$; * $p \leq .05$; ** $p \leq .01$

These tables demonstrate that the effects of the key variables of interest—recruitment and gatekeeping—remain largely unchanged when additional controls are added. As in the main models, recruitment is not related to women's representation, but legislative gatekeeping is negatively related. State party gatekeeping has a negative effect on women's presence as state legislators, though the effect is not always statistically significant (see table 6.A3). In no case is the effect of an additional, state-level contextual variable related to women's representation. The failure of these variables to have an independent effect on women's representation is probably the result of controlling for the previous level of women's representation.

---

session and base salary, is from the Council of State Governments (various years). Term-limit information is from the National Conference of State Legislatures (<www.ncsl.org>). Multimember district information is from the states and additional sources. Ideology measures come from state public opinion polls about general liberal/conservative ideology (Erikson, Wright, and McIver 1993) and gender role ideology (Brace et al. 2002).

TABLE 6.A3.   Summary of Legislative and State Party Practices with State Contextual Controls on Women's Presence as Legislators

	Legislative Party		State Party	
	Recruitment	Gatekeeping	Recruitment	Gatekeeping
Model 1	−.004	−.012*	.004	−.008
	(.005)	(.005)	(.007)	(.006)
Model 2	−.003	−.015*	.006	−.008
	(.006)	(.006)	(.006)	(.005)
Model 3	−.004	−.013*	.004	−.009[a]
	(.006)	(.006)	(.007)	(.005)
Model 4	−.002	−.010*	.004	−.012*
	(.005)	(.005)	(.006)	(.005)
Model 5	−.001	−.012*	.004	−.013*
	(.006)	(.006)	(.007)	(.006)
Model 6	−.003	−.013*	.005	−.008
	(.006)	(.006)	(.007)	(.005)

Note: N ranges from 47 to 70. Each row and each major column (legislative or state party) represents a separate analysis. Cell entries are parameter estimates with robust standard errors in parentheses. The dependent variable is the percentage of 2003 state representatives who are women, by party. All models include controls for party, women's representation last time, turnover, party balance of seats, and region. In addition, the following controls are added to specific models:

Model 1: social eligibility pool (working women) and political culture (moralistic)
Model 2: legislative professionalism (length of session, base salary), and multimember districts
Model 3: term limits
Model 4: ideology (Erikson, Wright, and McIver 1993)
Model 5: gender role ideology (Brace et al. 2002)
Model 6: 1992 women local elected officials (U.S. Department of Commerce, Bureau of the Census 1994)
[a] $p \leq .10$; * $p \leq .05$; ** $p \leq .01$

In a further check on the results, I limited the analyses to those states and parties where I have data for both the legislative and state parties, a total of forty-one cases. If I limit the analysis to these cases and include the legislative and state party activities within the same model, the results are largely similar to the main models in the chapter (see table 6.A4). Legislative party gatekeeping continues to have a negative effect, while state party activities are not related to women's representation.

The surveys provide additional insight into the effect of local party organizations. Both legislative and state party leaders were asked to characterize the recruitment and nomination activities of the local parties in their state. The survey questions were identical to the party leader reports of their own activities except that the questions concerned the activities of the local party. Thus, the surveys provide indirect measures of local party involvement in candidate recruitment and gatekeeping. These data provide further

TABLE 6.A4. Effect of Legislative and State Party Practices on Women's Presence as Candidates and Legislators, Reduced Sample

	Women Candidates	Women Legislators
Legislative party recruitment activities	−.006	−.009
	(.008)	(.007)
State party recruitment activities	−.006	.002
	(.010)	(.009)
Legislative party gatekeeping activities	−.018*	−.015*
	(.008)	(.007)
State party gatekeeping activities	.007	−.005
	(.005)	(.006)
Democrat	.048*	.040*
	(.021)	(.016)
Women's representation$_{(t-1)}$	.680**	.857**
	(.108)	(.094)
Turnover	.072	−.017
	(.065)	(.061)
Party balance of seats$_{(t-1)}$	−.016	−.037
	(.036)	(.034)
South	−.028	−.009
	(.018)	(.012)
Intercept	.087*	.077*
	(.033)	(.030)
N	40	40
R^2	.81	.88

Note: Cell entries are parameter estimates with robust standard errors in parentheses. The dependent variable in column 1 is the percentage of all 2002 general election candidates for state representative who are women, by party; column 2 is the percentage of 2003 state representatives who are women, by party. The analysis only includes those states and parties in which both legislative and state party leaders responded to the survey.

[a] $p \leq .10$; * $p \leq .05$; ** $p \leq .01$

evidence of a negative relationship between party organizational strength and women's representation (table 6.A5).

The first column of table 6.A5 examines the legislative party's reports of local party recruitment and gatekeeping activities on women's representation as candidates, whereas the second column examines the state party's reports. In two cases, local party activities are negatively related to women's presence as legislators, though the coefficient is only marginally statistically significant in the case of recruitment. Gatekeeping has a marginally significant and negative impact on women's presence as candidates.

Finally, as a robustness check on the analyses of existing measures of party organizational strength, I included a host of state-level contextual variables in the model. I included two models—one with the standard measure of ideology (Erikson, Wright, and McIver 1993) and one with the Brace et al.

TABLE 6.A5. Effect of Local Party Practices on Women's Representation

	Women Candidates		Women Legislators	
	Legislative Party's Report	State Party's Report	Legislative Party's Report	State Party's Report
Local party recruitment	.007	−.001	−.001	−.010[a]
activities	(.005)	(.008)	(.005)	(.006)
Local party gatekeeping	−.013[a]	.005	−.020*	−.002
activities	(.007)	(.010)	(.007)	(.006)
Democrat	.051**	.062**	.020	.017
	(.016)	(.021)	(.016)	(.013)
Women's	.601**	.541**	.888**	.858**
representation$_{(t-1)}$	(.064)	(.104)	(.080)	(.065)
Turnover	.034	−.001	−.064	−.079
	(.043)	(.075)	(.043)	(.056)
Party balance of	−.006	.010	−.016	−.011
seats$_{(t-1)}$	(.026)	(.031)	(.023)	(.019)
South	−.030**	−.015	−.022*	.001
	(.011)	(.018)	(.008)	(.011)
Intercept	.076**	.059	.079*	.075**
	(.025)	(.036)	(.034)	(.022)
N	61	53	61	53
R^2	.77	.67	.84	.86

Note: Cell entries are parameter estimates with robust standard errors in parentheses. The dependent variable in the first two columns is the percentage of all 2002 general election candidates for state representative who are women, by party. The dependent variable in the last two columns is the percentage of all 2003 state representatives who are women, by party. Local party activities are based on legislative or state party reports.

[a] $p \leq .10$; * $p \leq .05$; ** $p \leq .01$

TABLE 6.A6. Summary of Party Effects on Women's Representation with State Contextual Controls

	State Party Organizations	Local Party Organizations	Traditional Party Organizations
Model 1	−1.987*	−.2366	−.4175*
	(.789)	(.494)	(.161)
Model 2	−1.968*	.0329	.0346
	(.844)	(.419)	(.174)

Note: N ranges from 1,117 to 1,266. Each cell represents a separate analysis. The dependent variable is the percentage of women state representatives, by party, from 1973 to 2003. State party organizations and local party organizations are from C. Cotter et al. 1984; traditional party organizations is from Mayhew 1986. All models include controls for party (Democrat), women's representation last time, turnover, party balance of seats, and region.

Model 1 includes controls for social eligibility pool (working women) and political culture (moralistic), legislative professionalism (length of session, base salary), multimember districts, and ideology (Erikson, Wright, and McIver 1993).

Model 2 includes controls for social eligibility pool (working women) and political culture (moralistic), legislative professionalism (length of session, base salary), multimember districts, and gender role ideology (Brace et al. 2002).

[a] $p \leq .10$; * $p \leq .05$; ** $p \leq .01$

(2002) measure of gender ideology. Because the ideology measures are not available in all states, only forty-six states are included in the analyses with the ideology measure and only forty-four states are in the analyses with the gender ideology measure. In both cases, I also control for the social eligibility pool, political culture, professionalism, and multimember districts.

The results remain largely unchanged from those presented in the chapter (see table 6.A6). State party organizations continue to have a negative effect, but it becomes statistically significant rather than marginally significant. Local party organizations remain unrelated to women's representation. Finally, traditional party organizations are negatively related and statistically significant in the model that includes ideology. However, traditional party organizations are not related to women's representation in the model with gender ideology.

CHAPTER 7

Conclusion

Whether women are present in state legislatures has important normative implications: legislative bodies that look like the people arguably contribute to democratic legitimacy. The presence of women in office can also enhance the representation of women's interests. Women's descriptive representation provides the potential rather than the guarantee that women's substantive representation will be facilitated. But a growing body of scholarship indicates that women legislators tend to be more likely than men to view women as an important constituency group and are more likely to introduce legislation intended to benefit women. Moreover, because state legislative office is one rung on the career ladder climbed by ambitious politicians, whether women run for the state legislature has long-term consequences for women's access to higher offices.

The proportion of female state legislators has generally risen since the 1970s. However, the proportion of women legislators may not increase in the future. In light of the recent stasis in women's representation, Carroll has argued,

> At a minimum, the leveling off is evidence that increases over time are not inevitable; there is no invisible hand at work to insure that more women will seek and be elected to office with each subsequent election. (2004: 396)

The assumption that women's representation will automatically increase with time overlooks the causal mechanisms that bring women into the legislature. Women and men tend to win their races at similar rates, yet focusing on this gender parity in competitiveness obscures the stark gender imbalance in who seeks office.

I begin this chapter by reviewing the evidence from previous chapters about how parties affect women's representation in the state legislatures. I then turn to a brief analysis of several additional states that supplement the case studies and shed further light on the relationship between parties and the recruitment of women for public office. In the remainder of the chapter, I discuss the implications of my findings for scholarship on political parties, gender and politics, and state politics and suggest questions for future research.

POLITICAL PARTIES, GENDER, AND REPRESENTATION

The conventional wisdom holds that strong political parties and greater party control over the nomination will lead to an increase in women's representation. However, I have argued that women are less likely to run for and hold state legislative office where parties are stronger. I used a multi-method approach to analyze this relationship between parties and women's candidacies. I conducted interviews in six states about candidate recruitment and perceptions of the barriers and opportunities facing women as candidates. Three mail surveys—a national survey of legislative party leaders, a national survey of state party leaders, and a survey of state legislative candidates in Ohio—investigated party practices across the country. While past studies have inferred party leader support for women candidates based on the types of races in which women run, I presented direct evidence of party leader beliefs about women candidates. I combined these approaches with a time-series, cross-section analysis of women's representation in the states.

I found little consensus among party leaders about the electability of women state legislative candidates. Proponents of women candidates as well as scholars of women and politics generally believe that when women run, women win. Yet, the interview and survey data in chapter 4 demonstrate that party leaders commonly believe women might have difficulty winning election to the House from some districts in their state; indeed, some party leaders believe that many such districts exist. These party leader beliefs about the hearts and minds of voters call into question the underlying assumptions of existing theories about parties and women's representation.

Candidate gender is one piece of information that party leaders may use to weigh the strengths and weaknesses of a potential candidate and the fit of a candidate for a district. In this sense, gender is not unlike other candidate characteristics such as race, ethnicity, occupation, and age, all of which party leaders may use to evaluate potential candidates. Some party leaders believe that women have a net electoral advantage because of gender stereotypes that benefit women. This advantage has generated more interest than might otherwise arise in women's candidacies, creating important opportunities for women. Because voters perceive women politicians as more honest than men or because women are perceived as better at handling particular issues, the party may stand to gain by recruiting women candidates.

At the same time, the interviews demonstrated that party leader perceptions about the electoral advantage of a woman candidate are often contingent. Interest in women candidates may depend on finding a particular type of woman candidate, not just any woman candidate. Moreover, in some states, survey respondents believe that men have an electoral advantage over women. Thus, to the extent that women potential candidates believe they face unfavorable electoral contexts, women may not misunderstand or misperceive their support among party leaders. Some legislative and state party leaders believe that men have an advantage, while others, in roughly equal proportion, believe women have an advantage. This distribution of party leader attitudes appears to balance out on average, suggesting a level playing field for women candidates. However, a qualitative difference between the status of women and men potential candidates is that party leaders do not necessarily think that women are electable in all state legislative districts. Party leaders want to field winning candidates and anticipate voter reaction to candidates as a means of doing so. The case studies also demonstrate that party leader beliefs about women candidates may change; in some cases, leaders believe that women no longer have an electoral advantage, though they did so in the past.

Elections in the United States today are usually regarded as candidate centered and political parties as relatively unimportant. Yet, chapter 3 demonstrates that political parties retain a significant role. Both the interviews and surveys of legislative and state party leaders reveal that parties are important players in shaping who runs for office. Parties may formally or informally support candidates in the primary or induce candidates to run at all. Party attempts to influence the nomination are less common than efforts to encourage candidates to run, but parties do engage in these gatekeeping practices. Where there is more competition and the legislature is more professionalized, legislative party leaders are more likely to seek to influence the selection of the party nominee. Thus, parties are already much more engaged in candidate selection than is often realized.

Perceptions of how women fare in these party efforts to field and select candidates depend very much on the state. Chapter 5 demonstrates that interview subjects in some states frequently mentioned an old boys' network, with women commonly arguing that women are overlooked in the candidate recruitment process. Some respondents argued that men tend to know other men; gender-based recruitment patterns are therefore a by-product of gender-based networks. However, others argued that men do not think of women as candidates or believe that women are not as well suited for politics as men. Where recruitment and gatekeeping practices are more tightly linked, these networks and attitudes appear to further disadvantage women.

Scholars often argue that strengthening political parties will lead to an increase in women's representation. However, I find in chapter 6 that party organizational strength is typically negatively related to women's representation. In particular, the parties' gatekeeping activities decrease rather than increase women's representation. Where parties are more involved in the selection of candidates, fewer women are the party's nominees and state legislators. Recruitment, another measure of party organizational strength, is not related to where women run for and hold office. Thus, in theorizing about the relationship between party organizational strength and women's representation, it is necessary to investigate party activities at the state level and analyze the consequences of recruitment as well as gatekeeping activities.

The interview evidence suggests that two mechanisms drive the negative effect of gatekeeping. First, party leader doubts about women's electability decrease the likelihood that women will be the party nominees for important races. Second, closed, more selective processes are negatively related to women's representation because of the gendered aspects of informal networks. Past scholars have argued that women have sufficient power within parties to influence candidate selection. Yet the interviews demonstrated that who serves as party leaders matters. In some states, interview subjects argued that women are less likely to be recruited and regarded as ideal candidates because of an old boys' network. The fact that women are underrepresented in party leadership positions across the country diminishes the likelihood that women will be recruited.

The Ohio case should have illustrated the manifold benefits of political parties: of the six state case studies, Ohio has the strongest legislative caucuses and state party organizations. Nevertheless, women candidates in Ohio believe that the parties are much more likely to recruit men than women to run for the legislature. Interview subjects also commonly argued that barriers to women's candidacies remain within the political parties. Ironically, a greater share of women candidates than men candidates report running for office because they were recruited by the party, perhaps because many people in Ohio believe that women currently have an electoral advantage.

The pipeline of women in lower offices, long identified as an important factor by scholars of women and politics, provides a significant source of candidates for higher levels. Today, women remain underrepresented in local elected office. In some states, this local experience is an important qualification for seeking a seat in the state legislature. However, most state legislators have no such prior experience. Indeed, the party leaders I surveyed rated an individual's past community involvement as the most important qualification for the legislature. In this respect, the pool of women with the informal qualifications to become candidates appears sufficient: studies of the mass public reveal only small gender differences in informal, community participation (Burns, Schlozman, and Verba 2001). Thus, a primary focus on the pool of eligible women will not account for women's underrepresentation: in most states, the pool of women eligible to seek state legislative office is more than sufficient.

The evidence assembled here suggests that it would be premature to conclude that gender is unrelated to understanding the dearth of women candidates. Despite tremendous social change and generational replacement, today's young elected officials are overwhelmingly likely to be men rather than women (Mandel and Kleeman 2004). Precisely because women have been so much less likely than men to seek public office, gender remains a factor in party assessments of a candidate's viability. Moreover, because women are relatively new to electoral politics and have yet to achieve parity with men, party leaders tend to be men rather than women. The extent to which gender structures social networks varies across states, which may explain the absence of any systematic relationship between party recruitment activity and women's representation. But the case studies provide initial evidence of the circumstances in which strong parties can indeed facilitate women's representation. The benefits of recruitment seem to depend, at a minimum, on the belief that women are at least as electable as men.

The shortcomings of existing accounts of women's underrepresentation are cause for new research approaches. I relied primarily on party leaders, legislators, and women's groups in the case-study states to understand the electoral opportunities and constraints potential women candidates face. I treated each state's interview subjects as experts about the impact of informal recruitment practices on women in their state. In all six states, I supplemented the interviews with additional research, and in one state, I conducted a state legislative candidate survey. Although I interviewed a very diverse set of respondents in each state, they do not constitute a random sample. But this qualitative evidence, combined with the other methodological approaches I have employed, provides important insights into the informal processes by which state legislative candidates emerge.

Many women reach their decisions to run for office the way that men do: women may run for the legislature because they have always wanted to be in politics. Yet women's political careers have often relied on alternative networks and different agents of recruitment than men's careers have. Given the myriad ways in which gender remains consequential for social life, it is not clear that solely relying on political parties will solve the problem of women's underrepresentation. In their pursuit of public office, women have challenged received views about what a typical politician looks like and what qualifications officeholders need. Women have frequently gained political experience in female-dominated organizations. These gender differences in backgrounds and paths to office suggest that the problem of women's underrepresentation will take more than reforms such as term limits or stronger parties.

In addition to the existence of open seats, women's representation depends on gender-based networks and gender-conscious political recruitment. In short, the problem of women's underrepresentation in public office is related to politics. What organizations or interest groups are involved in candidate recruitment? Who holds leadership positions in the parties? Which individuals are perceived to be competitive? Answering these questions helps to explain who is recruited and who ultimately runs and serves.

GENDER, CANDIDATE-CENTERED ELECTIONS, AND WEAK PARTY ENVIRONMENTS

My findings suggest that we reconsider the view that women candidates are necessarily worse off in weak party environments. In this section, I turn to interview data from several additional states to examine why strong parties may not be necessary for increasing women's representation. Past scholars have argued that women are at a disadvantage in candidate-centered elections. The absence of party involvement in the nomination does not necessarily mean that women will run, of course, with Alabama a case in point. But one advantage to such an environment is that candidates do not need the party's permission to enter primaries.

Recruitment by the party arguably plays a critical role in candidacy because "the party game is the only game in town" (Baer 1993: 565). However, a cursory examination of state legislative recruitment in several additional states suggests that recruitment need not occur through the party to benefit women.[1] A weak party system does not preclude concerted efforts by interest groups and informal networks to recruit women candidates. Interest groups may be very active in candidate recruitment, efforts that may or may not occur in tandem with the political parties. A decentralized, informal process of candidate recruitment can yield women candidates.

Differences across states in party organizational strength and the typical routes by which candidates are recruited have important implications for women's representation. While scholars have suggested that the direct primary and informal recruitment patterns disadvantage women, such is not necessarily the case. More closed, selective processes whereby parties seek to limit candidate entry or party leaders coalesce behind one primary candidate do not appear to facilitate women's representation. Instead, women appear to be better off when they can take the case for their candidacy directly to voters in the primary. A decentralized recruitment process also provides the opportunity for interest groups as well as parties to encourage women to run.

First, evidence from states such as Maine and California confirms the utility of distinguishing party recruitment activities from party gatekeeping activities. For example, interview subjects think that the absence of parties as gatekeepers in Maine benefits women. Assistant Senate Democratic Leader Sharon Treat explained that a relatively weak party structure enables women without ties to the party to seek office: "I think that that tends to benefit the women, because the women weren't strongly part of the party structure, at least ten years ago. And so it makes it possible to get into politics without having those connections."

The parties do not restrict the nomination in Maine state legislative races but apparently act as gatekeepers for statewide office. These party efforts are

---

1. I interviewed women state legislators from California, Georgia, Maine, New Hampshire, and Washington at the CAWP 2001 Forum for Women State Legislators. At that time, Washington ranked first in the nation for women's representation, with women comprising 39 percent of the legislature (<www.cawp.rutgers.edu>). California ranked thirteenth, with 28 percent; Georgia ranked thirtieth, with 21 percent; Maine ranked eighth with 30 percent; and New Hampshire ranked eleventh with 29 percent.

thought to hurt women in both parties. One legislator observed that the old boys' network selects candidates for the governor's office: "Women that were totally qualified for leadership were closed out, because the boys sat in the room and decided that they wanted one of their own, even though the person they may have chosen was not as qualified." For the legislature, however, the party does not discourage candidates.

Second, evidence from these states suggests that recruitment remains vital to women's representation. According to Treat, "It's very important to have people go out and *find* women that are activists and maybe not in the traditional party structure, that are good candidates, and to encourage them and to give them help." Recruitment of women in particular does not necessarily occur through the parties, however. Maine legislative leaders look for candidates who can win and do not necessarily focus on recruiting women. Speaking about her role in leadership, Treat argued,

> I wouldn't say that we're particularly trying to recruit women. We're really just looking for who can win. We'd love to see the same number of women or more women. But [in] some of these districts, particularly because of term limits, we're losing senators who are Democrats in Republican areas. And finding people who have the similar personal qualities to be able to win in a district that is fundamentally not on your side is a real challenge.

Some of the interest groups to which the Democratic caucus turns have a reputation for recruiting women. For example, one important ally of the Democratic party is the Dirigo Alliance, which Treat helped to found in 1987. This coalition of groups, including Maine National Organization for Women and the Maine Women's Lobby, recruits progressive candidates for the legislature.

The Senate caucus does not recruit women candidates specifically. Yet Treat expressed concern about the consequences of women's departure from legislative leadership as a result of term limits:

> The leadership is more male than female, and that's who's doing the recruiting. It's not that they're against women. But you know, who do you go to? You think about your friends, the people you know, who you're connected with. So I think there's issues there.

Women do not appear to be at a disadvantage in California, where candidate recruitment is even more decentralized than in Maine. Assembly member Virginia Strom-Martin described the primary as a "free-for-all" in which "everybody tries to promote their own candidate."[2] Groups of legislators and like-minded interest groups commonly recruit candidates to enter the primary. For example, Senator Sheila Kuehl has weekly contacts with other progressive legislators and advocacy groups—for example, attorneys, environmentalists, and labor unions—to discuss potential candidates for open seats. The legislative caucuses only support candidates in the general election, though individual leaders might back particular candidates in primaries.

Kuehl explained that winning party endorsements can be very useful in campaign mailings:

> So we do a lot in the mail. And when you target Democratic voters, if you can list six Democratic clubs in the district [that] have endorsed you, then Democratic voters think you're the best Democrat. And so those endorsements are extremely important. But they're gained by organizing. They're not necessarily gained because of working in the Democratic clubs personally. It was simply that I had the same values that the Democratic clubs were looking for.

Thus, winning support from local party clubs is important to winning the primary in some districts, but past party involvement per se is not critical.

In this candidate-centered environment, no guarantee exists that women's representation will increase. Individuals who would like to see more women in the legislature cultivate women's candidacies, which may be a multiyear process. As Strom-Martin explained,

> You just have to make a concerted effort and you have to start early with trying to recruit and talk people into thinking about it. They have to get into the mind-set that they can even do it and know that they can have the support once they do make up their mind. That's key. It's one thing to tell somebody to make that kind of commitment. It's another thing to say, "And I will help you with resources." I think that's what our charge is now.

Kuehl also helps women potential candidates position themselves for state legislative candidacy. These efforts entail identifying women several years prior to the election and recruiting them to run.

---

2. Skalaban (1997: 33) argues, "Party politics in California is best described as a partisan network of groups and individuals who move in and out of the political system depending on the issue or election involved. The formal party organizations are part of the network but in no way dominate it, nor could the party organizations even be considered the most important players."

Washington, which has a much less professionalized legislature than California's, led the nation in women's representation at the time of my interviews. The existence of the blanket primary in Washington, in which Democratic and Republican candidates compete in the same primary, has not precluded both parties from creating more sophisticated party organizations (Appleton and Depoorter 1997). Much recruitment for the legislature takes place through the local party, state party, and the legislative caucuses. As Representative Sharon Tomiko Santos explained, "It's a little bit of everything." Like most states, the caucuses have campaign committees that assist the party with recruitment. The state parties recruit candidates as well, sometimes coordinating efforts with the legislature. According to Representative Ruth Kagi, local officeholding is not "a necessity at all." Nor is it necessary to have come through the party structure. And although the party actively recruits, these efforts do not necessarily imply gatekeeping. Much as the party might like to avoid a primary, doing so may not be feasible. For example, outgoing members commonly try to find their replacements. These handpicked successors do not necessarily get the parties' nominations, however; according to House co-speaker pro tempore Val Ogden: "You can't stop anyone who says, 'Hey, I'd like to do this too.'"

Meanwhile, whether candidate gender should matter in recruitment is a matter of some debate in Washington. Carolyn Edmonds, a representative from an area of the state with a twenty-five-year tradition of electing women to the legislature, explained, "A common refrain you hear up in my district is that if you're a man, don't bother to run because you won't get elected. But like I said, this is a luxury that I have that very few women do." This is the same area of the state where U.S. Senators Patty Murray and Maria Cantwell began their political careers. Edmonds believes this unusual tradition gives her an advantage: "In my particular district, there's a predisposition to electing Democratic women, which has given me a significant advantage [over] a woman that runs in a district that's never elected a woman." However, leaders in both the Democratic and Republican parties sharply criticized outgoing women state legislators' desire to recruit women to take their seats.[3] This example speaks to women's efforts to ensure that women

3. "'That any sort of political seat should be reserved for one gender or one race is a ridiculous, anachronistic idea. We've gotten so far beyond that,' said Chris Vance, state Republican Party leader. 'The idea a seat is reserved for women is nuts, and unnecessary'"; "'For any given race, are we looking for women, because women are being replaced? I would say

continue to run for the legislature as well as to the controversy that surrounds such gender-conscious recruitment.

In sum, parties are not the only institutions that can encourage women to seek office. In a weak party environment, interest groups and individuals can organize and work to increase women's representation. Indeed, pessimism about the parties' failure to recruit more women to run for office led Carroll and Strimling (1983) to argue that alternative means of recruitment were needed and to suggest that women's organizations take up this task:

> Women's organizations also can play a critical role in encouraging women already active in political organizations, political parties, or their communities to take the next step and run for office. Because the political parties as the traditional mechanisms for candidate recruitment have not sought out and encouraged large numbers of women to run for winnable seats, an alternative recruitment mechanism is needed. (10)

Since the early 1970s, women's groups have increased the pool of potential candidates by training women, recruited women to run for office, and helped women win election by channeling resources to women's campaigns (Mandel 1981; Hartmann 1989; Burrell 1994; Rozell 2000; Duerst-Lahti 1998). The women's movement has also legitimated women's political ambitions (Mueller 1982). Women's groups, networks, and political action committees (PACs) remain an important support system for women candidates. New groups such as Iowa's Women in Public Policy continue to form to increase women's representation. The national PAC EMILY's List recently launched a new campaign to train Democratic pro-choice women candidates for the state legislature in response to the declining number of women state legislators ("Creating a New Generation" 2001).

It is important to acknowledge that the involvement of women's groups in electoral politics introduces new dilemmas. Deciding which woman candidate to support and whether issue criteria should trump interest in electing more women to office can create divisions within and among women's organizations (Mandel 1981; Barakso 2004). Moreover, my party leader surveys and the state legislative candidate surveys conducted by other scholars demonstrate that parties are more actively involved in candidate recruitment

---

no,' said Kurt Fritts, executive director of Washington's Senate Democratic Campaign Committee. 'It's a factor only to the extent a woman candidate might be a better profile in that particular race. It's always candidate-specific'" (Buck 2002).

than are interest groups. Thus, the interest group solution to women's representation is not clear-cut.

The ways in which gender continues to inform the path to public office suggest that the level of women's representation is shaped by the condition of those mechanisms that bring women into the electoral arena, including the parties' interest in fielding women candidates. Although the party is one institution that can facilitate candidacy, it is not the only such institution.

IMPLICATIONS

Current debates about American party politics center on the condition of the parties and their relevance in contemporary elections. Have party organizations grown stronger in recent years, or are they just busier (e.g., Coleman 1996; Fiorina 2002)? Much evidence suggests that party organizations are growing stronger, although the form of the party organization, including the increasing importance of the legislative caucuses, has changed (Gierzynski 1992; C. Rosenthal 1995; Shea 1995; Aldrich 2000). My findings contribute to this debate. In many states, the party in the legislature bears primary responsibility for candidate recruitment. Not only the parties themselves believe that parties are significant: candidate surveys and interviews with state legislators confirm the parties' important role.

Whether party leaders seek to influence the nomination depends on the state. Thus, the party's importance to structuring the context and decision making of potential candidates varies across states. Some studies have concluded from candidate surveys that parties play a minor role in state legislative elections (e.g., Frendreis and Gitelson 1999). However, I believe that the pressing question for party scholars is whether parties are more influential in that decision-making process in some states than in others, not whether parties are more influential than personal factors. Personal factors, such as whether individuals have the support of their families, are both idiosyncratic and universal. In contrast, the state and legislative party surveys demonstrate that party activities vary systematically across states.

The interviews I conducted with party leaders illustrated a wide range of party involvement in candidate recruitment. In some states, party leaders recruit candidates two years before the election; in other states, the party plays almost no role in these activities. Whether interest groups are central to party recruitment activities and whether interest groups actively recruit candidates on their own also depended on the state. The party turns to interest groups for help in recruitment in Colorado, Iowa, and North Carolina. Interest groups in Alabama are more likely to conduct candidate efforts independent of the parties. Legislative factions and interest groups in California recruit candidates in an extremely decentralized fashion. In short, because the recruitment process is not the same across the state legislatures, the states should be disaggregated when analyzing the parties' role in elections. Studies of political ambition should incorporate this variation across the American states in the political parties' roles.

Consideration of descriptive representation does not typically form part of contemporary debates about strong parties. Scholars of women and politics commonly theorize that strengthening political parties can benefit women, adding yet another rationale for why strong parties can strengthen democracy. Strong parties may enhance representation by offering voters a clear choice and more effectively tying public preferences to policy outcomes (Committee on Political Parties 1950). However, such parties may not lead to greater descriptive representation of previously underrepresented groups. Indeed, they may have the opposite effect. Therefore, recent evidence of growing party organizational strength may not bode well for women's representation.

Groups such as EMILY's List believe that increasing women's representation depends on supporting women in primaries, even in the wake of criticism that primaries weaken the party's chances in the general election. Thus, women's groups and PACs remain unwilling to leave the selection of the party's nominee to the party. My interviews confirm that party women see advantages to organizing outside the party. For example, the pro-choice Democratic women's PACs Hope Chest in Ohio and Lillian's List in North Carolina were modeled self-consciously after EMILY's List. Just as EMILY's List operates independently of the national party, these state PACs are independent of their state parties.

My analysis of state legislative recruitment patterns suggests that previously excluded groups are unlikely to benefit from a more closed nominating system. The legacy of being a historically excluded and underrepresented group, the continued underrepresentation of women as candidates, and the scarcity of women in party leadership combine to put women at a disadvantage when the candidate selection process is more closed. Despite its drawbacks, a more decentralized, candidate-centered system enables women to enter primary contests without needing permission from party leaders.

Women's groups and PACs can then mobilize on behalf of those primary candidates.

Putting the choice of electing women candidates to primary voters has the advantage of eliminating one potential barrier to women's candidacies: the danger that party leaders, anticipating voter bias, will preclude or discourage women from running. Many of the women I interviewed in those states where parties engage in gatekeeping practices believe that party leaders misperceive the electability of women candidates. As Norris and Lovenduski have argued, informal, centralized recruitment can be problematic for increasing women's representation:

> In informal-centralised systems of recruitment, if party leaders wish to promote certain groups or individuals to balance the ticket, they have considerable power to do so. Through patronage, party leaders can improve the position of candidates on party lists to create a balanced ticket, or place them in good constituencies. As a result under this system of "benevolent autocracy" change can be implemented relatively quickly, although without institutional safeguards the gains can be quickly reversed. On the other hand, if the leadership resists change to the status quo, they can block opportunities for challengers. (1995: 200)

The absence of party lists in the United States makes it more difficult for women to use a strategy of pressing the parties to increase women's representation. For example, Darcy, Welch, and Clark (1994: 158) argue that one reason women may fare better in multimember districts is that the parties will face more pressure to nominate women: "Since women are a legitimate grouping with political relevance, slate makers will be under greater pressure to include them as candidates as the number to be nominated increases." Matland and Studlar (1996: 709) note, "In proportional representation systems . . . parties balance their tickets by including viable female candidates on the party list in order to appeal to a broad portion of the electorate. Ticket balancing is impossible, however, in single-member districts where only one person carries the party banner." The nomination of lists of candidates makes it easier to ensure women's representation. Cross-national studies of women's representation highlight the importance of women's activities within party organizations to win quotas and other policies to facilitate the election of women (e.g., Lovenduski and Norris 1993). Electoral rules may therefore play a critical role in women's ability to press for gender balance. It is not clear that party nominating conventions that yield one nominee for single-member districts would enhance women's representation.[4]

Diversity in politics is arguably socially desirable; several party leaders I interviewed argued a premium exists today on being inclusive. Yet the case studies provided scant evidence that one party sought to recruit more women as a way of competing with the other party. Thus, I found that the mechanism of party contagion identified by scholars in comparative politics has little impact on the parties' recruitment strategies. The public's interest in having "more" women in office does not necessarily imply interest in gender parity (Sanbonmatsu 2003). Similarly, at the level of elite politics, diversity may mean including a token woman in a legislative caucus or in leadership.

The case studies evidenced less competition between the Democratic and Republican parties to field women candidates than might be expected. In addition, the six case-study states offered little indication that women's groups constitute central participants in the parties' efforts to field candidates. Nevertheless, the main criterion driving the recruitment process is finding the candidate who can win. Even among party leaders sympathetic to increasing women's representation, winning remains the primary goal.

Past scholarship has suggested that a change in majority party status can facilitate women's election to office. Given the barrier of incumbency, a change in the majority party could yield more open seats and hence more opportunities for women candidates (Darcy and Beckwith 1991). I found some support for the view that women's opportunities are related to majority party status. For example, the minority party in particular has incentives to seek out nontraditional candidates in its efforts to win a majority. However, the negative effects of gatekeeping suggest that heightened competition between the two parties may not lead to an increase in women's representa-

---

4. One of my interview subjects from Washington was skeptical about the prospect of party nominating conventions. The state has been working to find an acceptable replacement for its blanket primary since the Supreme Court ruled in 2000 that the blanket primary infringed on the parties' right to freedom of association. The Republican party has pledged to adopt party nominating conventions if party primaries are not allowed. Many scholars of women and politics have advocated party reforms such as conventions as a way of increasing women's representation. However, one Republican woman, Representative Shirley Hankins, worried that this type of party influence might be problematic: "I think it says to me when you start doing that if you are not the kind of Republican they want you to be, in some areas you will never ever get nominated to run for office. That limits my right to make a choice for myself at the ballot box."

tion precisely because the stakes for both parties increase with greater competition. Because of concern about women's electability, party competition may not create favorable settings for women's representation.

As the Republican party has become more successful in state legislative elections and won control of more legislative chambers, the percentage of women as a share of all Republican legislators has declined. At the same time, the Democratic party, which has been losing seats, is seeing women become a larger share of its caucuses across the country. Why such is the case is not clear. In general, the two parties exhibited fairly similar levels of recruitment and gatekeeping activities.

The party gap in women legislators may be a function of the gender gap in voting behavior: women voters are more likely to identify as Democrats than as Republicans (Kenski 1988; Bendyna and Lake 1994; Kaufmann and Petrocik 1999). The Democratic party has also been more ideologically committed to diversity and has been more likely than the Republican party to mandate equal representation on party committees (J. Freeman, forthcoming). The interaction of gender and party stereotypes may matter as well. Republican voters may be more skeptical of women candidates than Democratic voters because women candidates are stereotyped as more liberal than men (Matland and King 2002). Thus, Republican voters may perceive Republican women candidates as insufficiently conservative. Finally, more mobilization on behalf of women candidates has taken place through women's groups and PACs affiliated with the Democratic party, suggesting that Democratic women may have stronger networks and access to more campaign resources than Republican women (Burrell 1994). An interesting aspect of the case studies, however, is that the parties' reputations regarding women's representation often defied predictions: in all of the case-study states, Republican women had achieved many firsts for women in politics.

In the early part of the twentieth century, Democratic and Republican leaders moved to incorporate women into the national parties, hoping that women would recruit other women to the party fold. Today, though their presence within the parties is well established as activists, women remain significantly underrepresented in party leadership positions. Were women to gain a greater leadership role within local, state, and legislative party organizations, the likelihood that women would be recruited to run for the legislature should increase. More research is needed to explain why women have not had more success in winning positions of party leadership (Baer 2003).

The case studies illustrate the importance of state boundaries for women's opportunities in politics in two respects: state boundaries shape the context in which women candidates run and define the composition of the state electorate.[5] Parties are one feature of the state context. Each state's history and experiences with women candidates shape the context facing women potential candidates. State boundaries also have implications for women's candidacies because of compositional effects: the demographics of the state make some places more sympathetic to women candidates than others. In sum, women have not been equally likely to become candidates across the fifty states precisely because they provide different opportunities and constraints for women candidates.

FUTURE RESEARCH

Several limitations of this study warrant mention and attention in future research. First, the case studies and party leader surveys were conducted at one point in time, and the six cases only begin to capture the diversity across the states. Although the longitudinal, quantitative analysis confirmed my main conclusions, scholars will need to investigate whether the negative impact of party activities on women's representation persists in the future.

Another strategy that could be employed in future research would be to survey potential state legislative candidates of both sexes and then compare the experiences of these potential candidates with the parties across states.[6] National surveys of potential candidates can shed light on the typical recruitment experience; however, understanding who runs for state offices ultimately requires state-level measures. Because the eligible pool of candidates for the legislature is notoriously difficult to define and varies across states, such a survey poses significant methodological hurdles.[7] However, my findings suggest that studying the experiences of women potential can-

5. See Gimpel and Schuknecht 2003 on theories of composition versus context in political geography.

6. Examples of potential candidate studies include Fox and Lawless 2004; Niven 1998; and the Candidate Emergence Study.

7. It is important to consider, for example, how the legislative caucuses define the pool of potential state legislative candidates. Moncrief, Squire, and Jewell (2001: 62) summarize what recruiters seek in state legislative candidates: "Recruiters stress that a good candidate should have standing in the community; this means being well known, having a good reputation, and having a record of organizational leadership."

didates on a state-by-state basis is critical. For example, I would expect that whether men and women potential candidates are equally likely to report being recruited by the party depends on the state. In states where the party does not perceive women to be at an electoral disadvantage and in states where women hold party leadership roles, women potential candidates should be more likely to be asked to run than in other states.

The interviews raised a number of important concerns that lay beyond the scope of my study. One enduring issue is the disproportionate share of responsibilities that continue to define women's family roles. These responsibilities make it more challenging for women to pursue careers in politics—or in any field, for that matter. The conundrum of balancing family life with a political career was a constant feature of my interviews, which respondents often described as a personal juggling act or a structural inequality based in traditional gender role arrangements. But some interview subjects also viewed it as a problem of voter attitudes. Even when women find ways to accommodate family and candidacy, anticipation of voter criticism may still discourage women from seeking office. Thus, not only gender roles but voter beliefs about gender roles have implications for women's candidacies. As Ogden explained, voter questions about women's family lives always loom in the background: "I know for younger women [candidates], that whether [voters] ask it, that is a question that is always in the back of people's minds. Who is taking care of your children?" Thus, beliefs about women's roles remain consequential for women's participation in elite politics.

Past studies have investigated voters' inferences based on a candidate's gender, but less is known about the intersection of additional characteristics such as parental status. Do voters penalize women who run for office when their children are young? Or do potential women candidates misperceive the extent to which voters will criticize their choices? Women candidates for governor and U.S. senator have been less likely than men to feature their families in their campaign advertisements (Bystrom et al. 2004). Can women candidates use their family situation to their advantage under some conditions?

Because most studies do not find a relationship between gender and fund-raising, I did not anticipate the extent to which interview subjects would identify campaign finance as a factor that disproportionately discourages women from running for office. Many interview subjects argued that fund-raising no longer constitutes the barrier for women candidates that it once was; others argued that fund-raising is difficult for men and women alike. However, many other respondents identified fund-raising as a major obstacle—

if not *the* major obstacle—to women's candidacies. Interview subjects believe that cultural norms make it more difficult for women to raise money for themselves rather than for a cause. In addition, because men and women candidates come from different networks and occupations, those interviewed perceived men as having much better access to donor networks and interest groups. One legislator from a southern state explained,

> What happens is that, men, if I'm in the legislature, I have a leadership position, and if I have a friend or someone who I think should run, then I funnel money to that candidate through people I know who come to me for various insight or help on legislation. So the network has always been from male to male, because all the lobbyists are male, CEOs of companies are male, rotary clubs are male. So there's just been a line of money.

Fund-raising was also argued to have long-term implications for women's political careers. Women may have less access to important committee assignments and leadership positions if they enter the legislature from backgrounds in education and social services rather than through connections to particular industries or interest groups.

Recent research suggests that to achieve the same electoral result, women may need more campaign funds and qualifications than men (Herrick 1996; Hoffman, Palmer, and Gaddie 2001). Success in fund-raising may also depend on the state. Thompson, Moncrief, and Hamm (1998) found that women state legislative candidates were disadvantaged in campaign finance in professional legislatures but in other states attracted financial support at rates similar to if not better than men. Moreover, although most analyses of candidate success at the state legislative and congressional levels find that women fare as well as men, women appear to have a disadvantage in statewide races (Delano and Winters 2002). These relationships among funds, qualifications, and elections merit further investigation.

Across the case-study states, some respondents observed that women were less savvy than men about building political careers, perhaps because women were more likely than men to have come to politics through concerns about issues. Because of a lack of connections or a lack of foresight, women may not pay sufficient attention to the game of politics, with consequences for their ability to seek leadership positions and achieve higher office. Assembly member Hannah Beth Jackson of California, for example, argued,

> Women are so concerned about policy that we frequently are left in the dust because the game is still a game of power and politics. And we have

to start being more willing to play that game, not necessarily in the same way, but to recognize that policy is critical and it's what motivates me, but you can't ignore the other side of it or else we will just find ourselves marginalized again.

The status of women within the legislature was another topic of concern (Kathlene 1994; Smooth 2001). In some cases, interview subjects perceived no barriers in the electoral process but had different reactions to the legislature. Some women observed that many men in the legislature were uncomfortable working with women or were unwilling to share power. Women legislators commonly related challenges they face in gaining the respect of their colleagues—feeling excluded, needing to prove themselves, facing sharp questioning when they speak on the floor, and so on. These experiences with discrimination within the legislature can be politicizing, leading women to advocate for increasing the presence of women within their institutions. Some men also argued that women face a glass ceiling inside the legislature, even in liberal places such as Colorado and Massachusetts.

Surveys confirm that many women state legislators feel they lack equal access to leadership roles (CAWP 2001c). Moreover, women who achieve leadership positions may not be typical women legislators: some interview respondents believe that women in leadership are less likely to advocate for women's interests than other women in the legislature. This is not a new problem confronting women in politics. Jo Freeman explains that after suffrage, the "women who succeeded in politics were those who ignored other women and depended on men for their advancement" (2000: 175). She describes the dilemma facing women in elective office:

> Women who attained political influence through male sponsors were more likely to be accountable to their sponsors, or the party organizations through which they worked, rather than to women as an abstract group or the women's movement. For a group to hold members accountable to it for their actions is a long-standing problem faced by all identifiable groups, but it has been a particularly difficult one for women. Thus sponsorship by an insider in politics may be an individual route to influence, but it does not lead to group influence. In order to attain group influence, there must be an organized group supported by group consciousness. (232–33)

More attention must be paid to the relationship between the selection processes that bring women into the legislature and their behavior once there

(Githens 2003).[8] Research is also needed on whether the party is more or less likely to recruit women potential candidates who see their role as group representatives of women as well as on whether concern about women as a group affects their status in the legislature.[9] In short, studying women's candidacies can provide a window into how the public will is translated into public policy.

Voter attitudes about women candidates have changed dramatically, as have the attitudes of parties, interest groups, and women themselves. As a result, the composition of office seekers has become more descriptively reflective of the population as a whole. At the same time, precisely because society remains structured by gender, how gender will be related to office-holding in the future is uncertain. Women's representation will, of course, depend on whether women put themselves forward as candidates. But women's representation will also depend on the choices and strategies of other political actors and institutions, including the political parties.

8. For example, J. Black and Erickson (2000) look at candidate backgrounds and their success rates.

9. See Dovi 2002 for possible criteria in selecting the "descriptive representatives" of women as a group.

APPENDIX

I conducted a total of 244 interviews. Almost all interviews were conducted in person, and most were tape-recorded; eighteen interviews were conducted by phone. I took notes during the interviews and at the end of each day of my fieldwork. Interviews usually lasted between half an hour and one hour, although interviews with party leaders and women's groups usually lasted at least an hour. Most of the interviews were conducted on the record. Of the 227 interviews in the case-study states, about 190 were tape-recorded.

I wrote to interview subjects to request an interview. In most cases, at the end of interviews I asked respondents to suggest other interview subjects. I contacted some of these individuals by telephone only.

The interview schedule differed somewhat according to the type of interview subject—a state party or state legislative leader, a state legislator, or some other respondent. The interviews with legislative and state party leaders and staff primarily concerned party involvement in state legislative races and candidate recruitment. The interview questions included the following topics: the party's role, if any, in candidate recruitment; the division of responsibilities for state legislative elections among the local, state, and legislative parties; the activities of any legislative campaign committees; party preferences with regard to avoiding primaries; formal or informal pre-primary endorsements; party assistance to state legislative candidates in the general election; the change over time, if any, in party activities in state legislative races; and the typical path to the state legislature.

The interviews with state legislators and candidates concerned their personal decisions to seek their seats and whether they had been recruited to run.

I also asked legislators about any experiences in recruiting other candidates. The interviews with women's groups addressed how and why the groups formed, how the groups were received, and how the groups assist women candidates.

One question common to all interview subjects concerned their perceptions of any barriers or opportunities facing women in their state as candidates or potential candidates for the legislature. Time permitting, I asked additional questions of all subjects about state legislative elections and women's candidacies, including whether majority party status, term limits (if applicable), or legislative professionalism affected candidate interest in serving in the legislature and whether those factors differentially affected potential candidates by party or gender. I asked respondents if they thought that voters reacted to candidate gender in any way or if they thought that voters were indifferent to candidate gender.

I also asked respondents whether they had observed any individuals, networks, or organizations involved in conscious efforts to recruit women candidates; whether the path to the legislature differed for women and men or for Democratic and Republican women; whether women had more opportunities as candidates within one party or the other; and whether any barriers or opportunities facing women candidates had changed over time. I also gave respondents an opportunity to speculate on why more women did not run for or serve in the legislature.

SAMPLE INTERVIEW SCHEDULE OF STATE LEGISLATORS, OHIO

How did you first decide to seek your seat?
    Did anyone encourage you to run? If yes: Who recruited you?
Had you held elective office or party office before you sought your seat?
In your area, is the local party involved in candidate recruitment?
    Is there often a favorite candidate? Is it important to seek support from particular leaders in the primary?
Have you helped to identify other candidates for the legislature, either formally or informally?
Do you think the majority (minority) status of your party affects who runs for the legislature?
    What effect, if any, do you think term limits have had on who runs?
    Has the type of candidate who runs for the legislature changed over time?
Have you noticed anything different about the paths that men and women take to the legislature?
    What about the paths of Democratic women versus Republican women?
Have you observed any conscious efforts—formal or informal—to recruit women for the legislature?
    Are there any women's groups or networks that are important in the state?
    Do you think that women legislators try to recruit other women? Why or why not?

Do you think women candidates or potential candidates for the legislature face any particular barriers or opportunities compared to men?

Do you think voters react to candidate gender in any way? Or are voters indifferent to candidate gender?

Why do you think there aren't more women serving in the legislature?

Do you have any experiences with women who chose not to run?

Is there anyone else I should speak with?

SAMPLE INTERVIEW SCHEDULE OF STATE LEGISLATIVE LEADERS AND PARTY OFFICIALS AND STAFF, OHIO

Could you tell me everything the party does for state legislative candidates?

How involved is the party in candidate recruitment? In how many races?

How does this recruitment process work? Who makes the decisions?

Where do you look for candidates? Are there any groups or networks that are particularly important in helping the party with recruitment?

What is the division of labor among the state party, the county parties, and the legislative caucus?

What resources does the state (legislative) party provide in the primary and general elections?

How has the state party role changed over time? How has the caucus role changed over time?

Are the party's efforts more organized now than in past years?

How has the state (legislative) party's involvement in candidate recruitment changed over time?

How many county parties make preprimary endorsements? Which counties?

About what percentage of counties have informal or formal gatekeepers?

How common is it for interest groups affiliated with the parties to recruit state legislative candidates?

How important is it for state legislative candidates to come from the party structure?

About what percentage of candidates come from outside versus inside the party structure?

About what percentage of candidates have held prior office?

Do you think the majority (minority) status of your party affects who runs for the legislature?

What effect, if any, do you think term limits have had on who runs?

Has the type of candidate who runs for the legislature changed over time?

Have you noticed anything different about the paths that men and women take to the legislature in terms of past experience or occupation?

What about the paths of Democratic and Republican women?

Do you think women face any particular barriers or opportunities as candidates or potential candidates for the legislature?

Are there any important groups or networks that consciously identify women candidates?

Do women legislators seek out women candidates?

Do you think voters react to candidate gender in any way?

Do you take gender into account when slating candidates?

Have you seen any change over time in women's opportunities in Ohio?

Why do you think women do not make up half of the General Assembly today?

Is there anyone else I should speak with?

SAMPLE INTERVIEW SCHEDULE OF WOMEN'S INTEREST GROUP
LEADERS, OHIO

What was the impetus for starting your organization? What was its original purpose? Who
was involved? How is it structured?

Is candidate recruitment part of your mission?

Do you think women in the party or as candidates for the legislature generally face any
particular barriers or opportunities compared to men?

How has this changed over time?

Have you observed any conscious efforts—formal or informal—to recruit women per se?

Are there any other women's groups or networks that are important in helping women
win election to the legislature?

Do you think that women legislators try to recruit other women? Why or why not?

Do you think women have more opportunities to become candidates in one party or the other?

Why do you think there aren't more women serving in the legislature?

Do you have any experiences with women who chose not to run?

What has changed for women candidates in Ohio over time?

LIST OF INTERVIEW SUBJECTS

Titles are current at the time of the interview. An asterisk (*) indicates that the interview
was conducted at the CAWP Forum for Women State Legislators in California. A dagger
(†) indicates that the interview was conducted by telephone. Unless otherwise indicated,
I conducted all interviews in the state capital.

Alabama

Tim Baer, executive director, Republican Party†
Ann Bedsole, former legislator†
Representative Barbara Boyd
Tom Butler, Senate majority leader
Marty Connors, chair, Republican Party
Representative Priscilla Dunn
Senator Sundra Escott-Russell
Senator Vivian Davis Figures
Marsha Folsom, executive director, Democratic Party
Representative Betty Carol Graham
Representative Jeanette Greene
Ken Guin, House majority leader
Representative Laura Hall
Representative Perry O. Hooper Jr.
Danne Howard, lobbyist
Dr. Paul Hubbert, Alabama Education Association
Charles McDowell Lee, secretary of the Senate
Representative Mary Sue McClurkin
Senator Wendell Mitchell
Demetrius Newton, House speaker pro tempore
Susan Parker, state auditor
Redding Pitt, chair, Democratic Party

Representative John W. Rogers Jr.
Representative Sue Schmitz
J. T. "Jabo" Waggoner, Senate minority leader
David White, *Birmingham News*

Colorado

Senator Norma Anderson
John Andrews, Senate minority leader
Bob Beauprez, chair, Republican Party†
Representative Alice Borodkin
Mary Dambman, former legislator
Doug Dean, speaker of the House
Rob Fairbank, House majority caucus chair
Mike Feeley, former Senate minority leader
Senator Joan Fitz-Gerald
Beth Ganz, former executive director, Democratic Party
Senator Ken Gordon
Dorothy Gotlieb, former legislator
Dan Grossman, House minority leader†
Peggy Kerns, former House minority leader
Sharron Klein, chair, Denver Democratic Party
Tim Knaus, chair, Democratic Party
Representative Alice Madden
Barbara Margolis, Democratic Women's PAC†
Representative Rosemary Marshall
Dianne Maywhort, lobbyist
Carolyn McIntosh, Democratic Women's PAC
Mike Melanson, executive director, Democratic Party
Janna Mendez, former legislator (Boulder)
Sean Murphy, executive director, Republican Party
Marilyn Musgrave, Senate minority caucus chair
Senator Alice Nichol
Terry Phillips, assistant Senate majority leader
Terri Rayburn, Senate candidate
Senator Peggy Reeves
Representative Pam Rhodes
Dorothy Rupert, former legislator (Boulder)
Representative Todd Saliman
Lola Spradley, House majority leader
Gloria Tanner, former legislator
Senator Penfield Tate
Jennifer Veiga, assistant House minority leader
Dottie Wham, former legislator
Representative Suzanne Williams
Representative Tambor Williams
Senator Sue Windels
Ruth Wright, former House minority leader (Boulder)

Iowa

Representative Andra Atteberry
Becky Beach, administrative assistant to the president of the Senate
Representative Carmine Boal
Nancy Boettger, assistant Senate majority leader
Leann Brunnette, founder and director, Iowa's Women in Public Policy (WIPP)
Polly Bukta, assistant House minority leader
Bill Dix, assistant House majority leader
Representative Barbara Finch
Tim Gannon, Iowa House campaign director
Representative Teresa Garman
Representative Jane Greimann
Michael Gronstal, Senate minority leader
Johnie Hammond, assistant Senate minority leader*
Jean Hessburg, executive director, Democratic Party
Geri Huser, House minority whip
Stewart Iverson Jr., Senate majority leader
Elizabeth Jacobs, House majority whip
Patty Judge, secretary of agriculture
Mary Kramer, Senate president
Representative Chuck Larson Jr., chair, Republican Party
Representative Vicki Lensing
Dick Myers, House majority leader
Charlotte Nelson, executive director, Iowa Commission on the Status of Women
Representative Janet Petersen
Marlys Popma, executive director, Republican Party
Dr. Sheila McGuire Riggs, chair, Democratic Party
Brent Siegrist, speaker of the House
Senator Maggie Tinsman*
Andy Warren, Legislative Majority Fund†
David Yepsen, *Des Moines Register*†

Massachusetts

Representative Cory Atkins
Suzanne Bump, former legislator*
Representative Carol Cleven
Representative Mark Falzone
Senator Susan Fargo
Jonathan Fletcher, interim executive director, Republican Party
Julie Granof, executive director, Massachusetts Caucus of Women Legislators
Representative Patricia Haddad
Lida E. Harkins, House majority whip
Kerry Murphy Healey, chair, Republican Party[1]
Robert L. Hedlund, third assistant Senate minority leader

1. Healey was elected party chair shortly after my interview. At the time of the interview, she was a candidate for party chair.

Philip Johnston, chair, Democratic Party†
Bradley H. Jones Jr., assistant House minority leader
Representative Jay Kaufman
Andrea Lee, Commonwealth Coalition
Francis L. Marini, House minority leader
Senator Therese Murray
Representative Shirley Owen-Hicks
Representative Marie Parente
Representative Susan Pope
Mary S. Rogeness, third assistant House minority leader
Marni Schultz, Massachusetts Women's Political Caucus
Susan Shaer, executive director, Women's Action for New Directions†
Representative Karen Spilka†
John Stefanini, chief counsel, Speaker's Office
Representative Ellen Story
Roni Thaler, executive director, Massachusetts Women's Political Caucus
Susan Fenochietti Thomson, executive director, Democratic Party (Quincy)
Suleyken Walker, steering committee, Massachusetts Women's Political Caucus
Senator Dianne Wilkerson

North Carolina

Barbara Allen, chair, Democratic Party
Jan Allen, chair, Lillian's List
Representative Rex Baker
Debbie Beatty, executive director, Republican Party
Senator Phil Berger
James B. Black, speaker of the House
Gerry Bowles, former candidate
Elizabeth Farrior Buford, board of directors, Lillian's List
Representative Marge Carpenter
Bill Cobey, chair, Republican Party
Betsy Cochrane, former House minority leader, Senate minority leader†
Representative W. Pete Cunningham, assistant to the speaker
Leo Daughtry, House minority leader
Andrew T. Dedmon, House majority whip
Beverly Earle, House majority whip
Representative Ruth Easterling
Laura Edwards, cofounder, Lillian's List†
Lisbeth Evans, former chair, Democratic Party
Scott Falmlen, executive director, Democratic Party
James Forrester, Senate minority whip
Mary F. Forrester, former Gaston Republican chair; director, Concerned Women
    for America-NC
Senator Virginia Foxx
Representative Charlotte Gardner
Senator Linda Garrou
Jane Gray, counsel to the speaker
Joe Hackney, House speaker pro tempore

Senator Kay Hagan
Julia Howard, House minority whip
Representative Verla Insko
Representative Mary Jarrell
Representative Linda Johnson
Wooten Johnson, director, North Carolina House Committee
Senator Eleanor Kinnaird
Senator Jeanne Lucas
Elaine Marshall, secretary of state
Betty Rae McCain, former chair, Democratic Party†
Representative Marian McLawhorn
Norma Mills, counsel to Senate president pro tempore
Representative Frank Mitchell
Representative Mia Morris
Meg Scott Phipps, commissioner of agriculture
Representative Jean Preston
Jan Pueschel, former vice chair, Wake County Republican Party†
Tony Rand, Senate majority leader
Joel Raupe, assistant to Senate minority leader
Representative Wilma Sherrill†
Representative Fern Shubert
Caroline Valand, director, North Carolina Senate Committee
Representative Jennifer Weiss

Ohio

Representative Dixie Allen
Jan Allen, consultant
Representative Joyce Beatty
Robert Bennett, chair, Republican Party
Representative Tom Brinkman Jr.
Sarah Brown, Treasurer, Ohio Republican Party†
Steven Buehrer, House majority floor leader
Representative Mary Cirelli
Neil S. Clark, consultant
Michael Colley, Franklin County Republican Party chair
Senator Kevin Coughlin
Jo Ann Davidson, former speaker of the House
Bill DeMora, political director, Democratic Party
Greg DiDonato, assistant Senate minority leader
Jack Ford, House minority leader
Senator Linda Furney
Teri Geiger, chief of staff, Ohio Senate
Dr. Karen Gillmor, former legislator
Representative John Hagan
Representative Nancy Hollister
Janet Jackson, city attorney
Representative Edward Jerse
Bruce Johnson, Senate president pro tempore

Representative Peter Lawson Jones
Representative Merle Kearns
Joyce Garver Keller, former president, Ohio Women's Political Caucus
Representative Sally C. Kilbane
Melodee Kornacker, Hope Chest cofounder†
Representative Eileen Krupinski
Joan Lawrence, former legislator
David Leland, chair, Democratic Party
Joanne Limbach, lobbyist†
Patricia Logsdon, chair, Hope Chest steering committee
Patrick McLean, minority chief of staff, Ohio Senate
Senator Rhine McLin
Chris McNulty, executive director, Republican Party
Senator Priscilla Mead
Betty Montgomery, attorney general
Joy Padgett, former legislator
Sally Perz, former legislator
Jon Peterson, House assistant majority whip
Representative Linda Reidelbach
Representative Arlene Setzer
Erin Sullivan, House minority whip
Representative Barbara Sykes
Charleta Tavares, former legislator
Robin Thomas, Hope Chest cofounder
Jim Tilling, former chief of staff, Ohio Senate
James Trakas, House majority whip
Antoinette Wilson, consultant, House Democratic caucus
Representative Anne Womer Benjamin

CAWP Forum for Women State Legislators, 2001, Dana Point, California

CALIFORNIA

Senator Dede Alpert
Assembly member Hannah-Beth Jackson
Senator Sheila Kuehl
Assembly member Virginia Strom-Martin

GEORGIA

Representative Kathy Ashe
Representative Georganna Sinkfield

MAINE

Senator Mary Cathcart
Sharon Treat, assistant Senate Democratic leader
Representative Elizabeth Watson

NEW HAMPSHIRE

Representative Betty Hall

WASHINGTON

Representative Carolyn Edmonds
Rosa Franklin, Senate president pro tempore
Representative Shirley Hankins
Representative Ruth Kagi
Representative Patricia Lantz
Val Ogden, co-speaker pro tempore
Representative Sharon Tomiko Santos

MAIL SURVEY PROCEDURES

The mail surveys were conducted by the Ohio State University Center for Survey Research. The surveys were sent to three discrete samples in 2002: state party leaders, state legislative leaders, and Ohio candidates.

The legislative leader sample consists of members of the Democratic and Republican House (or Assembly) leadership teams in forty-nine states. A total of ninety-five legislative caucuses in forty-nine states were contacted. (According to the state Web sites and the National Conference of State Legislatures Web site, three minority parties do not have leadership positions: the Louisiana Republicans, the Mississippi Republicans, and the Texas Republicans. Nebraska is excluded because it is unicameral and nonpartisan.) I had the resources to survey approximately five leaders from each party in each state. Because the leadership structure varies across state legislatures and by majority party status, the total number of leaders I surveyed from each caucus varied. The maximum number of leaders surveyed in a single caucus was 10, the minimum was 1, and the average was 4.5 leaders per caucus. The sample includes the following top leadership positions in each state: speaker, speaker pro tempore, majority leader, and minority leader. I supplemented these top positions as needed with up to two additional leadership positions in the majority party and up to four additional leadership positions in the minority party, with the goal of surveying a total of five individuals. For example, if three people served as speaker pro tempore, then the top three positions yielded five individuals, and I did not continue down the leadership ladder. If more than one person served in one of the top positions, I surveyed all individuals holding that position (e.g., all assistant minority leaders). In no case did I contact individuals from more than five leadership positions in each caucus. In a few cases, I contacted more than five individuals because there were more than five people holding the top leadership positions.

Contact information was taken from the Council of State Governments leadership directory (Council of State Governments, *State Legislative Leadership, Committees, and Staff 2002*) as well state legislature Web sites. I supplemented this information with calls to the state legislatures. I also consulted the National Conference of State Legislatures' list of leadership positions ("Leadership Positions in State Legislatures," <www.ncsl.org/programs/leaders/positions.htm>).

The individual level response rate for legislative leaders was about 35 percent: 149 of 429 respondents completed the survey. At least one respondent from seventy-one of the ninety-five caucuses completed the survey, for a response rate at the caucus level of about 75 percent. Forty-five states are represented in the sample. A total of thirty-six Republican House leadership teams and thirty-five Democratic House leadership teams completed the survey. The following legislative parties participated in the study: Alabama (D), Alaska (R), Arizona (R), Arkansas (D), California (R), Colorado (D, R), Connecticut (D, R), Delaware (R), Florida

(D, R), Georgia (R), Hawaii (D, R), Idaho (D, R), Illinois (D, R), Indiana (D, R), Iowa (D, R), Kansas (D, R), Kentucky (D, R), Maine (D), Maryland (D, R), Massachusetts (D, R), Michigan (D, R), Minnesota (D), Mississippi (D), Missouri (D, R), Montana (D, R), New Hampshire (D, R), Nevada (D, R), New Jersey (D, R), New Mexico (D, R), New York (R), North Dakota (D, R), Ohio (R), Oklahoma (D, R), Oregon (D), Pennsylvania (D), South Carolina (R), South Dakota (D, R), Tennessee (D, R), Utah (D, R), Vermont (R), Virginia (R), Washington (D), West Virginia (D), Wisconsin (D, R), Wyoming (D, R).

The state party leader sample consists of the state party chair and executive director from the Democratic and Republican parties in all states (N = 193). (The N is short of 200 as a result of vacancies. In addition, the state party chair was also serving as the executive director in a few cases.) Names and contact information of the state party chair and executive director were taken from the Republican National Committee and Democratic National Committee Web sites as well as the Web sites of the state parties. In a few cases, I contacted the state party or consulted Lexis-Nexis for the name of the executive director. A few Democratic party organizations lack an executive director position; I therefore contacted the staff member whose title most closely resembled the position of executive director.

A total of sixty-eight respondents completed the survey of state party leaders, for a response rate of about 35 percent. Twenty-eight Democratic parties and twenty-eight Republican parties participated in the study, or about 56 percent of all state parties. Thirty-nine of the fifty states are included in the sample. The following state parties participated in the study: Alabama (D, R), Alaska (R), Arizona (D), Arkansas (R), California (D, R), Colorado (R), Delaware (D), Florida (R), Georgia (D), Hawaii (D, R), Idaho (R), Illinois (D), Iowa (D, R), Kansas (D, R), Kentucky (D), Louisiana (R), Maine (D, R), Massachusetts (D), Michigan (D, R), Minnesota (D, R), Mississippi (D, R), Missouri (D, R), Nebraska (R), Nevada (D), New Hampshire (R), New Jersey (R), North Carolina (D, R), North Dakota (D, R), Ohio (D, R), Oklahoma (D, R), Oregon (D, R), Pennsylvania (D), South Dakota (D, R), Tennessee (D, R), Utah (R), Virginia (R), Washington (D), Wisconsin (D), Wyoming (D).

The Ohio state legislative candidate sample consists of all candidates who entered the Democratic or Republican primaries for the Ohio House of Representatives and the Ohio Senate. I exclude candidates who won the nomination but dropped out of the race before the general election; I also exclude substitute candidates who ran in the general election but not the primary. Because the House leaders of both parties were already being surveyed for the legislative leader sample, I did not include those individuals in the candidate sample. The total number of Ohio candidates surveyed was 270, of whom 14 dropped out before the primary or general election, leaving 256 candidates; these candidates who withdrew are not included in my analyses. A total of 156 candidates completed the survey, for a response rate of about 61 percent.

The procedures for all three surveys were largely identical. Shortly after the November 2002 election, respondents received an advance letter notifying them that they would receive a questionnaire shortly. About one week later, respondents received a cover letter with the questionnaire and a self-addressed, stamped return envelope. This mailing was followed by a reminder postcard. Nonrespondents received another complete mailing with cover letter, questionnaire, and self-addressed stamped envelope during the first week of December. About two weeks after this mailing, nonrespondents received a reminder telephone call from the OSU Center for Survey Research. Each of the cover letters was tailored to the appropriate sample—state legislative leaders, state party leaders, or Ohio candidates. For example, the state legislative leader cover letter explained that the purpose of the study was to research party activities in state legislative elections and that the questions concerned the most recent elections for the House or Assembly in their state. The letter stated that the survey had been sent to members of the Democratic and Republican House/ Assembly leadership teams in all states. Respondents in all three samples were promised confidentiality and assured that the data would be analyzed in the aggregate. For the state legislative and state party surveys, the cover letter explained that I would be reporting a list of participating states and parties. Party leaders were also assured that their responses would not be linked to their state parties.

As of early January, the response rate among the state party leader sample remained lower than that of the other two samples. This lower response rate led to one additional, unplanned round of data collection for the state parties only. In mid-January 2003, nonrespondents from the state party leader sample received another mailing with a cover letter, questionnaire, and self-addressed stamped envelope. I placed reminder telephone calls to nonrespondents two weeks later. I called only state parties that had not yet participated in the study, and I did not call respondents if they were no longer at the state party (i.e., if the state party Web site or information obtained through Lexis-Nexis indicated that the party chair or executive director I had originally contacted was no longer serving). I made a total of seventy-six contacts with nonrespondents; as of February 3, 2003, 128 nonrespondents remained.

Survey of State Legislative Leaders

Thank you for responding to this survey. Your responses are completely confidential. The following questions concern election to the **House or Assembly of the state legislature** only. I will send you a summary of the survey results when the study is completed.

1. You are a …
   - ☐ State Party Chair ☐ State Party Executive Director
   - ☐ Member of House/Assembly leadership team (please specify position): _____
   - ☐ Other (please specify position): _____

2. How many years have you served in this position? _____

3. You are a… ☐ Democrat ☐ Republican ☐ Other: _____

4. Did the caucus leadership assist **House/Assembly candidates** with any of the following activities in the last election? (Please check all that apply)
   - ☐ Recruited candidates
   - ☐ Assisted candidates with fundraising
   - ☐ Made direct campaign contributions
   - ☐ Held get-out-the-vote drives
   - ☐ Shared voter lists with candidates
   - ☐ Conducted polls for candidates
   - ☐ Provided technical assistance with campaign materials
   - ☐ Created and mailed campaign materials
   - ☐ Created television ads for candidates
   - ☐ Loaned or paid campaign staff for candidates
   - ☐ Trained candidates or campaign staff
   - ☐ Other (please specify): _____

5. In your opinion, how important is it that a candidate from your party have the following qualifications in order to win election to the **House/Assembly**? (Please check one per row)

	Not important at all 1	Not too important 2	Somewhat important 3	Very important 4	Extremely important 5
Has held local elected office	☐	☐	☐	☐	☐
Has held local appointed office	☐	☐	☐	☐	☐
Has been active in the party	☐	☐	☐	☐	☐
Is a businessperson	☐	☐	☐	☐	☐
Is a teacher	☐	☐	☐	☐	☐
Is independently wealthy	☐	☐	☐	☐	☐
Is a community activist/ volunteer	☐	☐	☐	☐	☐

6. In your view, how active was each group in recruiting **House/Assembly candidates** for your party in the last election, on a scale from 1 to 5? (Please check one box per row)

	Not at all active 1	Not very active 2	Somewhat active 3	Fairly active 4	Very active 5
Most local party leaders	☐	☐	☐	☐	☐
The state party	☐	☐	☐	☐	☐
The legislative leadership	☐	☐	☐	☐	☐

7. In House/Assembly elections in recent years, in how many districts has the **caucus leadership**…

	Never	Very few seats	Some seats	Many seats	All seats
Encouraged a candidate to run	1☐	2☐	3☐	4☐	5☐
Encouraged a candidate not to run	1☐	2☐	3☐	4☐	5☐
Formally endorsed a candidate in a primary	1☐	2☐	3☐	4☐	5☐
Helped a challenged incumbent in a primary	1☐	2☐	3☐	4☐	5☐
Taken sides in a primary	1☐	2☐	3☐	4☐	5☐
Selected a candidate for a targeted race	1☐	2☐	3☐	4☐	5☐

8. In House/Assembly elections in recent years, in how many districts have **local party leaders** from your party…

	Never	Very few seats	Some seats	Many seats	All seats
Encouraged a candidate to run	1☐	2☐	3☐	4☐	5☐
Encouraged a candidate not to run	1☐	2☐	3☐	4☐	5☐
Formally endorsed a candidate in a primary	1☐	2☐	3☐	4☐	5☐
Helped a challenged incumbent in a primary	1☐	2☐	3☐	4☐	5☐
Taken sides in a primary	1☐	2☐	3☐	4☐	5☐
Selected a candidate for a targeted race	1☐	2☐	3☐	4☐	5☐

9. In your state, about how many House/Assembly seats are considered safe or very certain your party will win? _____ ☐ Don't know

In about how many seats do you expect close races between the 2 major parties? _____ ☐ Don't know

10. If the caucus leadership recruited candidates in the last election, for about how many total House/Assembly seats were candidates recruited? _____

10a. For how many House/Assembly seats was recruiting candidates a priority? _____

10b. Is there a staff person who assists the caucus leadership in recruiting candidates for the House/Assembly? ☐ No ☐ Yes, Full-time staff person ☐ Yes, Part-time staff person

10c. Who in your caucus recruits candidates for the House/Assembly? (Please check as many as apply)

₁☐ Member(s) of the leadership team

₂☐ Caucus campaign/reelection committee/fund

₃☐ Caucus recruitment chair or committee

₄☐ Entire caucus

₅☐ Other (please specify): _____

₆☐ Not applicable

₇☐ Don't know

10d. Does your caucus have a formal or informal chair in charge of candidate recruitment?

₁☐ No ₂☐ Yes; I am the chair ₃☐ Yes; I am not the chair

11. Over the past 8 years, the involvement of the caucus leadership in candidate recruitment has:

₁☐ Increased ₂☐ Decreased ₃☐ Stayed about the same ₄☐ Don't know

12. When a House/Assembly candidate is supported by most party leaders, the candidate's chances of winning the primary… ₁☐ Increase greatly ₂☐ Increase somewhat ₃☐ Stay the same ₄☐ Decrease greatly ₅☐ Decrease somewhat ₆☐ Don't know

13. In your view, is it usually better if the party avoids a primary in a House/Assembly district that is going to have a competitive general election? ₁☐ No ₂☐ Yes, usually ₃☐ Yes, sometimes ₄☐ Don't know

14. About what percentage of nonincumbent House/Assembly candidates come forward on their own to run without being asked by the party? ₁☐ 0 to 25% ₂☐ 25-50% ₃☐ 50-75% ₄☐ 75-100% ₅☐ Don't know

15. How often do interest groups recruit candidates for the House/Assembly?

₁☐ Never ₂☐ Very few seats ₃☐ Some seats ₄☐ Many seats ₅☐ All seats ₆☐ Don't know

16. Which interest groups are helpful to your party in recruiting candidates for the House/Assembly? (Please check all that apply)

☐ Labor/Union ☐ Business ☐ Women's Groups ☐ Christian Coalition

☐ Gun Owner ☐ Gun Control ☐ Pro-Life ☐ Pro-Choice

☐ Teachers ☐ Farmers ☐ Local/Community ☐ Environmentalists

☐ Lawyers ☐ Tax Relief ☐ Other (please specify): _____

17. Aside from leadership or caucus activities, how often do individual House/Assembly members recruit like-minded House/Assembly candidates to enter the primary in other districts?

    ₁☐ Never ₂☐ Very few seats ₃☐ Some seats ₄☐ Many seats ₅☐ All seats ₆☐ Don't know

18. About how many House/Assembly members from your caucus are likely to run for statewide or federal office at some point in the future?

    ₁☐ Very few ₂☐ Some ₃☐ Many ₄☐ Most ₅☐ Don't know

19. How often does an outgoing House/Assembly member from your party...

	Never	Rarely	Sometimes	Often	Always
Identify a possible successor	₁☐	₂☐	₃☐	₄☐	₅☐
Endorse or actively help a possible successor	₁☐	₂☐	₃☐	₄☐	₅☐

20. In races for the House/Assembly, other factors being equal, do you think that women candidates usually have an electoral advantage over men candidates, that men have an electoral advantage over women, or that neither has an advantage?

    ₁☐ women have some advantage

    ₂☐ men have some advantage

    ₃☐ neither has an advantage

    ₄☐ don't know

21. Are there districts in your state where it might be hard for a woman to win election to the House/Assembly?   ₁☐ Yes, many   ₂☐ Yes, a few   ₃☐ No   ₄☐ Don't know

22. Do you think that women usually make better candidates for the House/Assembly than men, that men usually make better candidates than women, or that there's no difference?

    ₁☐ Women better candidates ₂☐ Men better candidates ₃☐ No difference ₄☐ Don't know

23. If you are a current or former state legislator, how many terms have you served (through 2002) in either house of the legislature? _____

24. What is your year of birth? _____

25. Are you: ☐ Male   ☐ Female

26. What is your race or ethnic background? (Please check all that apply)
    ₁☐ White ₂☐ Black ₃☐ Hispanic ₄☐ Asian/Pacific Islander ₅☐ Native American ₆☐ Other _____

27. Your answers to this survey are confidential. Would you be willing to participate in a future telephone survey? ☐ No ☐ Yes; the best telephone number to reach me at is:_____

Thank you very much for your time. Please return this survey in the enclosed envelope.

Survey of State Party Leaders

'hank you for responding to this survey. Your responses are completely confidential. The following
uestions concern election to the **House or Assembly of the state legislature** only. I will send you a
ummary of the survey results when the study is completed.

. You are a ...

☐ State Party Chair   ☐ State Party Executive Director

☐ Member of House/Assembly leadership team (please specify position): _____

☐ Other (please specify position): _____

. How many years have you served in this position? _____

. You are a...   ☐ Democrat   ☐ Republican   ☐ Other: _____

. Did the state party assist **House/Assembly candidates** with any of the following activities in
the last election? (Please check all that apply)

☐ Recruited candidates   ☐ Provided technical assistance with campaign materials

☐ Assisted candidates with fundraising   ☐ Created and mailed campaign materials

☐ Made direct campaign contributions   ☐ Created television ads for candidates

☐ Held get-out-the-vote drives   ☐ Loaned or paid campaign staff for candidates

☐ Shared voter lists with candidates   ☐ Trained candidates or campaign staff

☐ Conducted polls for candidates   ☐ Other (please specify): _____

. In your opinion, how important is it that a candidate from your party have the following
qualifications in order to win election to the **House/Assembly**? (Please check one per row)

	Not important at all 1	Not too important 2	Somewhat important 3	Very important 4	Extremely important 5
Has held local elected office	☐	☐	☐	☐	☐
Has held local appointed office	☐	☐	☐	☐	☐
Has been active in the party	☐	☐	☐	☐	☐
Is a businessperson	☐	☐	☐	☐	☐
Is a teacher	☐	☐	☐	☐	☐
Is independently wealthy	☐	☐	☐	☐	☐
Is a community activist/ volunteer	☐	☐	☐	☐	☐

6. In your view, how active was each group in recruiting **House/Assembly candidates** for your party in the last election, on a scale from 1 to 5? (Please check one box per row)

	Not at all active 1	Not very active 2	Somewhat active 3	Fairly active 4	Very active 5
Most local party leaders	☐	☐	☐	☐	☐
The state party	☐	☐	☐	☐	☐
The legislative leadership	☐	☐	☐	☐	☐

7. In House/Assembly elections in recent years, in how many districts has the **state party**…

	Never	Very few seats	Some seats	Many seats	All seats
Encouraged a candidate to run	1☐	2☐	3☐	4☐	5☐
Encouraged a candidate not to run	1☐	2☐	3☐	4☐	5☐
Formally endorsed a candidate in a primary	1☐	2☐	3☐	4☐	5☐
Helped a challenged incumbent in a primary	1☐	2☐	3☐	4☐	5☐
Taken sides in a primary	1☐	2☐	3☐	4☐	5☐
Selected a candidate for a targeted race	1☐	2☐	3☐	4☐	5☐

8. In House/Assembly elections in recent years, in how many districts have **local party leaders** from your party…

	Never	Very few seats	Some seats	Many seats	All seats
Encouraged a candidate to run	1☐	2☐	3☐	4☐	5☐
Encouraged a candidate not to run	1☐	2☐	3☐	4☐	5☐
Formally endorsed a candidate in a primary	1☐	2☐	3☐	4☐	5☐
Helped a challenged incumbent in a primary	1☐	2☐	3☐	4☐	5☐
Taken sides in a primary	1☐	2☐	3☐	4☐	5☐
Selected a candidate for a targeted race	1☐	2☐	3☐	4☐	5☐

9. In your state, about how many House/Assembly seats are considered safe or very certain your party will win? _____ ☐ Don't know

In about how many seats do you expect close races between the 2 major parties? _____ ☐ Don't know

10. If the state party recruited candidates in the last election, for about how many total House/Assembly seats were candidates recruited? _____

    10a. For how many House/Assembly seats was recruiting candidates a priority? _____

10b. Is there a staff person who assists the state party in recruiting candidates for the
House/Assembly?   ☐ No ☐ Yes, Full-time staff person ☐ Yes, Part-time staff person

11. Over the past 8 years, the involvement of the state party in candidate recruitment has:
₁☐ Increased ₂☐ Decreased ₃☐ Stayed about the same ₄☐ Don't know

12. When a House/Assembly candidate is supported by most party leaders, the candidate's chances of
winning the primary… ₁☐ Increase greatly ₂☐ Increase somewhat ₃☐ Stay the same
₄☐ Decrease greatly ₅☐ Decrease somewhat ₆☐ Don't know

13. In your view, is it usually better if the party avoids a primary in a House/Assembly district that is
going to have a competitive general election? ₁☐ No ₂☐ Yes, usually ₃☐ Yes, sometimes ₄☐ Don't know

14. About what percentage of nonincumbent House/Assembly candidates come forward on their own to
run without being asked by the party? ₁☐ 0 to 25% ₂☐ 25-50% ₃☐ 50-75% ₄☐ 75-100% ₅☐ Don't know

15. How often do interest groups recruit candidates for the House/Assembly?
₁☐ Never ₂☐ Very few seats ₃☐ Some seats ₄☐ Many seats ₅☐ All seats ₆☐ Don't know

16. Which interest groups are helpful to your party in recruiting candidates for the House/Assembly?
(Please check all that apply)

☐ Labor/Union	☐ Business	☐ Women's Groups	☐ Christian Coalition
☐ Gun Owner	☐ Gun Control	☐ Pro-Life	☐ Pro-Choice
☐ Teachers	☐ Farmers	☐ Local/Community	☐ Environmentalists
☐ Lawyers	☐ Tax Relief	☐ Other (please specify): _____	

17. Aside from leadership or caucus activities, how often do individual House/Assembly members recruit like-minded House/Assembly candidates to enter the primary in other districts?

₁☐ Never ₂☐ Very few seats ₃☐ Some seats ₄☐ Many seats ₅☐ All seats ₆☐ Don't know

18. About how many House/Assembly members from your caucus are likely to run for statewide or federal office at some point in the future?

₁☐Very few ₂☐ Some ₃☐ Many ₄☐ Most ₅☐ Don't know

19. How often does an outgoing House/Assembly member from your party…

	Never	Rarely	Sometimes	Often	Always
Identify a possible successor	₁☐	₂☐	₃☐	₄☐	₅☐
Endorse or actively help a possible successor	₁☐	₂☐	₃☐	₄☐	₅☐

20. In races for the House/Assembly, other factors being equal, do you think that women candidates usually have an electoral advantage over men candidates, that men have an electoral advantage over women, or that neither has an advantage?

₁☐ <u>women</u> have some advantage

₂☐ <u>men</u> have some advantage

₃☐ <u>neither</u> has an advantage

₄☐ don't know

21. Are there districts in your state where it might be hard for a woman to win election to the House/Assembly?   ₁☐ Yes, many ₂☐ Yes, a few ₃☐ No ₄☐ Don't know

22. Do you think that women usually make better candidates for the House/Assembly than men, that men usually make better candidates than women, or that there's no difference?

₁☐ Women better candidates ₂☐ Men better candidates ₃☐ No difference ₄☐ Don't know

23. If you are a current or former state legislator, how many terms have you served (through 2002) in either house of the legislature? _____

24. What is your year of birth? _____

25. Are you: ☐ Male ☐ Female

26. What is your race or ethnic background? (Please check all that apply)

₁☐ White ₂☐ Black ₃☐ Hispanic ₄☐ Asian/Pacific Islander ₅☐ Native American ₆☐ Other _____

27. Your answers to this survey are confidential. Would you be willing to participate in a future telephone survey? ☐ No ☐ Yes; the best telephone number to reach me at is:_____

Thank you very much for your time. Please return this survey in the enclosed envelope.

Survey of State Legislative Candidates

Thank you for responding to this survey. Your responses to this survey are completely confidential. I will send you a summary of the survey results when the study is completed.

1. You are a: ☐ Democrat ☐ Republican ☐ Other (please provide:) _____

2. Are the <u>voters</u> in the district in which you ran in 2002:

₁☐ Much more likely to be Republicans than Democrats
₂☐ Somewhat more likely to be Republicans than Democrats
₃☐ About evenly divided between Republicans and Democrats
₄☐ Somewhat more likely to be Democrats than Republicans
₅☐ Much more likely to be Democrats than Republicans
₆☐ I don't know

3. How much did reapportionment after the 2000 Census change the boundaries of the district in which you ran in 2002?   ₁☐ not at all   ₂☐ somewhat   ₃☐ a lot   ₄☐ I don't know

4. Before you ran for the legislature for the first time, how active were you…

	Not at all active	**Not too active**	**Somewhat active**	**Very active**
in the <u>local</u> party:	₁☐	₂☐	₃☐	₄☐
in the <u>state</u> party:	₁☐	₂☐	₃☐	₄☐
in the <u>national</u> party:	₁☐	₂☐	₃☐	₄☐

5. Before you ran for the legislature for the first time, what public offices did you hold? (Please check all that apply)

	None	Local/ county	Judge- ship	State- wide	Local party	State party	National party
Appointed	☐	☐	☐	☐	☐	☐	☐
Elected	☐	☐	☐	☐	☐	☐	☐

5a. How many total years did you serve in: **Appointive** office? _____

Elective office (<u>excluding</u> the state legislature)? _____

6. Have you ever worked as a staff member in the office of an elected official?

₁☐ No   ₂☐ Yes, for a state legislator   ₃☐ Yes, other (please specify office): _____

7. When you ran for the state legislature for the first time, were you holding public office?

₁☐ No   ₂☐ Yes, elective office   ₃☐ Yes, appointive office

8. In thinking about your initial decision to run for the legislature, which of the following statements most accurately describes your decision: (Please check one)

₁☐	It was entirely my idea to run
₂☐	I had already thought seriously about running when someone else suggested it
	I had not seriously thought about running until…
₃☐	friends, family, co-workers, and/or acquaintances suggested it
₄☐	members of an association or organization suggested it
₅☐	party officials and/or legislative leaders suggested it
₆☐	local elected officials suggested it

9. When you were first deciding to seek a seat in the legislature, did you discuss your potential candidacy with any of the following party leaders?

Local party officials	☐ Yes	☐ No	☐ I do not recall
State party officials	☐ Yes	☐ No	☐ I do not recall
Local elected officials	☐ Yes	☐ No	☐ I do not recall
Leaders in the state legislature	☐ Yes	☐ No	☐ I do not recall

9a. If Yes: Did they encourage you to run, discourage you, or neither encourage nor discourage you?

	Encouraged	Discouraged	Neither	I do not recall
Local party officials	₁☐	₂☐	₃☐	₄☐
State party officials	₁☐	₂☐	₃☐	₄☐
Local elected officials	₁☐	₂☐	₃☐	₄☐
Leaders in state legislature	₁☐	₂☐	₃☐	₄☐

10. Did you have a primary opponent <u>when you ran for the legislature for the first time</u>?

₁☐ Yes   ₂☐ No   (If No: Please skip to Question 12)

11. If you had a primary opponent when you ran for the legislature for the first time, who did most party leaders endorse or informally support? (Please check one per row)

	Formally endorsed me	Informally supported me	Formally endorsed someone else	Informally supported someone else	Were neutral	I don't know
Most local party officials	1☐	2☐	3☐	4☐	5☐	6☐
Most state party officials	1☐	2☐	3☐	4☐	5☐	6☐
Most leaders in state legislature	1☐	2☐	3☐	4☐	5☐	6☐

12. In the most recent election, did the state party or legislative leadership target your race as one of the most important state legislative races to win this year?   ☐ Yes   ☐ No   ☐ I don't know

13. Did you have a campaign manager, coordinator, or director in the most recent election?
   1☐ No   2☐ Yes, part-time   3☐ Yes, part-time   4☐ Yes, full-time   5☐ Yes, full-time
                    volunteer   paid   volunteer   paid

14. Approximately how much was spent on your campaign in the most recent election, including your spending as well as any party or caucus spending on your race? (Leave blank if not applicable)

   Primary election $ _____   **General election $** _____

15. In races for the House/Assembly, other factors being equal, do you think that women candidates usually have an electoral advantage over men candidates, that men have an electoral advantage over women, or that neither has an advantage?
   1☐ <u>women</u> have some advantage
   2☐ <u>men</u> have some advantage
   3☐ <u>neither</u> has an advantage
   4☐ don't know

16. What about <u>most party leaders</u>? Do you think that most party leaders think women candidates usually have an electoral advantage over men candidates, that men have an electoral advantage over women, or that neither has an advantage?
   1☐ <u>women</u> have some advantage
   2☐ <u>men</u> have some advantage
   3☐ <u>neither</u> has an advantage
   4☐ don't know

17. In your district, how often do local/state party leaders or legislative leaders <u>discourage potential candidates</u> for the Ohio House or Senate from entering the primary?
   1☐ Never   2☐ Sometimes   3☐ Often   4☐ I don't know

18. In your district, how often do local party organizations <u>formally endorse</u> candidates for the Ohio House or Senate in the primary?

₁☐ Never   ₂☐ Sometimes   ₃☐ Often   ₄☐ I don't know

19. <u>In your view</u>, are men and women equally likely to be encouraged by your party to become candidates for the Ohio House and Senate?

₁☐ Yes, <u>men and women</u> are <u>equally</u> encouraged

₂☐ No, <u>women</u> are <u>sometimes</u> more encouraged

₃☐ No, <u>women</u> are <u>often</u> more encouraged

₄☐ No, <u>men</u> are <u>sometimes</u> more encouraged

₅☐ No, <u>men</u> are <u>often</u> more encouraged

₆☐ Don't know

Please answer the following background questions to complete the survey. Remember that your responses to this survey are confidential.

20. In general, how would you describe your political views?

₁☐ Extremely Liberal   ₂☐ Liberal   ₃☐ Slightly Liberal   ₄☐ Moderate/ middle of the road   ₅☐ Slightly Conservative   ₆☐ Conservative   ₇☐ Extremely Conservative

21. If you currently hold elective office, are you also employed in another occupation?

☐ No   ☐ Yes   **If Yes:** About how many hours per week do you usually spend at this job? _____

22. What is or was your occupation outside politics? (please specify:)_____

23. Do you have any children under 18 living at home? ☐ No ☐ Yes

24. What is your year of birth? _____

25. What was your approximate family income last year—before taxes?

₁☐ under $50,000   ₂☐ $50,000-$100,000   ₃☐ $100,000-$150,000   ₄☐ Over $150,000

26. How much formal schooling have you completed?

₁☐ Grade school or less   ₄☐ Some college

₂☐ Some high school   ₅☐ College graduate

₃☐ High school graduate   ₆☐ Graduate or professional degree

27. Are you: ☐ Male   ☐ Female

28. What is your race or ethnic background? (Please check all that apply)

₁☐ White ₂☐ Black ₃☐ Hispanic ₄☐ Asian/Pacific Islander ₅☐ Native American ₆☐ Other _____

Thank you very much for your time. Please return this survey in the enclosed envelope.

REFERENCES

Abramson, Paul R., John H. Aldrich, and David W. Rohde. 1987. "Progressive Ambition among United States Senators: 1972–1988." *Journal of Politics* 49 (February): 3–35.

Alabama Women's Initiative. 2002. *A Report on the Status of Women in Leadership in Alabama.* Birmingham: Alabama Women's Initiative.

Alan, Sara Jade. 1999. "See Jane Run. Run Jane Run! Gender Effects and Candidate Emergence in the U.S. House of Representatives." Paper presented at the Western Political Science Association Annual Meetings, Seattle.

Aldrich, John H. 1995. *Why Parties? The Origin and Transformation of Party Politics in America.* Chicago: University of Chicago Press.

Aldrich, John H. 2000. "Southern Parties in the State and Nation." *Journal of Politics* 63 (August): 643–70.

Alexander, Deborah, and Kristi Andersen. 1993. "Gender as a Factor in the Attribution of Leadership Traits." *Political Research Quarterly* 46 (September): 527–45.

Andersen, Kristi. 1996. *After Suffrage: Women in Partisan and Electoral Politics before the New Deal.* Chicago: University of Chicago Press.

Appleton, Andrew M., and Anneka Depoorter. 1997. "Washington." In *State Party Profiles: A Fifty-State Guide to Development, Organization, and Resources,* ed. Andrew M. Appleton and Daniel S. Ward, 341–49. Washington, DC: Congressional Quarterly.

Arceneaux, Kevin. 2001. "The 'Gender Gap' in State Legislative Representation: New Data to Tackle an Old Question." *Political Research Quarterly* 54 (March): 143–60.

Baer, Denise. 1993. "Political Parties: The Missing Variable in Women and Politics Research." *Political Research Quarterly* 46 (September): 547–76.

Baer, Denise L. 2003. "Women, Women's Organizations, and Political Parties." In *Women and American Politics: New Questions, New Directions,* ed. Susan J. Carroll, 111–45. Oxford: Oxford University Press.

Baer, Denise L., and David A. Bositis. 1988. *Elite Cadres and Party Coalitions: Representing the Public in Party Politics.* New York: Greenwood.

Baer, Denise L., and John S. Jackson. 1985. "Are Women Really More 'Amateur' in Politics Than Men?" *Women and Politics* 5 (summer–fall): 79–92.

Baldez, Lisa. 2004. "Elected Bodies: The Gender Quota Law for Legislative Candidates in Mexico." *Legislative Studies Quarterly* 29 (May): 231–58.

Barakso, Maryann. 2004. *Governing NOW: Grassroots Activism in the National Organization for Women.* Ithaca: Cornell University Press.

Bazar, Beth. 1987. *State Legislators' Occupations: A Decade of Change.* Denver: National Conference of State Legislatures.

Beckwith, Karen. 2002. "The Substantive Representation of Women: Newness, Numbers, and Models of Representation." Paper presented at the American Political Science Association Annual Meetings, Boston.

Bendyna, Mary E., and Celinda C. Lake. 1994. "Gender and Voting in the 1992 Election." In *The Year of the Woman: Myths and Realities,* ed. Elizabeth Adell Cook, Sue Thomas, and Clyde Wilcox, 237–54. Boulder: Westview.

Berkman, Michael B. 1994. "State Legislators in Congress: Strategic Politicians, Professional Legislatures, and the Party Nexus." *American Journal of Political Science* 38 (November): 1025–55.

Bernstein, Robert A., and Anita Chadha. 2003. "The Effects of Term Limits on Representation: Why So Few Women?" In *The Test of Time: Coping with Legislative Term Limits,* ed. Rick Farmer, John David Rausch Jr., and John C. Green, 147–58. Lanham, MD: Lexington Books.

Betts, Drew, and Thad Beyle. 2000. "NC State Senate Voting Results: 1968–1998." *North Carolina DataNet* 24 (March): 1–3.

Black, Gordon S. 1972. "A Theory of Political Ambition: Career Choices and the Role of Structural Incentives." *American Political Science Review* 66 (March): 144–59.

Black, Jerome H., and Lynda Erickson. 2000. "Similarity, Compensation, or Difference? A Comparison of Female and Male Office-Seekers." *Women and Politics* 21 (4): 1–38.

Bledsoe, Timothy, and Mary Herring. 1990. "Victims of Circumstances: Women in Pursuit of Political Office." *American Political Science Review* 84 (March): 213–23.

Brace, Paul. 1984. "Progressive Ambition in the House: A Probabilistic Approach." *Journal of Politics* (May): 556–71.

Brace, Paul, Kellie Sims-Butler, Kevin Arceneaux, and Martin Johnson. 2002. "Public Opinion in the American States: New Perspectives Using National Survey Data." *American Journal of Political Science* 46 (January): 173–89.

Brady, Henry E., Kay Lehman Schlozman, and Sidney Verba. 1999. "Prospecting for Participants: Rational Expectations and the Recruitment of Political Activists." *American Political Science Review* 93 (March): 153–68.

Bratton, Kathleen A. 2002a. "Critical Mass Theory Revisited: The Behavior and Success of Token Individuals in State Legislatures." Paper presented at the American Political Science Association Annual Meetings, Boston.

Bratton, Kathleen A. 2002b. "The Effect of Legislative Diversity on Agenda-Setting: Evidence from Six State Legislatures." *American Politics Research* 30 (March): 115–42.

Bratton, Kathleen A., and Kerry L. Haynie. 1999. "Agenda Setting and Legislative Success in State Legislatures: The Effects of Gender and Race." *Journal of Politics* 61 (August): 658–79.

Bratton, Kathleen A., and Rorie L. Spill. 2002. "Existing Diversity and Judicial Selection: The Role of the Appointment Method in Establishing Gender Diversity in State Supreme Courts." *Social Science Quarterly* 83 (June): 504–18.

Buchler, Justin, and Raymond J. LaRaja. 2002. "Do Party Organizations Matter? The Electoral Consequences of Party Resurgence." Paper presented at the Midwest Political Science Association Annual Meetings, Chicago.

Buck, Howard. 2002. "State Politicians Debate Issue of 'Gender Balance.'" *Columbian,* 2 June, A1.

Burns, Nancy, Kay Lehman Schlozman, and Sidney Verba. 2001. *The Private Roots of Public Action: Gender, Equality, and Political Participation.* Cambridge: Harvard University Press.

Burrell, Barbara C. 1990. "The Presence of Women Candidates and the Role of Gender in Campaigns for the State Legislature in an Urban Setting." *Women and Politics* 10 (3): 85–102.

Burrell, Barbara C. 1993. "Party Decline, Party Transformation, and Gender Politics: The USA." In *Gender and Party Politics,* ed. Joni Lovenduski and Pippa Norris, 291–308. London: Sage.

Burrell, Barbara C. 1994. *A Woman's Place Is in the House: Campaigning for Congress in the Feminist Era.* Ann Arbor: University of Michigan Press.

Bystrom, Dianne G., Mary Christine Banwart, Lynda Lee Kaid, and Terry A. Robertson. 2004. *Gender and Candidate Communication: VideoStyle, WebStyle, NewsStyle.* New York: Routledge.

Carey, John M., Richard G. Niemi, and Lynda W. Powell. 1998. "Are Women State Legislators Different?" In *Women and Elective Office: Past, Present, and Future,* ed. Sue Thomas and Clyde Wilcox, 87–102. New York: Oxford University Press.

Carey, John M., Richard G. Niemi, and Lynda W. Powell. 2000. *State Legislative Survey and Contextual Data, 1995: (United States) (Computer file).* ICPSR version. Columbus, OH: Kathleen Carr, Ohio State University, Polimetrics Lab (producer), 1995. Ann Arbor, MI: Interuniversity Consortium for Political and Social Research (distributor).

Carroll, Susan J. 1993. "The Political Careers of Women Elected Officials: An Assessment and Research Agenda." In *Ambition and Beyond,* ed. Shirley Williams and Edward L. Lascher Jr., 197–230. Berkeley: Institute of Governmental Studies Press, University of California.

Carroll, Susan J. 1994. *Women as Candidates in American Politics.* 2nd ed. Bloomington: Indiana University Press.

Carroll, Susan J., ed. 2001. *The Impact of Women in Public Office.* Bloomington: Indiana University Press.

Carroll, Susan J. 2002. "Representing Women: Congresswomen's Perceptions of Their Representational Roles." In *Women Transforming Congress,* ed. Cindy Simon Rosenthal, 50–68. Norman: University of Oklahoma Press.

Carroll, Susan J. 2003a. "Are U.S. Women State Legislators Accountable to Women? The Complementary Roles of Feminist Identity and Women's Organizations." Paper presented at the Gender and Social Capital Conference, St. John's College, University of Manitoba, Winnipeg.

Carroll, Susan J., ed. 2003b. *Women and American Politics: New Questions, New Directions.* Oxford: Oxford University Press.

Carroll, Susan J. 2004. "Women in State Government: Historical Overview and Current Trends." In *The Book of the States 2004,* 389–97. Lexington, KY: Council of State Governments.

Carroll, Susan J., and Krista Jenkins. 2001. "Unrealized Opportunity? Term Limits and the Representation of Women in State Legislatures." *Women and Politics* 23 (4): 1–30.

Carroll, Susan J., and Debra J. Liebowitz. 2003. "Introduction: New Challenges, New Questions, New Directions." In *Women and American Politics: New Questions, New Directions,* ed. Susan J. Carroll, 1–29. Oxford: Oxford University Press.

Carroll, Susan J., and Wendy S. Strimling. 1983. *Women's Routes to Elective Office: A Comparison with Men's.* New Brunswick, NJ: Center for the American Woman and Politics, Eagleton Institute of Politics, Rutgers University.

Carsey, Thomas, John Green, Rick Herrera, and Geoffrey Layman. 2003. "The New Party Professionals? An Initial Look at National Convention Delegates in 2000 and Over Time." Paper presented at the American Political Science Association Annual Meetings, Philadelphia.

Carson, Clara N. 1999. *The Lawyer Statistical Report: The U.S. Legal Profession in 1995.* Chicago: American Bar Foundation.

Caul, Miki. 1999. "Women's Representation in Parliament: The Role of Political Parties." *Party Politics* 5 (January): 79–98.

Caul, Miki. 2001. "Political Parties and the Adoption of Candidate Gender Quotas: A Cross-National Analysis." *Journal of Politics* 63 (November): 1214–29.

Caul, Miki, and Katherine Tate. 2002. "Thinner Ranks: Women as Candidates and California's Blanket Primary." In *Voting at the Political Fault Line: California's Experiment with the Blanket Primary,* ed. Bruce E. Cain and Elisabeth R. Gerber, 234–47. Berkeley: University of California Press.

CAWP (Center for the American Woman and Politics). 1992. *Women in State Legislatures 1992.* New Brunswick, NJ: National Information Bank on Women in Public Office, Eagleton Institute of Politics, Rutgers University.

CAWP (Center for American Women and Politics). 1999. *Women State Legislators: Leadership Positions and Committee Chairs 1999.* New Brunswick, NJ: National Information Bank on Women in Public Office, Eagleton Institute of Politics, Rutgers University.

CAWP (Center for American Women and Politics). 2001a. *Women in State Legislatures 2001.* New Brunswick, NJ: National Information Bank on Women in Public Office, Eagleton Institute of Politics, Rutgers University.

CAWP (Center for American Women and Politics). 2001b. *Women State Legislators: Leadership Positions and Committee Chairs 2001.* New Brunswick, NJ: National Information Bank on Women in Public Office, Eagleton Institute of Politics, Rutgers University.

CAWP (Center for American Women and Politics). 2001c. *Women State Legislators: Past, Present, and Future.* <www.cawp.rutgers.edu/pdf/research/StLeg2001Report.pdf>

CAWP (Center for American Women and Politics). 2003. *Women State Legislators: Leadership Positions and Committee Chairs 2003.* New Brunswick, NJ: National Information Bank on Women in Public Office, Eagleton Institute of Politics, Rutgers University.

CAWP (Center for American Women and Politics). 2004. *Sex Differences in Voter Turnout.* New Brunswick, NJ: National Information Bank on Women in Public Office, Eagleton Institute of Politics, Rutgers University.

CAWP (Center for American Women and Politics). 2005a. *Statewide Elective Executive Women 2005.* New Brunswick, NJ: National Information Bank on Women in Public Office, Eagleton Institute of Politics, Rutgers University.

CAWP (Center for American Women and Politics). 2005b. *Women in Elective Office 2005.* New Brunswick, NJ: National Information Bank on Women in Public Office, Eagleton Institute of Politics, Rutgers University.

CAWP (Center for American Women and Politics). 2005c. *Women in New Jersey Government.* New Brunswick, NJ: National Information Bank on Women in Public Office, Eagleton Institute of Politics, Rutgers University.

CAWP (Center for American Women and Politics). 2005d. *Women in State Legislatures*

2005. New Brunswick, NJ: National Information Bank on Women in Public Office, Eagleton Institute of Politics, Rutgers University.

Clark, Janet, R. Darcy, Susan Welch, and Margery Ambrosius. 1984. "Women as Legislative Candidates in Six States." In *Political Women: Current Roles in State and Local Government,* ed. Janet A. Flammang, 141–55. Beverly Hills, CA: Sage.

Clarke, Harold D., and Allan Kornberg. 1979. "Moving up the Political Escalator: Women Party Officials in the United States and Canada." *Journal of Politics* 41 (May): 442–77.

Coleman, John J. 1996. "Resurgent or Just Busy? Party Organizations in Contemporary America." In *The State of the Parties: The Changing Role of Contemporary American Parties,* ed. John C. Green and Daniel M. Shea, 367–84. Lanham, MD: Rowman and Littlefield.

Committee on Political Parties, American Political Science Association. 1950. *Toward a More Responsible Two-Party System: A Report of the Committee on Political Parties of the American Political Science Association.* New York: Rinehart.

Constantini, Edmond, and Kenneth H. Craik. 1977. "Women as Politicians: The Social Background, Personality, and Political Careers of Female Party Leaders." In *A Portrait of Marginality: The Political Behavior of the American Woman,* ed. Marianne Githens and Jewel L. Prestage, 221–40. New York: McKay.

Cook, Elizabeth Adell. 1994. "Voter Responses to Women Senate Candidates." In *The Year of the Woman: Myths and Realities,* ed. Elizabeth Adell Cook, Sue Thomas, and Clyde Wilcox, 217–36. Boulder, CO: Westview.

Costello, Cynthia B., and Anne J. Stone, eds. 2001. *The American Woman 2001–2002: Getting to the Top.* New York: Norton.

Cott, Nancy F. 1987. *The Grounding of Modern Feminism.* New Haven: Yale University Press.

Cotter, Cornelius P., James L. Gibson, John F. Bibby, and Robert J. Huckshorn. 1984. *Party Organizations in American Politics.* New York: Praeger.

Cotter, Patrick R. 1995. "Alabama: Activists in a Competitive Age." In *Southern State Party Organizations and Activists,* ed. Charles D. Hadley and Lewis Bowman, 111–25. Westport, CT: Praeger.

Cotter, Patrick R. 1997. "Alabama." In *State Party Profiles: A Fifty-State Guide to Development, Organization, and Resources,* ed. Andrew M. Appleton and Daniel S. Ward, 1–8. Washington, DC: Congressional Quarterly.

Council of State Governments. Various years. *The Book of the States.* Lexington, KY: Council of State Governments.

Cox, Elizabeth M. 1996. *Women State and Territorial Legislators, 1895–1995: A State-by-State Analysis, with Rosters of 6,000 Women.* Jefferson, NC: McFarland.

Cox, Gary W., and Chris Den Hartog. 2001. "Majority Status and Reelection in U.S. State Houses, 1970–1988." Paper presented at the American Political Science Association Annual Meetings, San Francisco.

"Creating a New Generation of Political Activists." 2001. *Notes from Emily* [EMILY's List], June. 1, 6, 7.

Crotty, William J. 1978. *Decision for the Democrats: Reforming the Party Structure.* Baltimore: Johns Hopkins University Press.

Crotty, William J. 1983. *Party Reform.* New York: Longman.

Crowley, Jocelyn Elise. 2004. "When Tokens Matter." *Legislative Studies Quarterly* 29 (February): 109–36.

Curtin, Michael F. 1996. *The Ohio Politics Almanac.* Kent, OH: Kent State University Press.

Dahlerup, Drude. 1998. "Using Quotas to Increase Women's Political Representation."

In *Women in Parliament: Beyond Numbers,* ed. Azza Karam, 91–106. Stockholm: International Institute for Democracy and Electoral Assistance.

Darcy, R., and Karen Beckwith. 1991. "Political Disaster, Political Triumph: The Election of Women to National Parliaments." Paper presented at the American Political Science Association Annual Meetings, Washington, DC.

Darcy, R., Charles D. Hadley, and Jason F. Kirksey. 1997. "Election Systems and the Representation of Black Women in American State Legislatures." In *Women Transforming Politics: An Alternative Reader,* ed. Cathy J. Cohen, Kathleen B. Jones, and Joan C. Tronto, 447–55. New York: New York University Press.

Darcy, R., and Sarah Slavin Schramm. 1977. "When Women Run against Men." *Public Opinion Quarterly* 41 (spring): 1–12.

Darcy, R., Susan Welch, and Janet Clark. 1994. *Women, Elections, and Representation.* 2nd ed. Lincoln: University of Nebraska Press.

Delano, Sophia, and Richard Winters. 2002. "Some Dynamics of Gender Gaps: A Multi-Methodological Analysis of Men/Women Voting for/against Men/Women Candidates for Elective Office." Paper presented at the Midwest Political Science Association Annual Meetings, Chicago.

Diamond, Irene. 1977. *Sex Roles in the State House.* New Haven: Yale University Press.

Dodson, Debra L. 1997. "Change and Continuity in the Relationship between Private Responsibilities and Public Officeholding: The More Things Change, the More They Stay the Same." *Policy Studies Journal* 25 (winter): 569–84.

Dodson, Debra L. 2006. *The Impact of Women in Congress.* New York: Oxford University Press.

Dodson, Debra L., and Susan J. Carroll. 1991. *Reshaping the Agenda: Women in State Legislatures.* New Brunswick, NJ: Center for the American Woman and Politics, Eagleton Institute of Politics, Rutgers University.

Dolan, Kathleen. 1998. "Voting for Women in 'The Year of the Woman.'" *American Journal of Political Science* 42 (January): 272–93.

Dolan, Kathleen. 2004. *Voting for Women: How the Public Evaluates Women Candidates.* Boulder, CO: Westview.

Dolan, Kathleen, and Lynne E. Ford. 1997. "Change and Continuity among Women State Legislators: Evidence from Three Decades." *Political Research Quarterly* 50 (March): 137–51.

Dovi, Suzanne. 2002. "Preferable Descriptive Representatives: Will Just Any Woman, Black, or Latino Do?" *American Political Science Review* 96 (December): 729–43.

Downs, Anthony. 1957. *An Economic Theory of Democracy.* New York: Harper and Row.

Duerst-Lahti, Georgia. 1998. "The Bottleneck: Women Becoming Candidates." In *Women and Elective Office: Past, Present, and Future,* ed. Sue Thomas and Clyde Wilcox, 15–25. New York: Oxford University Press.

Elazar, Daniel J. 1984. *American Federalism: A View from the States.* 3rd ed. New York: Harper and Row.

Erikson, Robert S., Gerald C. Wright, and John P. McIver. 1993. *Statehouse Democracy: Public Opinion and Policy in the American States.* Cambridge: Cambridge University Press.

Fastnow, Chris, and Dena Levy. 2001. "Poor Pennsylvania? Patterns and Causes of Women's Under-Representation in County Government." Paper presented at the Midwest Political Science Association Annual Meetings, Chicago.

Faucheux, Ron, and Paul S. Herrnson. 1999. "See How They Run: State Legislative Candidates." *Campaigns and Elections* 20 (August): 21–26.

Fiorina, Morris P. 2002. "Parties and Partisanship: A Forty-Year Retrospective." *Political Behavior* 24 (June): 93–115.

Fitzgerald, Barbara. 2003. "Reflections on a Glass Ceiling." *New York Times,* 10 August.

Flammang, Janet A. 1997. *Women's Political Voice: How Women Are Transforming the Practice and Study of Politics.* Philadelphia: Temple University Press.

Fleer, Jack D. 1994. *North Carolina Government and Politics.* Lincoln: University of Nebraska Press.

Fowler, Linda L. 1993. *Candidates, Congress, and the American Democracy.* Ann Arbor: University of Michigan Press.

Fowler, Linda L., and Robert D. McClure. 1989. *Political Ambition: Who Decides to Run for Congress.* New Haven: Yale University Press.

Fowlkes, Diane L., Jerry Perkins, and Sue Tolleson Rinehart. 1979. "Gender Roles and Party Roles." *American Political Science Review* 73 (September): 772–80.

Fox, Richard L. 1997. *Gender Dynamics in Congressional Elections.* Thousand Oaks, CA: Sage.

Fox, Richard L., and Jennifer L. Lawless. 2004. "Entering the Arena? Gender and the Decision to Run for Office." *American Journal of Political Science* 48 (April): 264–80.

Francia, Peter L., Paul S. Herrnson, John P. Frendreis, and Alan R. Gitelson. 2003. "The Battle for the Legislature: Party Campaigning in State House and State Senate Elections." In *The State of the Parties: The Changing Role of Contemporary American Parties,* 4th ed., ed. John C. Green and Rick Farmer, 171–89. Lanham, MD: Rowman and Littlefield.

Franke-Ruta, Garance. 2002. "EMILY's List Hissed: Fellow Democrats Criticize the Women Candidates' PAC." *American Prospect,* 23 September.

Freeman, Jo. 2000. *A Room at a Time: How Women Entered Party Politics.* Lanham, MD: Rowman and Littlefield.

Freeman, Jo. Forthcoming. "Gender Representation in the Democratic and Republican Parties." *Social Science Journal.*

Freeman, Patricia, and William Lyons. 1992. "Female Legislators: Is There a New Type of Woman in Office?" In *Changing Patterns in State Legislative Careers,* ed. Gary F. Moncrief and Joel A. Thompson, 59–73. Ann Arbor: University of Michigan Press.

Frendreis, John P., James L. Gibson, and Laura L. Vertz. 1990. "The Electoral Relevance of Local Party Organizations." *American Political Science Review* 84 (March): 225–35.

Frendreis, John P., and Alan R. Gitelson. 1999. "Local Parties in the 1990s: Spokes in a Candidate-Centered Wheel." In *The State of the Parties,* 3rd ed., ed. John C. Green and Daniel M. Shea, 135–53. Lanham, MD: Rowman and Littlefield.

Fulton, Sarah A. 2003. "Becoming A Woman of the House: A Model of Gender and Progressive Ambition." Paper presented at the Midwest Political Science Association Annual Meetings, Chicago.

Gerring, John. 2004. "What Is a Case Study and What Is It Good for?" *American Political Science Review* 98 (May): 341–54.

Gertzog, Irwin N. 1995. *Congressional Women: Their Recruitment, Integration, and Behavior.* 2nd ed.. Westport, CT: Praeger.

Gertzog, Irwin N. 2002. "Women's Changing Pathways to the U.S. House of Representatives: Widows, Elites, and Strategic Politicians." In *Women Transforming Congress,* ed. Cindy Simon Rosenthal, 95–118. Norman: University of Oklahoma Press.

Gibson, James L., Cornelius P. Cotter, John F. Bibby, and Robert J. Huckshorn. 1983. "Assessing Party Organizational Strength." *American Journal of Political Science* 27 (May): 193–222.

Gibson, James L., John P. Frendreis, and Laura L. Vertz. 1989. "Party Dynamics in the

1980s: Change in County Party Organizational Strength, 1980–1984." *American Journal of Political Science* 33 (February): 67–90.

Gierzynski, Anthony. 1992. *Legislative Party Campaign Committees in the American States.* Lexington: University Press of Kentucky.

Gimpel, James G., and Jason E. Schuknecht. 2003. *Patchwork Nation: Sectionalism and Political Change in American Politics.* Ann Arbor: University of Michigan Press.

Githens, Marianne. 2003. "Accounting for Women's Political Involvement: The Perennial Problem of Recruitment." In *Women and American Politics: New Questions, New Directions,* ed. Susan J. Carroll, 33–52. Oxford: Oxford University Press.

Gottschlich, Anthony J. 2002. "Former Candidate Calls GOP Leaders Bullies; Threats Used to Force Him Out of Race, He Says." *Dayton Daily News,* 10 June.

Green, John C., and Daniel M. Shea. 1997. "Ohio." In *State Party Profiles: A Fifty-State Guide to Development, Organization, and Resources,* ed. Andrew M. Appleton and Daniel S. Ward, 253–58. Washington, DC: Congressional Quarterly.

Hallett, Joe. 2000. "GOP Must Heal Itself after Fractious Primary, Ideological Wounds Linger." *Columbus Dispatch,* 9 April.

Hamm, Keith, and Gary Moncrief. 1999. "Legislative Politics in the States." In *Politics in the American States: A Comparative Analysis,* 7th ed., ed. Virginia Gray, Russell L. Hanson, and Herbert Jacob, 144–90. Washington, DC: CQ Press.

Handlin, Amy H. 1998. *Whatever Happened to the Year of the Woman? Why Women Still Aren't Making it to the Top in Politics.* Denver: Arden.

Hardy-Fanta, Carol, ed. 2003. *Women in New England Politics: A Profile and Handbook for Action.* Boston: Center for Women in Politics and Public Policy, John W. McCormack Graduate School of Policy Studies, University of Massachusetts, Boston.

Hartmann, Susan M. 1989. *From Margin to Mainstream: American Women and Politics since 1960.* New York: Knopf.

Harvey, Anna L. 1998. *Votes without Leverage: Women in American Electoral Politics, 1920–1970.* Cambridge: Cambridge University Press.

Herrick, Rebekah. 1996. "Is There a Gender Gap in the Value of Campaign Resources?" *American Politics Quarterly* 24 (January): 68–80.

Herrnson, Paul S. 1988. *Party Campaigning in the 1980s.* Cambridge: Harvard University Press.

Hershey, William. 2002. "Tape of Phone Call Enlivens House Contest; GOP Aide Says Race Played Role in Redistricting." *Dayton Daily News,* 1 May.

Hertzke, Allen D. 1994. "Vanishing Candidates in the 2nd District of Colorado." In *Who Runs for Congress?* ed., Thomas A. Kazee, 82–100. Washington, DC: Congressional Quarterly.

Hill, David B. 1981. "Political Culture and Female Political Representation." *Journal of Politics* 43 (February): 159–68.

Hirsch, Eric. 1996. *State Legislators' Occupations, 1993 and 1995.* Denver: National Conference of State Legislatures.

Hoffman, Kim U., Carrie Palmer, and Ronald Keith Gaddie. 2001. "Candidate Sex and Congressional Elections: Open Seats before, during, and after the Year of the Woman." *Women and Politics* 23 (1–2): 37–58.

Hogan, Robert E. 2001. "The Influence of State and District Conditions on the Representation of Women in U.S. State Legislatures." *American Politics Research* 29 (January): 4–24.

Htun, Mala. 2004. "Is Gender Like Ethnicity? The Political Representation of Identity Groups." *Perspectives on Politics* 2 (September): 439–58.

Huckshorn, Robert J. 1976. *Party Leadership in the States.* Amherst: University of Massachusetts Press.

Huddy, Leonie, and Nayda Terkildsen. 1993. "Gender Stereotypes and the Perception of Male and Female Candidates." *American Journal of Political Science* 37 (February): 119–47.

Iverson, Stewart, Jr. 2002. "Iverson: Strong Field of Candidates Will Help Republicans Build on Majority in Iowa Senate; 35 Republicans File Nomination Papers for Senate Seats." Press release. March 15.

Jacobson, Gary C., and Samuel Kernell. 1983. *Strategy and Choice in Congressional Elections.* 2nd ed. New Haven: Yale University Press.

Jewell, Malcolm E., and Sarah M. Morehouse. 2001. *Political Parties and Elections in American States.* 4th ed. Washington, DC: Congressional Quarterly.

Jewell, Malcolm E., and Marcia Lynn Whicker. 1994. *Legislative Leadership in the American States.* Ann Arbor: University of Michigan Press.

Johnson, Marilyn, and Susan Carroll. 1978. *Profile of Women Holding Office II.* New Brunswick, NJ: Center for the American Woman and Politics, Eagleton Institute of Politics, Rutgers University.

Jones, Mark P. 2004. "Quota Legislation and the Election of Women: Learning from the Costa Rican Experience." *Journal of Politics* 66 (November): 1203–23.

Kahn, Kim Fridkin. 1994. "Does Gender Make a Difference? An Experimental Examination of Sex Stereotypes and Press Patterns in Statewide Campaigns." *American Journal of Political Science* 38 (February): 162–95.

Kahn, Kim Fridkin. 1996. *The Political Consequences of Being a Woman: How Stereotypes Influence the Conduct and Consequences of Political Campaigns.* New York: Columbia University Press.

Kanter, Rosabeth Moss. 1977. *Men and Women of the Corporation.* New York: Basic Books.

Kathlene, Lyn. 1994. "Power and Influence in State Legislative Policymaking: The Interaction of Gender and Position in Committee Hearing Debates." *American Political Science Review* 88 (September): 560–76.

Kaufmann, Karen, and John Petrocik. 1999. "The Changing Politics of American Men: Understanding the Sources of the Gender Gap." *American Journal of Political Science* 43 (July): 864–87.

Kazee, Thomas A., ed. 1994. *Who Runs for Congress?* Washington, DC: Congressional Quarterly.

Kenski, Henry C. 1988. "The Gender Factor in a Changing Electorate." In *The Politics of the Gender Gap,* ed. Carol Mueller, 38–59. Newbury Park, CA: Sage.

Key, V. O. 1949. *Southern Politics in State and Nation.* New York: Knopf.

Key, V. O. 1956. *American State Politics: An Introduction.* New York: Knopf.

Klausen, Jytte, and Charles S. Meier, eds. 2001. *Has Liberalism Failed Women? Assuring Equal Representation in Europe and the United States.* New York: Palgrave.

Koch, Jeffrey W. 2000. "Do Citizens Apply Gender Stereotypes to Infer Candidates' Ideological Orientations?" *Journal of Politics* 62 (May): 414–29.

Kurtz, Karl T. 1992. "Understanding the Diversity of American State Legislatures." *APSA Legislative Studies Newsletter Extension of Remarks* 16:2–5.

Lawless, Jennifer L. 2004. "Women, War, and Winning Elections: Gender Stereotyping in the Post September 11th Era." *Political Research Quarterly* 57 (September): 479–90.

Leeper, Mark Stephen. 1991. "The Impact of Prejudice on Female Candidates: An Experimental Look at Voter Inference." *American Politics Quarterly* 19 (April): 248–61.

Leonard, Lee. 2000a. "GOP Deal Doesn't Sit Well with Some; The Plan, Which Lines Up

Ohio House Speakers for Two Years, Was Called 'Just Plain Arrogance.'" *Columbus Dispatch,* 13 January.

Leonard, Lee. 2000b. "Old Style, New System." *Columbus Dispatch,* 3 December.

Loevy, Robert D. 1997. "Colorado." In *State Party Profiles: A Fifty-State Guide to Development, Organization, and Resources,* ed. Andrew M. Appleton and Daniel S. Ward, 39–46. Washington, DC: Congressional Quarterly.

Lovenduski, Joni, and Pippa Norris, eds. 1993. *Gender and Party Politics.* London: Sage.

Maddox, H. W. Jerome. 2004. "Working Outside of the State House (and Senate): Outside Careers as an Indicator of Professionalism in American State Legislatures." *State Politics and Policy Quarterly* 4 (summer): 211–26.

Maestas, Cherie, L. Sandy Maisel, and Walter J. Stone. 1999. "Stepping Up or Stopping? Candidate Emergence among State Legislators." Paper presented at the Southwest Political Science Association Annual Meetings, San Antonio, TX.

Maggiotto, Michael A., and Ronald E. Weber. 1986. "The Impact of Organizational Incentives on County Party Chairpersons." *American Politics Quarterly* 14 (July): 201–18.

Maisel, L. Sandy, Linda L. Fowler, Ruth S. Jones, and Walter J. Stone. 1990. "The Naming of Candidates: Recruitment or Emergence?" In *The Parties Respond: Changes in the American Party System,* ed. L. Sandy Maisel, 137–59. Boulder, CO: Westview.

Maisel, L. Sandy, and Walter J. Stone. 1997. "Determinants of Candidate Emergence in U.S. House Elections: An Exploratory Study." *Legislative Studies Quarterly* 22 (February): 79–96.

Maisel, L. Sandy, Walter J. Stone, and Cherie Maestas. 2001. "Quality Challengers to Congressional Incumbents: Can Better Candidates Be Found?" In *Playing Hardball: Campaigning for the U.S. Congress,* ed. Paul S. Herrnson, 12–40. Upper Saddle River, NJ: Prentice Hall.

Mandel, Ruth B. 1981. *In the Running: The New Woman Candidate.* New Haven, CT: Ticknor and Fields.

Mandel, Ruth B., and Debra Dodson. 1992. "Do Women Officeholders Make a Difference?" In *The American Woman,* ed. Sara E. Rix, 149–77. New York: Norton.

Mandel, Ruth B., and Katherine E. Kleeman. 2004. *Political Generation Next: America's Young Elected Leaders.* New Brunswick, NJ: Eagleton Institute of Politics, Rutgers University.

Mansbridge, Jane. 1999. "Should Blacks Represent Blacks and Women Represent Women? A Contingent 'Yes.'" *Journal of Politics* 61 (August): 628–57.

Margolis, Diane. 1980. "The Invisible Hands: Sex Roles and the Division of Labor in Two Local Political Parties." In *Women in Local Politics,* ed. Debra Stewart, 22–41. Metuchen, NJ: Scarecrow.

Martin, David L. 1994. *Alabama's State and Local Governments.* 3rd ed. Tuscaloosa: University of Alabama Press.

Matland, Richard E. 1994. "Putting Scandinavian Equality to the Test: An Experimental Evaluation of Gender Stereotyping of Political Candidates in a Sample of Norwegian Voters." *British Journal of Political Science* 24 (April): 273–92.

Matland, Richard E., and Deborah Dwight Brown. 1992. "District Magnitude's Effect on Female Representation in U.S. State Legislatures." *Legislative Studies Quarterly* 17 (November): 469–92.

Matland, Richard E., and David C. King. 2002. "Women as Candidates in Congressional Elections." In *Women Transforming Congress,* ed. Cindy Simon Rosenthal, 119–45. Norman: University of Oklahoma Press.

Matland, Richard E., and Donley T. Studlar. 1996. "The Contagion of Women Candidates in Single-Member District and Proportional Representation Electoral Systems: Canada and Norway." *Journal of Politics* 58 (August): 707–33.

Mayhew, David R. 1986. *Placing Parties in American Politics: Organization, Electoral Settings, and Government Activity in the Twentieth Century.* Princeton: Princeton University Press.

McLean, Joan. 1994. "Strategic Choices: Career Decisions of Elected Women." Ph.D. diss., Ohio State University.

Merriam, Charles E. 1922. *The American Party System: An Introduction to the Study of Political Parties in the United States.* New York: Macmillan.

Mileur, Jerome M. 1997. "Massachusetts." In *State Party Profiles: A Fifty-State Guide to Development, Organization, and Resources,* ed. Andrew M. Appleton and Daniel S. Ward, 146–53. Washington, DC: Congressional Quarterly.

Moncrief, Gary F., Peverill Squire, and Malcolm E. Jewell. 2001. *Who Runs for the Legislature?* Upper Saddle River, NJ: Prentice Hall.

Mueller, Carol. 1982. "Feminism and the New Women in Public Office." *Women and Politics* 2 (fall): 7–21.

Nechemias, Carol. 1985. "Geographic Mobility and Women's Access to State Legislatures." *Western Political Quarterly* 38 (March): 119–31.

Nechemias, Carol. 1987. "Changes in the Election of Women to U.S. Legislative Seats." *Legislative Studies Quarterly* 12 (February): 125–42.

Nelson, Albert. 1991. *The Emerging Influentials in State Legislatures: Women, Blacks, and Hispanics.* Westport, CT: Praeger.

Niven, David. 1998. *The Missing Majority: The Recruitment of Women as State Legislative Candidates.* Westport, CT: Praeger.

Norrander, Barbara, and Clyde Wilcox. 1998. "The Geography of Gender Power: Women in State Legislatures." In *Women and Elective Office: Past, Present, and Future,* ed. Sue Thomas and Clyde Wilcox, 103–17. New York: Oxford University Press.

Norris, Pippa. 1993. "Conclusions: Comparing Legislative Recruitment." In *Gender and Party Politics,* ed. Joni Lovenduski and Pippa Norris, 309–30. London: Sage.

Norris, Pippa. 1997. "Introduction: Theories of Recruitment." In *Passages to Power: Legislative Recruitment in Advanced Democracies,* ed. Pippa Norris, 1–14. Cambridge: Cambridge University Press.

Norris, Pippa, and Joni Lovenduski. 1995. *Political Recruitment: Gender, Race, and Class in the British Parliament.* Cambridge: Cambridge University Press.

Pew Center on the States. 2003. *The Pew Center on the States State Legislators Survey: A Report on the Findings.* Princeton Survey Research Associates. Available at <http:www.stateline.org/specialreport/Pew%20state%20legislators%20%238288.pdf>.

Phillips, Anne. 1991. *Engendering Democracy.* University Park: Pennsylvania State University Press.

Phillips, Anne. 1995. *The Politics of Presence: The Political Representation of Gender, Ethnicity, and Race.* New York: Oxford University Press.

Plutzer, Eric, and John F. Zipp. 1996. "Identity Politics, Partisanship, and Voting for Women Candidates." *Public Opinion Quarterly* 60 (spring): 30–57.

Prysby, Charles. 1997. "North Carolina." In *State Party Profiles: A Fifty-State Guide to Development, Organization, and Resources,* ed. Andrew M. Appleton and Daniel S. Ward, 234–43. Washington, DC: Congressional Quarterly.

Reingold, Beth. 2000. *Representing Women: Sex, Gender, and Legislative Behavior in Arizona and California.* Chapel Hill: University of North Carolina Press.

Riker, William H. 1982. "The Two-Party System and Duverger's Law: An Essay on the History of Political Science." *American Political Science Review* 76 (December): 753–66.

Roederer, Charlie. 1999. "Voting for the North Carolina General Assembly: Election Trends from 1968 to 1998." *North Carolina DataNet* 23 (December): 1–3.

Rohde, David W. 1979. "Risk-Bearing and Progressive Ambition: The Case of Members of the United States House of Representatives." *American Journal of Political Science* 23 (February): 1–26.

Rosenstone, Steven J., and John Mark Hansen. 1993. *Mobilization, Participation, and Democracy in America.* New York: Macmillan.

Rosenthal, Alan. 1989. "The Legislative Institution: Transformed and at Risk." In *The State of the States,* ed. Carl E. Van Horn, 69–101. Washington, DC: CQ Press.

Rosenthal, Cindy Simon. 1995. "New Party or Campaign Bank Account? Explaining the Rise of State Legislative Campaign Committees." *Legislative Studies Quarterly* 20 (May): 249–68.

Rosenthal, Cindy Simon, ed. 2002. *Women Transforming Congress.* Norman: University of Oklahoma Press.

Rosenwasser, Shirley M., and Jana Seale. 1988. "Attitudes toward a Hypothetical Male or Female Presidential Candidate—A Research Note." *Political Psychology* 9 (December): 591–98.

Rozell, Mark J. 2000. "Helping Women Run and Win: Feminist Groups, Candidate Recruitment, and Training." *Women and Politics* 21 (3): 101–16.

Rule, Wilma. 1981. "Why Women Don't Run: The Critical Contextual Factors in Women's Legislative Recruitment." *Western Political Quarterly* 34 (March): 60–77.

Rule, Wilma. 1990. "Why More Women Are State Legislators: A Research Note." *Western Political Quarterly* 43 (June): 437–48.

Sanbonmatsu, Kira. 2002a. *Democrats, Republicans, and the Politics of Women's Place.* Ann Arbor: University of Michigan Press.

Sanbonmatsu, Kira. 2002b. "Gender Stereotypes and Vote Choice." *American Journal of Political Science* 46 (January): 20–34.

Sanbonmatsu, Kira. 2002c. "Political Parties and the Recruitment of Women to State Legislatures." *Journal of Politics* 64 (August): 791–809.

Sanbonmatsu, Kira. 2003. "Gender-Related Political Knowledge and the Descriptive Representation of Women." *Political Behavior* 25 (December): 367–88.

Sapiro, Virginia. 1981. "Research Frontier Essay: When Are Interests Interesting? The Problem of Political Representation of Women." *American Political Science Review* 75 (December): 701–16.

Sapiro, Virginia. 1981–82. "If U.S. Senator Baker Were a Woman: An Experimental Study of Candidate Images." *Political Psychology* 3 (spring–summer): 61–83.

Sapiro, Virginia. 1983. *The Political Integration of Women: Roles, Socialization, and Politics.* Urbana: University of Illinois Press.

Schattschneider, E. E. 1942. *Party Government.* New York: Rinehart.

Schlesinger, Joseph A. 1966. *Ambition and Politics: Political Careers in the United States.* Chicago: Rand McNally.

Schlesinger, Joseph A. 1975. "The Primary Goals of Political Parties: A Clarification of Positive Theory." *American Political Science Review* 69 (September): 840–49.

Schlozman, Kay Lehman, and Carole Jean Uhlaner. 1986. "Candidate Gender and Congressional Campaign Receipts." *Journal of Politics* 48 (February): 30–50.

Seligman, Lester G. 1961. "Political Recruitment and Party Structure: A Case Study." *American Political Science Review* 55 (March): 77–86.

Seligman, Lester G., Michael R. King, Chong Lim Kim, and Roland E. Smith. 1974. *Patterns of Recruitment: A State Chooses Its Lawmakers.* Chicago: Rand McNally.

Seltzer, Richard A., Jody Newman, and Melissa Vorhees Leighton. 1997. *Sex as a Political Variable: Women as Candidates and Voters in U.S. Elections.* Boulder, CO: Rienner.

Shea, Daniel M. 1995. *Transforming Democracy: Legislative Campaign Committees and Political Parties.* Albany: State University of New York Press.

Siegrist, Brent. 1999. "Women in Politics: GOP Track Record Excels." Press release. October 1.

Skalaban, Andrew. 1997. "California." In *State Party Profiles: A Fifty-State Guide to Development, Organization, and Resources,* ed. Andrew M. Appleton and Daniel S. Ward, 32–39. Washington, DC: Congressional Quarterly.

Smooth, Wendy G. 2001. "African American Women State Legislators: The Impact of Gender and Race on Legislative Influence." Ph.D. diss., University of Maryland at College Park.

Sorauf, Frank J. 1963. *Party and Representation: Legislative Politics in Pennsylvania.* New York: Atherton.

Squire, Peverill. 1988. "Career Opportunities and Membership Stability in Legislatures." *Legislative Studies Quarterly* 13 (February): 65–82.

Squire, Peverill. 1992. "Legislative Professionalization and Membership Diversity in State Legislatures." *Legislative Studies Quarterly* 17 (February): 69–79.

Squire, Peverill. 1997. "Another Look at Legislative Professionalization and Divided Government in the States." *Legislative Studies Quarterly* 22 (August): 417–32.

Squire, Peverill, and Gary F. Moncrief. 1999. "The Road Less Traveled: Recruitment Patterns among Women State Legislative Candidates." Paper presented at the Western Political Science Association Annual Meetings, Seattle.

Squire, Peverill, and Gary F. Moncrief. 2004. "Run, Jane, Run: Recruitment Patterns among Women State Legislative Candidates." Paper presented at the Western Political Science Association Annual Meetings, Portland, OR.

Stone, Walter J., and Alan I. Abramowitz. 1983. "Winning May Not Be Everything, but It's More than We Thought: Presidential Party Activists in 1980." *American Political Science Review* 77 (December): 945–56.

Stone, Walter J., and L. Sandy Maisel. 2003. "The Not-So-Simple Calculus of Winning: Potential U.S. House Candidates' Nomination and General Election Prospects." *Journal of Politics* 65 (November): 951–77.

Stone, Walter J., L. Sandy Maisel, and Cherie D. Maestas. 2004. "Quality Counts: Extending the Strategic Politician Model of Incumbent Deterrence." *American Journal of Political Science* 48 (July): 479–95.

Straayer, John A. 2000. *The Colorado General Assembly.* 2nd ed. Boulder: University Press of Colorado.

Swers, Michele L. 1998. "Are Congresswomen More Likely to Vote for Women's Issue Bills Than Their Male Colleagues?" *Legislative Studies Quarterly* 23 (August): 435–48.

Swers, Michele L. 2002. *The Difference Women Make: The Policy Impact of Women in Congress.* Chicago: University of Chicago Press.

Thomas, Sue. 1994. *How Women Legislate.* New York: Oxford University Press.

Thomas, Sue, Rebekah Herrick, and Matthew Braunstein. 2002. "Legislative Careers: The

Personal and the Political." In *Women Transforming Congress,* ed. Cindy Simon Rosenthal, 397–421. Norman: University of Oklahoma Press.

Thomas, Sue, and Susan Welch. 2001. "The Impact of Women in State Legislatures: Numerical and Organizational Strength." In *The Impact of Women in Public Office,* ed. Susan J. Carroll, 166–81. Bloomington: Indiana University Press.

Thompson, Joel A., and Gary F. Moncrief. 1992. "The Evolution of the State Legislature: Institutional Change and Legislative Careers." In *Changing Patterns in State Legislative Careers,* ed. Gary F. Moncrief and Joel A. Thompson, 195–206. Ann Arbor: University of Michigan Press.

Thompson, Joel A., Gary F. Moncrief, and Keith E. Hamm. 1998. "Gender, Candidate Attributes, and Campaign Contributions." In *Campaign Finance in State Legislative Elections,* ed. Joel A. Thompson and Gary F. Moncrief, 117–38. Washington, DC: Congressional Quarterly.

Tobin, Richard J., and Edward Keynes. 1975. "Institutional Differences in the Recruitment Process: A Four-State Study." *American Journal of Political Science* 19 (November): 667–82.

U.S. Department of Commerce, Bureau of the Census. 1994. *1992 Census of Governments: Popularly Elected Officials.* Vol. 1, no. 2. Washington, DC: U.S. Government Printing Office.

U.S. Department of Commerce, Bureau of the Census. 2002. *2000 Census of Population and Housing, Summary Population and Housing Characteristics.* PHC-1-1. Washington, DC: U.S. Government Printing Office.

U.S. Department of Labor, Bureau of Labor Statistics. Various years. *Geographic Profile of Employment and Unemployment.* Washington, DC: U.S. Government Printing Office.

Verba, Sidney, Kay Lehman Schlozman, and Henry E. Brady. 1995. *Voice and Equality: Civic Voluntarism and American Politics.* Cambridge: Harvard University Press.

Volgy, Thomas J., John E. Schwarz, and Hildy Gottlieb. 1986. "Female Representation and the Quest for Resources: Feminist Activism and Electoral Success." *Social Science Quarterly* 67 (March): 156–68.

Ware, Alan. 1988. *The Breakdown of Democratic Party Organization, 1940–1980.* New York: Oxford University Press.

Welch, Susan. 1978. "Recruitment of Women to Public Office." *Western Political Quarterly* 31 (September): 372–80.

Werner, Brian L. 1993. "Bias in the Electoral Process: Mass and Elite Attitudes and Female State Legislative Candidates, 1982–1990." Ph.D. diss., Washington University.

Werner, Brian L. 1997. "Financing the Campaigns of Women Candidates and Their Opponents: Evidence from Three States, 1981–1990." *Women and Politics* 18 (1): 81–97.

Werner, Brian L. 1998. "Urbanization, Proximity, and the Intra-State Context of Women's Representation." *Women and Politics* 19 (2): 81–93.

Werner, Emmy. 1968. "Women in the State Legislatures." *Western Political Quarterly* 21 (March): 40–50.

Whitman, Mebane Rash. 1996. "The Evolution of Party Politics: The March of the GOP Continues in North Carolina." In *North Carolina Focus: An Anthology on State Government, Politics, and Policy,* ed. Mebane Rash Whitman and Ran Coble, 173–80. Raleigh: North Carolina Center for Public Policy Research.

Williams, Christine B. 1990. "Women, Law, and Politics: Recruitment Patterns in the Fifty States." *Women and Politics* 10 (3): 103–23.

Wilson, James Q. 1962. *The Amateur Democrat: Club Politics in Three Cities.* Chicago: University of Chicago Press.

Wolbrecht, Christina. 2000. *The Politics of Women's Rights: Parties, Positions, and Change.* Princeton: Princeton University Press.

Zipp, John F., and Eric Plutzer. 1985. "Gender Differences in Voting for Female Candidates: Evidence from the 1982 Election." *Public Opinion Quarterly* 49 (summer): 179–97.

INDEX